CW01218952

The Tilson Case

The Tilson Case
Church and state in 1950s Ireland

DAVID JAMESON

CORK UNIVERSITY PRESS

First published in 2023 by
Cork University Press
Boole Library
University College Cork
CORK
T12 ND89
Ireland

Reprinted 2023

© David Jameson, 2023

Library of Congress Control Number: 2023932111
Distribution in the USA: Longleaf Services, Chapel Hill, NC, USA

All rights reserved. No part of this book may be reprinted or reproduced or utilised in any electronic, mechanical or other means, now known or hereafter invented, including photocopying and recording or otherwise, without either the prior written permission of the publishers or a licence permitting restricted copying in Ireland issued by the Irish Copyright Licensing Agency Ltd., 25 Denzille Lane, Dublin 2.

British Library Cataloguing in Publication Data
A CIP record for this book is available from the British Library.

ISBN: 978-1-78205-560-0

Printed by Hussar Books in Poland.
Print origination & design by Carrigboy Typesetting Services
www.carrigboy.co.uk

COVER IMAGE – Mid-twentieth-century Dublin Corpus Christi procession with the King's Inns in the background. *Courtesy of The National Library of Ireland, Wiltshire Collection* (WIL 46 [11])

www.corkuniversitypress.com

For Mariea

'Do you know the Greek word for *endogamein*? It means to marry within the tribe. And the word *exogamein* means to marry outside the tribe. And you don't cross those borders casually – both sides get very angry.'

Brian Friel, *Translations*

Contents

LIST OF FIGURES	viii
LIST OF ABBREVIATIONS	ix
PREFACE	x
ACKNOWLEDGEMENTS	xii
INTRODUCTION	1

PART 1. THE BACKGROUND: SOCIAL, THEOLOGICAL, POLITICAL

1.	Historical Antecedents: Mixed-marriage disputes in Ireland	19
2.	*Ne Temere*, the 'Promises' and the Dispensation	37
3.	The Birds' Nest	50
4.	The Catholic Ethos and the Church/State Consensus	67

PART 2. THE TILSONS AND THE COURTS

5.	Paternal Supremacy and the Irish Courts	81
6.	The Affidavits and the High Court Case	89
7.	George Gavan Duffy	106
8.	The High Court Judgment	120
9.	The Supreme Court Appeal	136

PART 3. THE AFTERMATH

10.	Reaction to the Court Judgments	163
11.	Reconciliation	196
CONCLUSION		205
NOTES		220
BIBLIOGRAPHY		243
INDEX		255

List of Figures

1. The Birds' Nest Orphanage, Dún Laoghaire, County Dublin [early twentieth century]. *Image courtesy of Dun Laoghaire-Rathdown Local Studies Department*
2. Charles Casey, who was attorney general in 1950. *Image courtesy of St Vincent's Castleknock College, Dublin*
3. John A. Costello TD (on right) with papal nuncio Gerald O'Hara and General Richard Mulcahy TD, (c. 1952). *Image courtesy of the National Library of Ireland* (IND, R 0152)
4. Mr Justice George Gavan Duffy, (c. 1950). *Image courtesy of the National Library of Ireland* (VTLS 299312)
5. Rev. W.L.M. Giff. *Image courtesy of* The Irish Times
6. Seán MacBride (*right*) with Cecil Lavery. Lavery sat on the Supreme Court bench for the Tilson case. *Image courtesy of Ms Caitriona Lawlor*
7. John Charles McQuaid, archbishop of Dublin. *Image courtesy of the Dublin Diocesan Archives*
8. *L to R*, Alan, Paul and David Tilson on Summer holidays in Oldcastle, 1949. *Private collection*
9. The three Tilson children leaving the Birds' Nest accompanied by their mother and solicitor, George McGrath. *Image courtesy of the* Daily Express *(Irish edition)*
10. Letter sent by David Tilson from the Birds' Nest to his mother. *Private collection*
11. Reunited in London: Ernest and Mary Tilson. *Private collection*

List of Abbreviations

DDA	Dublin Diocesan Archives
DIB	*Dictionary of Irish Biography*
ICM	Irish Church Missions
IR	*Irish Reports*
MSH	Mrs Smyly's Homes
NAI	National Archives of Ireland
NAIT	National Archives of Ireland, Tilson Infants file

Preface

My late father was born and raised as a Presbyterian and my mother is a devout Catholic. They married in 1959 and all their children were raised as Catholics. Though my father converted to Catholicism before his marriage – much to the annoyance of his parents – I believe that throughout his life he always identified himself as Protestant and, indeed, that he died as a Protestant. I asked him one day about his religion and he replied, 'It's very hard to change what you are brought up with.'

Many years ago, when we were living in a rural part of County Westmeath, my mother's nephew, a Catholic priest of whom she was very proud, decided to pay us a visit. He got lost among the myriad of back roads in our townland and eventually stopped his car outside a small cottage. An old man emerged, and, pleasantly surprised to see a man of the cloth at the end of his path, obligingly gave him directions to the 'Jamesons'. But as the priest was about to drive away, the old man unlatched the gate, hurried onto the road and beckoned to the priest to lower his car window. 'I was thinking, Father, I should warn you: I think those Jamesons are Protestants.'

Identifying the starting point of any journey in life is fraught with danger but this one may have begun when my parents married or, perhaps, when I was reading history as an undergraduate at UCD and the eminent historian Tom Bartlett warned us that as historians we were 'duty bound to interrogate assumptions'. Or it may have begun when I was researching for my doctoral degree in 2010 when I ran my finger up and down the list of 'Tilsons' in the telephone directory and stopped at 'A. Tilson'. I asked the lady who answered the phone if her husband had been in a Protestant orphanage as a child and if his parents had gone to court over the matter. When we sat down at their kitchen table the following day, Alan Tilson told me that I was the first person to contact the family about the issue in almost sixty years. He shared his memories of the Birds' Nest, showed me their scrapbook of press cuttings and the letter that his brother David had written to his mother from the Birds' Nest in June 1950. He then told me that his parents reunited many years after the court cases and lived out

Preface

their days together until their deaths in Dublin in the early 1990s. I realised then that there was much more to the Tilson case than landmark court judgments or the Catholic *Ne Temere* decree.

At his kitchen table that day I promised Alan Tilson that I would eventually write a comprehensive and even-handed account of the Tilson case. And I promised myself that, in the process, I would interrogate all the assumptions. I hope I have honoured both pledges.

DAVID JAMESON
Dun Laoghaire, County Dublin
and Ballinahoun, County Clare
January 2023

Acknowledgements

I am extremely grateful to Alan and Judy Tilson, without whose reflections, insights and help this book would not have been possible. I wish also to thank them for permission to reproduce family photographs in their possession. Maria O'Donovan and Mike Collins at Cork University Press must also be especially thanked for their forbearance and professionalism and for helping me bring this project to fruition. I am also very grateful to their peer reviewers; though they remain anonymous, their suggestions for improvement have added real value to the book.

My heartfelt thanks to my friend and mentor Professor Emeritus Joe Ruane, who has taught me much about the writing of social history – not least that truth and meaning is more likely found in the nuances and subtleties. This book has been improved by his wise counsel and many stimulating observations. I also owe a special debt of gratitude to Mr Justice Gerard Hogan, who has been generous to a fault with his time and very formidable expertise over many years. I am greatly indebted to Professor Jarlath Killeen of the School of English, Trinity College for awarding me a Visiting Research Fellowship, without which this project would have proven much more difficult.

I must especially thank my agent, Jonathan Williams, for his superb judgment, for the meticulous care he took when reading the original manuscript and whose belief in this project has been resolute from the very beginning. It says much of the man that despite facing his own challenges in recent times, he remained a constant source of advice and encouragement. Also, for painstakingly reading various drafts of the text and making valuable criticisms and observations, I thank my dear friends Avril Patterson and Guy Woodward. I would also like to say a particular word of thanks to Aonghus Meaney, Cork University Press' very efficient copy-editor, for his first-rate work.

This book grew out of my PhD thesis and I am grateful to the Irish Research Council for awarding me a postgraduate scholarship to assist with my doctoral research. I am indebted to many others for their help over the past few years: the late Linda Barrington of Smyly Trust Services and Olive Stewart and David Martin of the Irish Church Missions; Very Rev. Fachtna McCarthy of St Mary's church, Haddington Road, Dublin 4; Monsignor Maurice Dooley; the staff at the Library of Trinity College Dublin and at the National Library of Ireland; Deirdre O'Connell and Gregory O'Connor at the National Archives of Ireland; Damien Burke at the Irish Jesuit Archives; Monsignor Gearóid Dullea and Anna Porter at the St Patrick's College Maynooth Archives; Carmel Connell at the Meath Diocesan Archives; Barbara Bonini and Elizabeth Kirwan at the National Photographic Archives and Don Harper of Artwerk. But I must especially thank Noelle Dowling of the Dublin Diocesan Archives, who has been unfailingly generous with her time and expertise and who alerted me to the McQuaid/Marchetti-Selvaggiani letter that was uncovered at the eleventh hour of this project. For sharing their experiences of their own mixed marriages or those of their parents, I am most grateful to Imogen Stuart, Edna Longley, Father Peter McVerry and John Finucane MP. Thanks also to Faber & Faber for permission to reprint the lines from Brian Friel's *Translations* used as an epigraph for this book.

For helping me find my métier all those years ago, I owe a special debt of gratitude to Seamus Leahy, my English teacher at Rockwell College. I wish also to thank the inspirational scholars and academics I was privileged to engage with as an undergraduate at UCD, such as Lindsey Earner-Byrne, Michael Laffan, Tom Bartlett, Andrew Carpenter, Ron Callan, Brian Donnelly and Declan Kiberd. At the School of English, Trinity College, I am equally grateful to my former teachers and colleagues: Gerald Dawe, Aileen Douglas, Paul Delaney, Eve Patten, Nicholas Grene, Brian Cliff and Sam Slote.

With deep gratitude I acknowledge the help of Joe Cleary of Yale University who was the external examiner for my doctoral degree, and who recognised the research potential of this subject at a very early stage. I also thank Daithí Ó Corráin of DCU, Dominic Bryan of Queen's University Belfast and Niall Meehan of Griffith College who have all shared their wisdom and have offered much sound advice. I am most grateful to Archbishop McQuaid's biographer, John Cooney, for his assistance, and the late Father Aidan Lehane CSSp for providing unique insights into the archbishop's personality. I owe a special debt of gratitude to the late Margaret MacCurtain; a most formidable woman and distinguished historian – who was known to have defied McQuaid's authority – she warned me to have the book published before she passed. Very, very sadly, this was not to be.

Outside of research and scholarship, I am most grateful to Dr Charles McCreery and Professor Richard Sheahan at the Blackrock Clinic who skilfully restored my sinus rhythm and got me back on the road, literally; also, Dr Amy Watchorn for, among many things, showing me the cosmos in a sycamore tree. I am heavily indebted to others for providing support, advice and, indeed, friendship over many years: my late father, John, my sister Alison and mother Eleanor, my aunt Norma McMaster, my running buddy and confidant Michael Gilleran, Lar Endersen, David Swanton, Des McDermott, Sheela Headon, Rev. Andrew Smith and his wife Tara, Mark Moran, Aengus Oates and Críostóir O'Flaherty. But my greatest debt is to my precious daughters Ruth and Jodie and my wife and soul mate, Mariea. Thank you for your love and support and for living through the highs and lows of this journey with such understanding. *Ab imo pectore.*

Introduction

ERNEST AND MARY TILSON

In the late summer and autumn of the 'Holy Year' 1950, Ireland became a house divided. This story began nine years earlier on 10 December 1941, when Ernest Neville Tilson, a twenty-four-year-old Protestant, married Mary Josephine Barnes, an eighteen-year-old Catholic, in St Mary's church on Haddington Road, Dublin.[1] The wedding took place under fraught conditions: Mary Barnes was pregnant and her mother, Annie, a 'very religious and pious' Catholic, vehemently opposed the marriage because of Tilson's religion.[2] In an effort to ensure that the marriage proceeded or simply to quell tensions, Tilson signed a Catholic Church pledge agreeing to raise any children of the marriage as Catholics. He subsequently reneged on that promise in 1950 when he removed three of his four sons to the Protestant-run Birds' Nest orphanage in Dún Laoghaire, County Dublin, intending to educate them as Protestants. To recover her sons, Mary Tilson took a case to the High Court; her husband later appealed in the Supreme Court that court's ruling in her favour. In terms of their own religious behaviour, neither Ernest Tilson nor his wife were overly pious, yet their dispute – which received widespread newspaper coverage in Ireland, Britain and the United States – polarised Ireland along confessional lines and became the '*cause célèbre* of the 1950s'.[3]

Ernest Tilson was born on 3 March 1917 at 8 Church Street, Oldcastle, County Meath, to parents David and Harriette (*née* Forsyth). He had an older sister, Martha (known as Mitty), and a younger brother, Tom. The family ran a small tailoring business where David, his wife and daughter worked, while Tom was employed as a lorry driver with Great Northern Railways. All the children attended the non-denominational Gilson Endowed School just across the road from their house, but David and Harriette Tilson were dedicated Protestants and raised their children accordingly. Oldcastle, like most rural Irish towns at the time, was overwhelmingly Catholic: in 1936 there were 2,580 Catholics and 125 non-Catholics in the parish.[4] There is some evidence of confessional antagonism in the town in the late 1940s: a local resident recalled how the Protestant owner of Porters shop placed a notice in the window advertising a job vacancy, which read: 'WANTED: SHOP ASSISTANT. No Catholics Please'.[5]

It has been suggested that there were three communities in Oldcastle for much of the twentieth century: the Catholic community and two Protestant communities, the latter of which were divided between a prosperous middle-class and a working-class group. The middle-class group consisted of families like the Porters or Trinnears who owned substantial agri-supplies and hardware stores in the town, or individuals such as the veterinary surgeon, Desmond O'Neill. These people are buried in the pastoral Loughcrew Protestant graveyard, which is situated alongside an old church on a rolling hill among tall trees. The working-class group consisted of people like the Tilsons, who lived from hand to mouth for much of their lives: one Catholic resident recalled that Mitty, then eleven or twelve years old, once knocked on her back door and borrowed sixpence to buy a loaf of bread. Like other working-class Protestants in the area, the Tilsons did not qualify for burial at Loughcrew; they are buried in the mostly Catholic St Bridget's Cemetery, in a separate division to Catholics and 'beside the paupers area'.[6] David, Harriette, Mitty and Tom were buried in a single grave and the inscription on their headstone simply reads: 'Tilson and Forsyth Family, Church Street, "In Heavenly Love Abiding"'. They were not of landed or ascendancy stock.

The Tilsons appear to have been well regarded in Oldcastle by Catholics and by their co-religionists. One Catholic resident, who was a close friend of Mitty, stated: 'Make no mistake about it, we liked the Tilsons. They were decent, hardworking people.'[7] At around seventeen years of age, Ernest Tilson left Oldcastle for Dublin where he secured employment with Dublin Corporation as a gardener. It was there, in the parks department, that he met his supervisor, John Barnes, who would introduce him to his daughter, Mary.

Mary Josephine Barnes was born on 4 August 1923 at 11 Turner's Cottages in Ballsbridge, Dublin, to parents John and Annie (*née* Drum).[8] She had four sisters, Berna, Ena, Phyllis and Lily and one brother, Joe. Both her parents were Catholics (as noted, Annie was particularly devout) and the children were raised in accordance with that tradition. The family would later move next door to 12 Turner's Cottages. This arc of terraced cottages, just off Shelbourne Road, was built in the mid-nineteenth century by the renowned ironmaster and engineer Richard Turner for his employees at the Hammersmith ironworks in Ballsbridge. Turner's notable works include the east wing of the palm house at the National Botanic Gardens at Glasnevin; Bellevue at Enniskillen; the wings of the palm house at Belfast Botanic Gardens and the palm house at the Royal Botanic Gardens at Kew.[9] The house builder George Crampton took over the site of the Hammersmith ironworks in 1891 and equipped it with builders' workshops;[10] in turn, he too used Turner's Cottages to accommodate his labourers. The census of Ireland shows that there were twenty-six cottages there in 1911.

Although recalled as a tight-knit community with an intense community spirit, Turner's Cottages was tenement housing and was colloquially known as 'The Gut'. The cottages were two-storey with four large rooms, each of which often housed one family. In fact, the 1911 Census of Ireland shows that the twenty-six cottages were subdivided into four- or five-room units, with a total occupancy of over 380 people – an average of over fourteen per cottage. Household return forms state that most male residents were employed as general labourers and most women as domestic servants or charwomen. The vast majority of the residents were Roman Catholic, though the occupants of two cottages listed themselves as Church of Ireland.[11]

Most of the houses did not have a kitchen and people often cooked on an open fire in one of the rooms. Coal was fetched in prams from a nearby yard and stored beneath the stairs. Residents shared a tap, situated to the rear of one of the houses, for drinking water and washing clothes, which were hung to dry on lines worked with pulleys that stretched from one side of the street to the other.[12] Proper sanitation was an ongoing problem: people queued to use the outside toilet and washed themselves in front of the fire in their rooms. A local government enquiry into poor sanitation in the Pembroke area in 1913 (John and Annie Barnes' marriage certificate shows that Annie lived at number 11 in 1917) heard that Turner's Cottages was 'in a very bad state of insanitation' and 'deserved to be demolished'.[13]

Until its demolition in the early 1970s, Turner's Cottages was also renowned for petty criminality: such was its reputation that if a crime was committed in the locality, it became the first port of call for the police. On 14 April 1936 Mrs Winifred Donegan of 11 Turner's Cottages was charged with larceny of a bag of coal valued at 5s. District Officer Dunphy gave evidence in the District Court and described how he had searched her house and found 'the balance of a bag of coal under some turf in Mrs. Donegan's room'. Mary Barnes' father, John, who was living next door at the time in number 12, gave evidence in the trial and said that, although he had seen 'the "raid" on the coal lorry ... neither Mr. or Mrs. Donegan had handled the coal'. The judge ordered the bag of coal to be returned to the Donegans.[14] On 26 May 1939 William Donegan (the same family?) and James Whelan of Turner's Cottages were charged with breaking and entering Coles' licensed premises in Ballsbridge and stealing goods to the value of £2 11s. 6d. Whelan was charged separately with breaking and entering the house of Captain Sydney Darling in the grounds of the Royal Dublin Society and stealing 12s. 6d. Both were sentenced to six months' imprisonment with hard labour.[15] In March 1943 John Byrne of Turner's Cottages was harshly sentenced by District Justice Mangan to a month's imprisonment for the larceny of cabbage plants from plots at Merrion Road. Showing that there was little tolerance for petty theft at the time, Mangan warned that 'those found guilty of theft from plots could expect no mercy'.[16] Perhaps somebody had stolen the judge's rhubarb plants?

After their marriage, Ernest and Mary Tilson moved into 12 Turner's Cottages. From the beginning, the couple had no room of their own and shared living accommodation with Mary's parents, three of her sisters, her brother and her aunt. Later, Mary's mother received permission (probably from the local housing authority) to sub-let one room to them. Although the cottage had only four rooms, which, when their youngest child, Neville, was born in 1946, were shared by thirteen people, much was made in the couple's sworn affidavits about living occasionally in 'our part' of the house or in Mary's 'parents' part' of the house. In his courtroom defence nine years after he moved into Turner's Cottages, Ernest stated in his affidavit to the High Court that conditions at number 12 were 'cramped and uncomfortable and an unsuitable place to raise children'. Alan Tilson and his sister-in-law, Judy, who was also raised in Turner's Cottages, however, have been at pains to stress that they enjoyed happy childhoods there and share fond memories of the working-class area.[17]

Four boys were born of the marriage, David, Alan, Paul and Neville, and all were baptised and educated initially in Catholic schools. The union was not a happy one, however, with husband and wife at times living apart. In 1949 Mary summonsed Ernest for maintenance; six months later the District Court effected a reconciliation, which saw the couple resuming life together at their home at Turner's Cottages and Ernest undertaking to pay her £4 per week. He would later claim that his wife was neglecting their children, while she would claim that he had physically assaulted her and was not providing financial support for the family, but the point on which the marriage eventually foundered was his placing of the children in the Protestant-run Birds' Nest orphanage.[18] This determining event not only saw a mother losing her children, but it also represented a clear breach of the promise Ernest had given concerning the Catholic upbringing of his children.

Since the issue was perceived to be primarily concerned with religious difference, it is necessary at the outset to consider what we mean by 'religion' in the context of the case. Although Ernest's and Mary's parents were devout in their religious practices and raised their children accordingly, neither son nor daughter was ardently observant in their own practice, though Mary did raise her children as Catholics, and they attended mass each Sunday and received the sacraments on a regular basis. For his part, Ernest attended Church of Ireland services on a much less frequent basis. As Robbie McVeigh has observed, 'Religious conviction and organisation is part of what makes up Protestantness and Catholicness but it is not definitive.'[19]

Some elements of their religions were intertwined or would overlap. Both Ernest and Mary always identified themselves as Protestant and Catholic respectively and maintained their association with their own religious tradition up to the time of their deaths in the 1990s. Religion for them was about being part of a particular ethnic or cultural group. Although they may not have been aware of it, religion was a discreet boundary marker between them or an inconspicuous way of signifying cultural or ethnic difference. And to borrow Claire Mitchell's terms, the boundary marker might 'ebb and flow' and be more significant at different times or in different circumstances, for example when Mary's mother strenuously objected to the marriage because Ernest was a Protestant, or when Ernest decided he wanted to raise his children as Protestants.[20] When Ernest took this course of action, he was effectively removing them from his wife's ethnic or religious grouping and placing them in his own. It will be shown that, while religious difference would be a key component of the court cases, it was far from the only cause of the dispute.

Religion or religious difference, of course, can also intersect with social class. At first glance, social class does not seem to have been a complicating factor in the couple's relationship for both Ernest and Mary shared similar working-class backgrounds. In terms of mixed marriages, however, Jack White has argued that 'there is at least a vestige of the old snobbery: Catholics, in the colonial ethos, are socially inferior persons'.[21] As part of his religious grouping, did Ernest hold any stereotypical perceptions of Catholics? For instance, did he somehow see them as 'inferior and unwashed', and was this perception given further traction when he was living among Catholics in the trying conditions at Turner's Cottages? We know that Ernest was raised by upright members of the Church of Ireland in Oldcastle, but did his parents feel that he was marrying beneath himself and his family when Mary Barnes became pregnant in 1941? We do not have the answers to these questions, but we do know that people in marriages often silently carry the burden of such matters and that they might never see the light of day. Or they might simmer beneath the surface for many years only to emerge in times of discord and strife.

REVIEW OF SOURCES

Drawing on archival material, previously unseen documentary sources, oral testimonies and reliable secondary sources, this book provides a new account of the Tilson case. The methodology adopted by the author reflects the fact that the case is examined from two perspectives. On one level, it is about a bitter domestic dispute between a Protestant man and a Catholic woman which resulted in court proceedings over the custody of their children. This book can therefore be seen as a case study of a working-class couple in a mixed marriage in mid-twentieth-century Ireland. On another level, the analysis of the dispute is concerned with the Catholic and Protestant Churches, the state and, indeed, with Irish society. This is because when Ernest Tilson took the extreme measure of placing his children in a Protestant orphanage, and when his wife initiated legal proceedings to retrieve them, they, unknowingly, unleashed forces well beyond their control or understanding. Collectively, the primary sources accessed are a wellspring of new data that helped the author navigate the complexities of the case, while secondary sources provided valuable background material which underpin the main arguments and central aims of the book.

Extensive interviews have been conducted with Tilson family members and people connected to the case, and access has been gained to personal correspondence relating to the matter. Alan is the only surviving son of Ernest and Mary, and not only does he hold clear memories of his time spent in the Birds' Nest orphanage, but his testimonies have illuminated many other relevant issues, such as family life in Turner's Cottages and his parents' reconciliation. Paul Tilson, who is now deceased, was placed in the orphanage along with his two brothers, and his widow Judy has provided valuable recollections of her conversations with her husband and his aunt, Mitty Tilson. Mitty – Ernest's sister – lived through the court cases and the widespread publicity that followed, and also experienced the trauma of the boycott of her family and her tailoring business.

Introduction   7

The Tilson family scrapbook has also proven to be an important repository of information. It was apparently assembled in late 1950 by one of Mary Tilson's sisters, and that it bears the title 'The Tilson Case' on its front cover indicates, perhaps, a conscious recognition, on the part of its compiler, of its future historical importance. The scrapbook contains abundant newspaper cuttings relating to the court cases, not only from newspapers such as the *Irish Independent* and the *Sunday Press*, which has ceased publication, but also from British newspapers, such as the *Sunday Dispatch* and *News Chronicle*, which have also ceased publication. There are also numerous letters contained in the scrapbook which can be readily divided between the shockingly honest and those that offer a subjective version of events. For instance, there is the heart-rending letter (reproduced later in this book) written by eight-year-old David Tilson to his mother from the Birds' Nest telling her that 'we are getting on well hear [*sic*]', and then there are letters to Mary Tilson, sent by Catholic mothers from all over Ireland assuring her that the Catholic Church was on her side and reminding her to pray to Our Lady.

Tilson case files held by Smyly's Trust Services/Mrs Smyly's Homes and the Irish Church Missions have been made available to the author and provide important new information about the Tilson family, and also about the internal dynamics of these organisations. Files held by the Irish Church Missions explain how Ernest's defence in the High Court and the Supreme Court was spearheaded and funded through the efforts of that organisation's superintendent, Rev. W.L.M. Giff. Correspondence in these files also discloses what became of Ernest in the aftermath of his legal defeat in the courts. Files held by Smyly's Trust Services/Mrs Smyly's Homes also contain important material, such as the admission forms that Ernest completed for his sons which were countersigned by Giff, correspondence relating to the case between lawyers and the trustees of the orphanage, and letters of support from individual Protestants across Ireland.

Archival sources have also played an important role in research. The National Archives of Ireland holds the affidavits sworn by Ernest and Mary Tilson in preparation for the High Court and Supreme Court proceedings. These testimonies, which are signed and dated by both parties, are supposedly 'statements of facts' and provide each of the protagonists' versions of events covering the period from their marriage in 1941 to the court hearings in 1950. Elsewhere, the papers of Cardinal John D'Alton at the Ó Fiaich Memorial Library and Archive in Armagh has a collection of newspaper cuttings and notes about the court hearings in a folder marked 'Tilson Case'; the 'Canon Law Faculty minutes' for 1951 held at St Patrick's College in Maynooth yielded information on the outcome of that faculty's re-examination of the 'marriage promises' in the wake of the Tilson judgments; and the papers of Edward Cahill SJ at the Jesuit Archives in Dublin gave insights into the power and influence of Catholic lay organisations in the 1950s.

The *Irish Reports*, the authoritative series of Irish case law from 1808 to the present, published by the Incorporated Council of Law Reporting for Ireland, provided invaluable and veritable accounts, not only of the Tilson hearings in the High Court and Supreme Court but also of other legal disputes discussed in this book. A further important mainstay of the research has been online newspaper archives. The *Irish Newspaper Archives* and *The Irish Times* and *Weekly Irish Times* databases provided details of the mixed-marriage dispute cases discussed in Chapter 1 along with day-by-day accounts of the Tilson court hearings. Coverage of the judgments in British, American and Australian newspapers were accessed on newspaper archive.com, britishnewspaperarchive.co.uk, newspapers.com and the Times Digital Archive websites. Copies of the *Church of Ireland Gazette* held in the Church of Ireland Representative Body Library in Churchtown, County Dublin, shed valuable light on how legal costs on the Protestant side were funded, as well as Protestant reaction to the judgments.

Historical studies by Thomas Bartlett, Alvin Jackson, J.J. Lee and Roy Foster were invaluable in establishing the historical background to the Tilson case, while the distinguished scholarship of Kurt Bowen, Tom Garvin, J.H. Whyte and Joseph Ruane added sharper focus to the matter of religiosity and church–state relations in Ireland. From a legal perspective, the works of Gerard Hogan and J.M. Kelly offered perspicacious, yet accessible, interpretations of the court cases examined, while monographs by J.P Casey, Paul Bartholomew, Alan Joseph Shatter and G.M. Golding yielded important legal background information. The book owes much to the *Dictionary of Irish Biography* (2009), which provided biographical information on many of the key participants, and also to exceptional recent scholarship, such as Eugenio F. Biagini's and Mary E. Daly's *The Cambridge Social History of Modern Ireland* (2017) and Richard Bourke's and Ian McBride's *The Princeton History of Modern Ireland* (2016); the relevant essays in these works were indispensable as the author evaluated the multiple themes and entanglements of the case.

As often happens with research projects, the author ran up several blind alleys. For example, the then minister for external affairs, Seán MacBride,

Introduction

was undoubtedly well attuned to the Tilson case owing to the amount of media coverage it received and because Ernest Tilson's mother, Harriette, wrote to him about the matter – as did Norman Porter of the National Union of Protestants on several occasions. It is odd, therefore, that there are no references to the case in MacBride's personal papers, nor in the Minister for External Affairs files at the National Archives of Ireland. References to the case are also absent from contemporary Dáil debate records and from minutes of cabinet and government meetings in Department of the Taoiseach files. It is also strange that there are no references to the issue in John A. Costello's or George Gavan Duffy's papers – both of which are held in the University College Dublin Archives. Meanwhile, an intensive search of the 1940s marriage files at St Mary's church – the church in which Mary Barnes and Ernest Tilson were married – showed that their marriage file is missing.

Stranger still is the dearth of material relating to the case in the Dublin Diocesan Archives. Ernest and Mary Tilson married in Dublin and lived in that city; three of their four children were placed in a Dublin orphanage and their dispute was then heard before Dublin-based courts and was aired extensively in newspapers at home and abroad. Given archbishop of Dublin John Charles McQuaid's propensity for involving himself in most controversies – even if they were none of his business – it is inconceivable that there is not a weighty file on the matter in these archives. On that note, it should be pointed out that there is a substantial amount of material relating to the Fethard-on-Sea boycott (discussed briefly later in this Introduction) at the same location.

In fact, exhaustive searches of the Diocesan Archives – assisted, it must be said, by the very helpful archivist Noelle Dowling – yielded only two documents: one contained a single-line reference to the aforementioned re-examination of the 'marriage promises' by the Faculty of Canon Law at Maynooth, and the other, a letter from McQuaid to Cardinal Francesco Marchetti-Selvaggiani in Rome, written just four weeks after judgment was handed down in the Supreme Court. That letter, and the cardinal's response, contain new revelations about the Tilson case and are dealt with in detail later in this book. All that said, the deficiency of material relating to such a high-profile case in some archives or repositories creates the impression of an official veil of secrecy being drawn over the matter in 1950 – as though it was being handled by a small and very tight-lipped sub-committee. Sometimes, though, what is absent speaks as loudly as that which is present.

Although written from a legal perspective, Gerard Hogan's seminal 1998 article 'A Fresh Look at Tilson's Case' offers the most thorough examination available of the case. Apart from its legal intricacies, Hogan also shines a light on why the Supreme Court at the time should have 'shouldered some of the blame for the misconceptions which the *Tilson* judgment engendered'.[22] Perhaps owing to a lack of clarity from that court, or a lack of information generally, or indeed as a means of serving the popular narrative that Ireland was *totally* controlled by the Catholic Church in the 1950s, most other commentators and historians have also tended to focus on the legal aspects, albeit solely through the narrow lens of Mr Justice Gavan Duffy's judgment in the High Court – and his language used when delivering it – and have fixated on his reference to the 'special position' of the Catholic Church in the constitution. Many others make no reference to the fact that Gavan Duffy also relied on Articles 41 and 42 and they also erroneously conflate the case with the Catholic *Ne Temere* decree. Indeed, it appears to have been lost on some commentators that the Supreme Court relied solely on Article 42.1 of the 1937 constitution (which referred to the family as educator) when reaching its verdict, and not Article 44.1.2 (which referred to the special position of the Catholic Church). On the 'special position' of the Catholic Church, which was enshrined in the constitution and later removed, Hogan notes that there is nothing unique about this, since countries such as Poland (Catholic), Spain (Catholic), Greece (Greek Orthodox) and Norway (Lutheran) all chose to insert similar references in their constitutions. Hogan concludes that the 'absence of any detailed and legal commentary regarding the drafting of the constitution itself has handicapped fair historical evaluation' and that too little attention has been paid to the contributions of constitutional experts such as John Hearne and Maurice Moynihan.[23]

Marianne Elliott, for example, has argued that Mr Justice Gavan Duffy 'ruled in favour of the Catholic mother, citing the special position of the Catholic Church in the constitution, which in his interpretation required judicial notice of canon law'[24] – an incorrect interpretation since the judge crucially added, 'I cannot decide those questions without full debate.' In fact, Gavan Duffy may have taken judicial notice of Catholic *practice*, 'though [he] did not make the concrete effect of his judgment depend on this'.[25] Like other historians, Elliott's commentary also fails to make any reference to the subsequent all-important Supreme Court judgment. Anti-Catholic polemicist Paul Blanshard, meanwhile, has tendentiously claimed that:

> The Catholic use of mixed marriage as a device for proselytising unborn children has been strengthened by an Irish Supreme Court ruling in the famous Tilson case ... The Tilson case is of immense significance to American and British non-Catholics because it shows how the traditions of the British common law ... can be modified to establish Catholic marital principles.[26]

Blanshard here suggests that the Supreme Court ruling was also precedential in the United States, but in 1942 the New York civil courts, in *Ramon* v. *Ramon*, gave state backing to the same prenuptial agreement.[27] Moreover, the mixed marriage was never used by the Catholic Church as a 'proselytising device'; the Catholic Church always discouraged mixed marriages and its objections to them were strengthened in the aftermath of the Tilson case. Furthermore, in neither the High Court nor the Supreme Court was British common law 'modified to establish Catholic marital principles'.

Many assessments of the case have erroneously conflated the judgments with the Catholic *Ne Temere* decree. Padraig O'Malley has argued that the 'court judgment held that the written pledge to bring up the children as Catholics required by the *Ne Temere* decree of the non-Catholic party to a mixed marriage was legally enforceable in view of the Church's officially recognised "special position"'.[28] But *Ne Temere* did not demand, or even make reference to, written pledges in regard to the religious upbringing of children; nor when reaching its judgment, it has been noted, did the Supreme Court rely on the special position of the Catholic Church, as set out in the constitution. Tim Fanning in *The Fethard-on-Sea Boycott* (2010) similarly conflates the *Ne Temere* decree with Gavan Duffy's judgment when he incorrectly states: 'Given that these written agreements were designed to make sure children of mixed marriages were raised as Catholics, [Gavan Duffy's judgment] was an explicit recognition of *Ne Temere* in civil law ... the [Supreme Court] judgment was an endorsement by the state of *Ne Temere*.'[29] Fanning's claim is misleading since neither the High Court nor the Supreme Court recognised, endorsed or even considered the Catholic decree. In a similar vein, religious affairs correspondent of *The Irish Times*, Patsy McGarry, writing about the Tilson case in 1997 under the incendiary headline 'Decree Likened to "Social Genocide"', argued that 'what few people realise is that *Ne Temere* had the force of law in this state'.[30] But the decree never had such a binding force; in fact, in the Ussher case in Galway in 1910 the court ruled that *Ne Temere* did not have any standing in civil law.[31]

Like Elliott, Kurt Bowen's reading of the case creates the impression that Gavan Duffy based his judgment solely on Article 44.1.2: 'Gavan Duffy justified his new interpretation of the law by referring to the 1937 constitution which accorded a "special position" to the Catholic church.'[32] Robin Bury offers a similar reading of the High Court judgment when he argues that Gavan Duffy justified his decision by referring to 'Article 44 of the constitution, which recognised the "special position" of the Roman Catholic Church,'[33] while Terence Brown likewise observed that, as a result of the High Court judgment, promises made by non-Catholics in regard to the religious upbringing of their children were binding, 'by reason of the clause in the 1937 constitution that recognised the special position of the Catholic Church.'[34] In actual fact, the promises were binding because the Supreme Court decided that under Article 42.1 of the 1937 constitution *both* parents – not just the *father* – had the right to decide on the religious upbringing of their children.

The Tilson case constituted multiple factors and a variety of dimensions well beyond what was ventilated in the courtroom. Addressing historians and general readers alike, this book explores the case afresh in its social, cultural and theological contexts, examining its legal aspects and considering public and church reaction. By focusing on a mixed marriage, which took place in Dublin in 1941 between a Catholic and a Protestant from similar social backgrounds, this book examines issues such as the Catholic *Ne Temere* decree and the dispensation required for a mixed marriage; paternal supremacy and how fathers had the sole prerogative in determining the religious upbringing of their children; the Protestant Birds' Nest orphanage where Ernest placed his children; the hearings in the High Court and the Supreme Court; and finally, the fall-out from the Tilson case and how Ernest and Mary reconciled and lived out their days together as husband and wife.

The book also illuminates other matters of interest, such as how the High Court and Supreme Court used an incorrect age for Mary at the time of her marriage and how Ernest, while in Oldcastle, came to place his children in a Protestant orphanage, and who paid the legal costs of the case, given there was no free legal aid scheme at the time. All that said, the book has two central, inter-related aims: first, to interrogate the notion that there was collusion between church and state, or that outside influence was brought to bear in respect of the Tilson case's legal process. For decades, many Protestants, and many others, have harboured suspicions regarding how the case was dealt with in the courts; this book may confirm or, indeed,

Introduction

allay their suspicions. Second, the book shows how a domestic dispute, with multiple causes, was elevated to an event of national significance involving both churches, the state and wider society. When Ernest and Mary's quarrel reached courtroom level and received widespread newspaper coverage, the couple were relegated to the role of bit players; in turn, their dispute exposed many of Ireland's confessional fault lines and polarised the Catholic and Protestant communities over the matter.

Against the backdrop of historic tensions between Catholics and Protestants in Ireland, Chapter 1 surveys a number of mixed-marriage disputes that occurred during the twentieth century. These show that the Tilson case was far from an isolated event and underscore two of the key issues central to the case and, indeed, central to most mixed-marriage disputes: the baptism or the religious upbringing of the children, and objections to the marriage from family members or the wider community.

As noted, the Catholic pledge that Ernest signed before his marriage, agreeing to raise his children as Catholics, was a pivotal issue in the case. Chapter 2 examines why he was required to sign that pledge and why it was necessary for the Catholic Church to provide a dispensation for a couple of mixed religion intent on marriage. The chapter also offers a detailed analysis of the Catholic *Ne Temere* decree, which has been widely misunderstood and erroneously associated with the case. It is argued that the misinterpretation of the decree was initiated by the Church of Ireland clergyman Rev. J.A.F. Gregg (who would later become archbishop of Dublin and Armagh) and compounded by the reporting of the case in *The Irish Times*.

Ernest placed his three sons in the Protestant-run Birds' Nest orphanage in Dún Laoghaire in May 1950 to begin their Protestant education. They remained there for three months. He completed admission forms and these were countersigned by Rev. W.L.M. Giff of the Irish Church Missions. Chapter 3 offers a partial history of the Birds' Nest from its establishment in 1860 and also examines the role of the Irish Church Missions, responsible for the education of children in the orphanage. Close attention is also paid to Giff, who would play a central part in the court proceedings and indeed in the welfare of Ernest Tilson after the case.

Chapter 4 considers the case against its contemporary cultural and political contexts, addressing the strong Catholic ethos in mid-twentieth-century Ireland along with the church/state consensus. One of the most striking features of John A. Costello's interparty government, which was in power when the Tilson case came before the courts, was the intimate relationship it enjoyed with the Catholic Church. This chapter examines the

Catholic leanings of its members and argues that the interparty coalition was excessively deferential to the church. The 'Holy Year' of 1950 is also explored since this occasion captured the politico-religious *zeitgeist* when it brought together the hierarchy, politicians and the laity in a national celebration of Catholicism.[35]

Until the Tilson case, it remained the father's sole prerogative to determine the religious upbringing and education of his children, a convention known as 'paternal supremacy'. Ernest Tilson was, therefore, within his legal rights when he decided to raise his children as Protestants, even though they had been raised as Catholics for many of their formative years. Chapter 5 examines a series of cases concerned with the religious upbringing of children of mixed marriages which came before the Irish courts. These show that from the Meade case in 1870 to the Keenan case in 1949, Irish courts followed precedent and relied on civil law to uphold paternal supremacy, unless there was a danger to the welfare of the children. In light of this, it is suggested that Ernest Tilson and his legal team would have approached the High Court proceedings with a fair degree of confidence.

Following the removal of her children, Mary issued *habeas corpus* proceedings at the High Court to secure their return. The analysis of the Tilsons' sworn affidavits in Chapter 6 reveals a litany of claim and counterclaim consistent with marital breakdown. In the subsequent case heard by Mr Justice George Gavan Duffy, T.K. Liston SC, on behalf of Mary Tilson, argued that the governing concern was the welfare of the children, while W.H. Carson SC, for Ernest Tilson, relied on the principle of paternal supremacy and argued that the passing of the constitution did not affect the law pertaining to these matters as it stood before 1937.

Because the High Court judge George Gavan Duffy was a key player in the case Chapter 7 investigates his Catholic nationalist background, his career on the bench and his membership of the Catholic lay organisation An Ríoghacht. Although, as previously noted, historians have tended to focus on Gavan Duffy and his language used in the High Court, it is appropriate that this book also pays close attention to him. His ruling was ground-breaking, but had he decided to follow precedent and uphold the tradition of paternal supremacy, it is quite likely that that would have been the end of the matter. Or, to put it another way, given the fact that paternal supremacy was long established in law, it is unlikely that Gavan Duffy's decision would have been appealed had he ruled in favour of Ernest Tilson, the Protestant father.

Introduction

Chapter 8 provides a detailed account of Mr Justice Gavan Duffy's judgment, which has become the reference point for the Tilson case for many historians, despite the all-important Supreme Court appeal which followed. The judge argued that, although prenuptial agreements of this kind had previously been unenforceable, Articles 41, 42 and 44 of the 1937 constitution had placed them in a new setting and altered their status. Archbishop McQuaid appeared to be in a celebratory mood after judgment was delivered, and the revealing letter he sent to Cardinal Marchetti-Selvaggiani in the Vatican is also examined in this chapter. In the Supreme Court appeal hearing that followed, that court relied entirely on Article 42.1 of the 1937 constitution, but in Chapter 9 it is argued that the legacy of the case was more complex than this suggests: the attorney general, Charles Casey, appeared, perhaps inappropriately, for Mary Tilson during the appeal and the court hearing also raised the possibility that Catholics might have constitutional privilege over people of other religious denominations.[36]

The outcome of the case was hotly debated in the months after the court hearings: Chapter 10 explores the widespread press coverage of the case and its discussion in Catholic and Protestant publications such as *The Standard*, *The Catholic Bulletin*, *Fiat* and the *Church of Ireland Gazette*. Correspondence published in *The Irish Times* also illustrates the divergent Protestant and Catholic reactions to the case. The court rulings were also 'weaponised' in debates at the time over the partition of Ireland. In addition, this chapter deals with the many letters Mary received from people throughout Ireland after the Supreme Court case. These were sent by Irish mothers who felt duty-bound to support a fellow Catholic mother and to advocate the power of prayer, the rosary or Our Lady. The final chapter follows the lives and reconciliation of Ernest and Mary after the court hearings up to their deaths in the 1990s. The Conclusion suggests two endings to this story: the courts reached progressive decisions when they dispensed with the tradition of paternal supremacy, and thereby drew attention to the rights of women already enshrined in the 1937 constitution; however, it was the way in which the state went about making those decisions that causes concern.

It would be remiss not to refer to the Fethard-on-Sea boycott, which occurred seven years after the Tilson case in 1957 and which has been a fixation for many historians and laypeople to the present day. Briefly, the boycott – which exposed many of the same societal and confessional divisions as the Tilson case – arose after Sheila Cloney, a Protestant woman married to a Catholic man, left home with her two daughters rather than having to raise them as Catholics. Catholic Church condemnation of her actions resulted in a Catholic boycott of local Protestant businesses in the County Wexford village, which amounted to a localised episode of confessional antagonism in a rural community, which had approval at local church and episcopal level. The Tilson case (which, as noted, also resulted in a boycott of Protestant businesses) had a similar repudiated agreement at its core but it had other complexities. It involved legal proceedings in the High Court and Supreme Court, which implicated the state in the matter; it was also interpreted by many as a battle at national level between the Catholic and Protestant Churches. The nature and the outcome of the court proceedings raised awkward questions about the impartiality of Catholic judges at the time and suggest that the Catholic Church exerted undue influence on the workings of the state.

PART 1

The Background: Social, theological, political

CHAPTER 1

Historical Antecedents: Mixed-marriage disputes in Ireland

Mixed marriages have long been a vexed issue in Ireland. Although they have been frowned upon by both Christian traditions, in Ireland church condemnation of them is coupled with a troubled historical backdrop. Conquest and colonisation and the English Reformation established religion as a political identity whereby Protestantism became associated with a colonising alien force, and Catholicism became a symbol of dispossession. The problems surrounding mixed marriages in Ireland, therefore, stem not only from theological objections, but also from perceived political affiliations and from social prescriptions. Indeed, because these matters in Ireland are, more often than not, inextricably bound up together, mixed marriages often concurrently transgress religious, social and political lines.

The marriage of Belfast solicitor Pat Finucane, who was murdered at his home by loyalist paramilitaries in 1989, offers one such example, but also shows that not all mixed marriages end in disharmony. His son John, Sinn Féin MP for Belfast North, has described how his mother, Geraldine Mawhinney, a middle-class east Belfast Protestant, began a relationship with his father, a working-class Catholic nationalist from west Belfast, at a time when the Troubles were developing into full-blown sectarian warfare. The couple attended Trinity College Dublin in the early 1970s and met during a first-year arts course. As Justine McCarthy has observed, 'for Pat Finucane, the son of Belfast nationalists, growing up with two brothers destined to join the IRA and go to jail (one of them romantically involved with Mairead Farrell at the time she was shot dead by the SAS in Gibraltar in 1988), Trinity was less familiar territory'.[1] In any event, Trinity provided the couple with a space free of sectarian enmity, which allowed their relationship to flourish; had the couple remained in febrile Northern Ireland during the 1970s, their marriage would probably never have taken place, as Finucane implies: 'Trinity was a world away from Belfast in the 1970s. That had a lot to do with my parents' ... happy marriage.'[2]

This chapter examines a number of mixed marriage or interfaith relationship disputes, which occurred in Ireland during the twentieth century and show that while Mary and Ernest's quarrel was unique in that it ended up being played out in the High Court and Supreme Court, it was far from *sui generis*. Before looking at the 'lived experience' of these disputes, it is necessary to consider in more detail how mixed marriages transgress religious, social and political boundaries.

THE MIXED MARRIAGE AS A RELIGIOUS TRANSGRESSION

The Tilson marriage and its subsequent public scrutiny took place at a time when both Catholic and Protestant Churches strongly discouraged mixed marriages, and when the Catholic Church held and exercised significant social and political power in Ireland.[3] Catholic Church objections to mixed marriages are primarily grounded in the belief that marriage is a sacrament and that a marriage between a Catholic and a non-Catholic debases that sacrament. The *Catholic Encyclopedia* explains: 'As Christ raised wedlock to the dignity of a Sacrament, a marriage between a Catholic and a non-Catholic was rightly looked upon as degrading the holy character of matrimony.'[4] Until the second Vatican Council of 1962–5, the church insisted that mixed marriages be held in an 'unconsecrated building without religious celebration', indicating its profound hostility to them.[5]

We must assume, therefore, that the marriage of Ernest Tilson and Mary Barnes took place in the sacristy; that the priest was there solely as a witness; that he wore no vestments and that he did not celebrate mass or bless the couple. Their marriage would have been – to borrow Louise Fuller's terminology – 'a second-class affair'.[6] Preaching in St Saviour's church, Dublin in 1937, Rev. Louis Ryan left his congregation in no doubt regarding the church's position. 'Evil' is a strong term and it is noteworthy that many Catholic and Protestant clerics have insisted on using it when referring to these unions:

> Many of the children of the Church received a dispensation, but when it was granted the Church did not conceal her displeasure. It was symbolised in the gloom with which she surrounded such a union. The contracting parties were not allowed to marry in the church, not even in the sacristy. The Holy Sacrifice was not offered, no candle burned as an emblem of faith, and the priest was divested of every insignia of his sacred office. The evils of mixed marriage were too great, too fearful for words to express.[7]

Historical Antecedents: Mixed-marriage disputes in Ireland

On 21 June 1941 – just six months before the Tilson marriage took place – the *Strabane Chronicle* reported on a confirmation ceremony in Belfast, at which the Irish Catholic prelate, His Lordship Most Rev. Dr Mageean, also issued a stern warning against the 'evil' of mixed marriages:

> In certain dioceses of Ireland the evil of mixed marriages was unknown ... The mind of the Church was opposed to mixed company and mixed marriages, which were a source of sin and scandal, endangering the faith of the Catholic party and bartering that of the unborn children.[8]

The 1940s and '50s were decades of 'vigilance and fortress Catholicism'[9] and the Catholic Church often publicly denounced mixed marriages through the medium of the 'Lenten pastoral'. Again using the term 'evil', the Most Rev. Dr Morrisroe, bishop of Achonry, declared in 1941 – the year of the Tilson marriage – that 'Catholics are forbidden to marry those of an alien faith, because such unions lead to evil associations, as well as endangering the happiness of the domestic hearth'.[10] Archbishop McQuaid was particularly opposed to mixed marriages and declared in a 1944 Lenten pastoral that 'Stress is laid on the severity with which the Church prohibits mixed marriages'.[11] More covertly, an internal Catholic Church document records his unambiguous instructions to his clerics: 'The clergy will ... in accordance with the mind of the Church, exercise a particular vigilance in this matter. They will instruct the faithful concerning the dangers of mixed marriages, and strive, in all prudence and clarity, to ensure that Catholics marry Catholics.'[12]

Along similar lines, the 1950s class notes of Monsignor Frank Cremin left seminarians training for the priesthood at St Patrick's College, Maynooth in no doubt regarding the church's attitude to mixed marriages:

> The many evils arising from a mixed marriage are described in Arcanum and Casti Connubii. The difference of religion indangers [*sic*] the faith of the Catholic party and the Christian education of the children and, occasioning unlawful communicato in divinis, it tends to create religious indifference and it produces defections from the Church ... As long as there is proximate danger of perversion for the Catholic party <u>or</u> for the children, a mixed marriage is forbidden by divine law itself, and the Church cannot allow the marriage.[13]

On the question of Catholic Church objections to such unions, Owen Dudley Edwards argues that:

> What was involved here was the proclamation of religious apartheid. It was part of a world-wide policy on the part of the Roman Catholic authorities, but it was imposed most stringently in Ireland or by Irish clerics abroad ... the outlawry of mixed marriages, then, was a social matter of critical significance in the building of the religious ghetto walls.[14]

These are strong terms and provocative analogies, but, as noted, these marriages were also discouraged by the Protestant Churches. Two years after the Tilson marriage, in 1943, *The Irish Times* reported the views of the Rev. J.C. Robb, who was speaking at a youth conference in Dublin:

> Mr. Robb said he did not preach against mixed marriages because of any bitterness against the Catholic Church; but [he argued that] the two faiths were so different and so irreconcilable, and the Catholic preaching was so distinct and so hard, that it was impossible for a Protestant to marry a Roman Catholic and have a lasting happy marriage.[15]

Donald Akenson has accordingly taken issue with Dudley Edwards' use of the word 'apartheid' and has argued that it was not a matter of one group attempting 'to keep itself pure of contamination' from another group, but more accurate to think of it 'as [Catholics and Protestants in Ireland] having developed mutually acceptable boundary maintenance systems'.[16]

Although the Protestant Churches had no parallel legislation or body of canon law governing mixed marriages, they did have theological objections, which were rooted in their opposition to 'the teachings and the practices of the Catholic Church'.[17] These objections were also grounded in the belief that the faith of the children could be compromised in a marriage comprised of parents of different religions. As the Rev. J.A.F. Gregg explained in 1946, 'the disadvantage of mixed marriages was that they divided the family in its most sacred concerns'.[18] The Protestant Churches were also strongly opposed to the Catholic Church's insistence that any children born of them had to be raised as Catholics; it followed that these marriages were a threat to the survival of the Protestant community. In practice, if the only son of a Protestant family married a Catholic and all his children were raised as Catholics, within a few generations that Protestant family line faced extinction. Gregg again argued: 'We need all our young people to replenish our ranks as we older people pass away; the Church which cannot count on a stronger younger generation is doomed to early extinction.'[19]

THE MIXED MARRIAGE AS A SOCIAL TRANSGRESSION

Marriages between members of Protestant and Catholic communities were made more difficult because those who entered these relationships often transgressed social prescriptions. It is hardly surprising that when they did occur, they sometimes led to friction and animosity, not only between the parties in the relationships but also between families and members of their respective communities. In fact, historian Margaret MacCurtain has described the difficulties surrounding mixed marriages in Ireland in the past as a form of 'warfare' or a 'pitched battle'.[20]

Social networks or structures created an environment in Ireland, and elsewhere, where people were more inclined to enter endogamous relationships, marrying *within* their own community. Since social interaction between Catholics and Protestants was very limited, or even non-existent, people were much less inclined to enter exogamous relationships – that is, marrying *outside* of their community. Joseph Ruane has stated more frankly that 'a key function of exclusive social networks was the prevention of intermarriage'.[21] Catholics went to Catholic schools and were educated by Catholic teachers. Protestants followed similar patterns. In these environments, students tended to encounter only those exposed to interpretations or versions of history that were harmonious with their groups' particular dispositions. In the field of sport, Protestants tended to play rugby, hockey and cricket, while Catholics were more inclined to play hurling or Gaelic football.[22] Social events such as dances were also confessionalised; Catholics attended the disco in the local GAA club while Protestants went to the 'hop' in the tennis or hockey club. Exclusive social networks were also evident in the home, which was sometimes a 'tightly guarded realm'.[23] In his comparative study of Catholic–Protestant conflicts in France and Ireland, Joseph Ruane has argued that the day a Catholic entered a Protestant home was often identified as a day of significance in the history of the family; if it resulted in a mixed marriage, that 'meant a rupture in family relationships or the permanent presence of members of the other religion within the family circle'.[24]

Bitterness or hostility might also be expressed by the local priest or minister or by friends or neighbours, often because these people had vested interests: when the couple intermarried, they undermined the religious and cultural boundaries that had been created and maintained by their own grouping.[25] As a result of this breach, each grouping might feel more vulnerable, diminished or, as Mary Douglas has suggested, feel that 'a pollution [in the community] might have occurred'.[26] The consequence of the marriage invariably meant that the demarcation lines between both communities became more sharply drawn.

The notion that a mixed marriage created an impurity is registered in W.B. Yeats' *Purgatory* (1938). In the play, the Anglo-Irish lady of the 'big house', who is clearly a Protestant, transgresses religious as well as class boundaries when she marries a drunken Catholic stable lad. Her irresponsible deed not only sees the ruin of the cultural and aristocratic house but also gives rise to the pollution of a dynasty. After watching the ghosts of his parents re-enacting the events of their wedding night, the Old Man attempts to arrest the possibility of contamination of future generations by killing his own son with the same blade he used to kill his father. The final scene of the play, however, indicates that his nefarious deed has been unsuccessful; the haunting hoofbeats suggest that the sinners will remain in their purgatorial condition and that the Anglo-Irish caste has indeed been contaminated. Roy Foster has observed that in his first draft of the play, Yeats 'specifically suggested that [the stable lad] was a Catholic, highlighting the ascendancy fear of decay through mixed marriage'.[27]

THE MIXED MARRIAGE AS A POLITICAL TRANSGRESSION

The political divide between Catholics and Protestants in Ireland can be traced primarily to the Reformation and to the sixteenth- and seventeenth-century period of conquest and colonisation. The Reformation divided Christians into Catholics and Protestants and was largely responsible for breeding the fundamental religious bitterness that fuelled tensions between both groups.[28] Protestants saw Catholics as steeped in superstition and 'kept ignorant of the word of God by a despotic and intolerant clergy and papacy', while Catholics saw 'all strands of Protestantism [as] heresies from the One True Church'.[29] Meanwhile, conquest and colonisation in Ireland created an enduring distinction between 'settlers' and 'natives', which in turn was bound up with religion; 'settlers' were generally identified as Protestant, and 'natives' identified as Catholic. The division of Ireland into two separate and mutually antagonistic Protestant and Catholic communities came about in the mid-nineteenth century.[30] In part, this was due to historical events, but it was the campaign for emancipation and the repeal of the union on the Catholic side, and Orangeism, evangelicalism and the defence of the union on the Protestant side which finally established two distinct communities with robust political identities.

The notion of a personal relationship between a Catholic and a Protestant transgressing political lines has often been depicted in Irish fiction. Set during the War of Independence, Peadar O'Donnell's novel *The Knife* (1930) opens in a planter district in Ulster as the Catholic nationalist Godfrey Dhu's family has just acquired some Protestant land, using money inherited from a relative in Australia. The narrator states that 'it was part of the Orangemen's religion that the possession of soil must remain solid',[31] establishing a conflict between planter and native over which the eventually successful interfaith relationship in the novel is designed to prevail.

The Catholic protagonist Knife and his sister Nuala become heavily involved in armed resistance to British rule. Nuala is a stereotypical red-haired Irish rebel who sings Fenian songs, loves Ireland and hates Britain in equal measure, and who is courted by both Catholic James Burns and Protestant Sam Rowan. Even though the narrator warns that 'mixed seed means a mixed crop',[32] ultimately Nuala rejects the determined advances of Burns and settles on Rowan. The novel concludes with Rowan freeing Knife from jail, where he had been imprisoned by Free State forces during the Civil War. This act of political co-operation mirrors the successful interfaith relationship between Nuala and Rowan, as strife between Protestants and Catholics in the opening pages of the novel is replaced by harmony and co-operation between both communities by the novel's end. Moreover, the fact that Catholic and Protestant insurgents work together towards this conclusion suggests an optimism on O'Donnell's part in the possibility of a unified offensive against Britain.

At a national level, a series of political events that occurred between the sixteenth and twentieth centuries polarised the Protestant and Catholic communities and provided an impetus for violent conflict. These include the Desmond Rebellion of 1579, which was fought along distinct sectarian lines; the Ulster plantation in the early seventeenth century, which saw Catholic 'natives' lose their lands to Protestant 'settlers'; during the Ulster Rebellion of 1641, Catholics savagely avenged the perceived wrongs committed against them by Protestants; the arrival of Cromwell in Ireland in 1649 on a revenge mission, which became emblematic of the suppression and dispossession of Catholics; the Battle of the Boyne in 1690, which saw Protestant William III defeat the deposed Catholic monarch James II; the penal laws introduced during the seventeenth and eighteenth centuries, which were designed to eradicate the Catholic religion in Ireland and, significantly, included a law banning intermarriage between Protestants and Catholics; the 1798 Rebellion which, though not intended by its architects, ultimately became associated with violent sectarianism; the bitter and divisive nineteenth-century campaigns for tenant rights and home rule; and in the early twentieth century, the War of Independence (1919–21) and the Civil War (1922–23).[33]

But these were national political events, many of which have become part of Catholic and Protestant folklore. A less documented locus of conflict has been the issue of mixed marriages. In fact, these often-troubled unions are equally valid as registers of conflict between Catholics and Protestants in Ireland.

THE DISPUTES

The mixed-marriage or interfaith relationship dispute cases examined in this chapter were sourced from local and national newspapers, and reportage both reflects attitudes to mixed marriages and draws the reader's attention to Ireland's confessional division: the term 'mixed marriage' – often used in the article headline and then prodigiously throughout the text – is applied as a term of opprobrium, while the protagonists in the disputes are always labelled as either 'Catholic' or 'Protestant', embedding the notion that everybody belongs to one community or the other. All the cases were controversial, and some were sensational, and the reader may have been left to wonder what compelled the protagonists to cross religious, political or cultural boundaries in the first place. The accounts may also have been presented or interpreted as 'cautionary tales'; the Catholic or Protestant reader might well have put down the newspaper with a sense of relief, and thought *Thank God that wasn't me*.

The specific issues that have engendered most hostility between couples in mixed marriages have been the baptism or religious upbringing of the children of the marriage and objections to the unions by family, friends or members of the wider community. Some qualification is necessary, however. It is often the case that the issue of the baptism or the religious upbringing of children is at the foreground of a dispute, when, in fact, this obscures or conceals the real cause. Couples may have been experiencing marital discontent for multiple reasons, but the touchpaper for the falling out is the baptism or religious upbringing of their children. Some qualification is also necessary regarding objections to these unions by family, friends or the wider community. Again, censure might be related to the religious upbringing of children, but it could also be rooted in other factors, such

Historical Antecedents: Mixed-marriage disputes in Ireland

as sectarianism, history, politics, social class or landownership. Indeed, a family's or community's disapproval of a mixed marriage might be based on the interaction of a number of these factors.

THE RELIGIOUS UPBRINGING OF THE CHILDREN AS THE CAUSE OF THE DISPUTE – OR PERHAPS NOT?

In 1931 a Belfast court heard how a dispute arose between Sarah Jordan, a Protestant, and her Catholic husband, Henry Jordan. Sarah left her husband and sued him for maintenance. The couple had married at St Aidan's Protestant church in Belfast and had agreed before their marriage that any children would be raised in the Protestant faith. However, shortly after their first child was born and as Sarah was about to go out for a walk with the baby, her husband barred the door and refused to allow her to leave. Reflecting on the way in which the application of the Catholic *Ne Temere* decree supposedly validated all marriages involving Catholics, a Catholic priest arrived and, together with Henry, attempted to convince Sarah that her marriage was invalid and her child illegitimate because her marriage had not been celebrated in a Catholic church before a priest and two witnesses. The priest further explained to Sarah that her marriage could be validated in the eyes of the Catholic Church and her husband forgiven for living in sin if the couple would agree to remarry in a Catholic church. He also explained that the couple had an obligation to raise their children as Catholics. Further inflaming the familial discord, Henry's brother, who was sharing a bedroom with the couple, had apparently insisted on raising 'sectarian questions in the *bedroom*'.[34]

The judge was forthright in his views. He stated that he was not going to concern himself with the laws of the churches vis-à-vis marriages because 'in the eyes of the law of the land the parties were man and wife'. Moreover, he contended that 'nobody had the power to order Sarah Jordan to be remarried in the Roman Catholic Church'. He did take the view, however, that a ready solution to the dispute might be found in the ejection of Henry's brother from the family home. Explaining that 'the cause of the whole trouble was the defendant's brother living in the same house and, if he cleared out, the parties would get on well together', the judge adjourned the case for one month in the hope that a settlement might be reached.[35]

This case shows the imposition of the *Ne Temere* decree, as the Catholic priest impresses on the Protestant party the need to marry before a priest and two witnesses to guarantee the validity of the marriage. It also prefigures the Tilson case in arising from the religious upbringing of the children, but involving a range of other factors such as maintenance payments, family objections to the marriage, and living conditions. In fact, the judge's claim regarding Henry Jordan's brother anticipates Alan Tilson's assertion about his parents' marriage: 'if they had a house of their own [as opposed to the shared accommodation at Turner's Cottages] things might have worked out a lot differently'.[36]

Twenty years earlier in 1911, a dispute involving the religious upbringing of children in the village of Kilmurry, County Cork, became even more fraught, involving grave robbery and kidnap. Jonathan Shorten, a Protestant who had married a Catholic, Mary Brady, some years previously, suffered sectarian attacks when he refused to raise their children as Catholics, in accordance with Catholic teaching. A report in the London *Daily Express* observed that 'Mr. Shorten's persecution had been the outcome of a marriage',[37] while the *Southern Star* provided an account of the type of community-led sectarianism that arose out of the issue: 'Jonathan Shorten was engaged in turning in his cattle when a fusillade of stones was fired at him from the roadside and caused a stampede amongst his cattle.'[38] One local man was charged with throwing stones at Shorten and was taken to court, and, giving evidence, a Detective Inspector Walsh warned with masterful understatement that 'you had better keep away from that dangerous subject. Religious matters in Ireland have caused a lot of trouble in the country.'[39]

Events took a bizarre twist when one of the Shorten children, a boy aged six or seven, died unexpectedly. Since the local undertaker did not have a suitable coffin, Shorten walked the forty or so miles to Cork city in order to purchase one. When he returned home some days later, he discovered that his wife had interred their son in the Catholic graveyard in Kilmurry. Under the cover of darkness and unbeknownst to his wife, Shorten then exhumed his son's remains by lamplight and reinterred them in the Protestant graveyard at Kilbohane, after which he 'placed the empty coffin in the grave from which he had transferred his child'.[40]

Shorten's stratagem was revealed after the death of his wife two years later; as her grave was being dug, the same undertaker discovered that her son's corpse was missing. This scandal, added to the knowledge that Shorten's children were being educated at Kilmurry Protestant school against their mother's wishes, led to what was described in *The Irish Times* as a 'reign of terror' against Jonathan Shorten, culminating in the 'mysterious abduction' of his two eldest children, Sophia and Flossie.[41] When this was reported to the local police, the Catholic community, led by the parish priest, Rev. Canon O'Mahony, denied any involvement or wrongdoing. Rumours abounded that the children had been spirited away to the home of their maternal grandmother after Mary Brady's death. Shorten told a special correspondent of *The Irish Times*, who had been dispatched to establish the true facts, that his wife's family made 'the most determined efforts to induce the two eldest girls to forsake Protestantism'.[42]

O'Mahony was, by his own admission, 'entirely opposed to mixed marriages' and convened a special meeting to discuss the issue, at which he denounced Shorten by arguing that, even though he had supposedly converted to Catholicism before his marriage, he was merely 'masquerading as a Catholic' and had never attended mass or received the sacraments. O'Mahony did point out that Shorten's marriage was still valid in the eyes of the Catholic Church, however, and that Shorten had been overheard saying to his wife that 'I turned my coat with you, but I did not turn the lining of it'. Extraordinarily, the Census of Ireland for 1911, which was completed and signed by Jonathan Shorten on 2 April 1911, records his religion, and that of his wife and all his children (including Sophia and Flossie) as Church of Ireland;[43] although the family was divided, this entry shows that he wished them to be formally recorded as Protestant.

The canon then sought to link the issue to local unionist opposition to home rule, castigating both Shorten and those opposed to home rule in the same speech. O'Mahony claimed that recent desecration of the local Protestant church was a false flag operation carried out by unionists attempting to emphasise to members of the Eighty Club the dire possible consequences of home rule for Irish Protestants.[44] Responding to the allegation that members of the Catholic community had abducted the Shorten children and desecrated the church, O'Mahony told the meeting:

> All this system of calumny and slander has been used for the purpose of defeating Home Rule. Unionism has already a discreditable history in this country, and when the Irish people shall have obtained legislative independence, and when the history of the times shall be written, then it shall be held that in waging this last campaign against Irish rights, Unionism has sought to be advanced by the ignoble tactics of slander and misrepresentation (*cheers*).[45]

The meeting ended on a somewhat lighter note as Canon O'Mahony called to the platform Shorten's mother-in-law, Mrs Brady, to confirm to the audience that the children had not in fact been kidnapped: '"Did you abduct them?" the chairman asked. "I did," she replied. The Very Rev. Chairman – "You don't understand the meaning of the word."[46] The acrimony between the couple in this case seems to have begun with a religious conversion and then disagreement over the religious upbringing of the children. It rapidly worsened to involve a dispute over a burial place and the abduction of children, but also reflected the febrile political environment surrounding the campaign for home rule, and community-led sectarianism.

The baptism and religious upbringing of a baby of a mixed marriage was at the centre of another dispute the following year in Portadown, County Armagh. In 1912 the Protestant and Catholic communities of the town were divided by revelations at a sworn local government inquiry into a complaint of proselytism and ill-treatment by a patient against a staff nurse at Lurgan workhouse hospital.

Ellen Moore, the Catholic wife of Alexander Moore, a Protestant, was admitted to the maternity unit of the hospital and gave birth to a baby girl. She complained that, unbeknownst to her or her Protestant husband, and at the behest of a nurse, Margaret Hanrahan, her baby had been baptised by a priest into the Roman Catholic faith. It was alleged by other staff members at the hospital that Hanrahan was preoccupied or fixated with Moore's mixed marriage and with the notion of baptising Moore's baby into the Catholic Church. One nurse alleged that she found Moore in a distressed state and that Moore had told her that she 'wanted her baby to be brought up as a Protestant'. When this was brought to the attention of Hanrahan, she apparently replied that 'she was responsible for the child's soul'. The inquiry heard that, before the birth, Hanrahan was overheard saying to Moore: 'You must have this baby baptised a Catholic when it is born; no one will be the wiser of it.' Moore had been extremely reluctant to accede to Hanrahan's supplications; and the inquiry also heard that after Moore had requested medication, an outraged Hanrahan had responded: 'I would rather put you in a tar-barrel and roast you.'[47]

Apparently, Hanrahan then took the matter into her own hands. While Moore was under sedation, and as a Catholic priest was 'doing his rounds', Hanrahan allegedly approached him and advised that there was a 'baptism to be done'. He readily agreed, and after both had decided that 'Mary' was a suitable name, the baby was baptised in a corridor on a wooden box that the nurse had procured. When Ellen Moore awoke and discovered Hanrahan's ruse, she hid the card on which the baptism had been recorded beneath her pillow, 'because if her husband saw Roman Catholic on it, HE WOULD HAVE HER LIFE'.[48]

Three weeks later, after Moore and her baby were discharged from hospital, the baby was baptised in the local Protestant church by a Reverend Morrison, a Church of Ireland clergyman. However, the baby's previous Catholic baptism did come to light later, when Moore's horrified husband, a reservist in the British army, discovered it on a birth certificate, which he had sought in order to satisfy a condition of the British War Office. This case shows that the sacrament of baptism and the religious upbringing of a child could be a source of severe discord, and that people outside the family were prepared to interfere in these matters.

SOCIAL DISAPPROVAL OF MIXED MARRIAGES

When Joseph McKee, originally a Presbyterian, married Bertha McKee, a Catholic, in the border county of Monaghan on 6 October 1911, he incurred the wrath of his family and friends. The details of the marriage were eventually aired before the criminal and civil courts and the two cases generated 'an intense amount of feeling' within the local community, leading to 'an infuriated mob' (presumably Catholic) gathering outside the Protestant defendant's home.[49]

Shortly before his marriage, McKee, who was then nineteen and apprenticed to a drapery store in Castleblayney, 'took instruction in the Catholic religion and was received afterwards into the Roman Catholic Church'. The couple were married shortly afterwards, but on his return from their honeymoon McKee visited the home of two Protestant friends, Thomas Lunney and Robert Fleming, where he remained for six days, by all accounts consuming large quantities of whiskey. Interestingly, the Census of Ireland 1911 lists their occupations as 'tailor' and 'farmer' respectively and their religion as Church of Ireland. Criminal charges against them arose when Bertha McKee was physically assaulted and verbally abused by the two men as she attempted to reclaim her husband. The court heard how, when she entered the house where her husband was staying, in order to convince him to return with her, somebody apparently murmured 'pope' and 'popery'; Lunney then said that he 'would not let him [her husband] go home with a Papist'. He next attempted to eject Mrs McKee from the house, threatening that he 'would break her neck for a Papist [*sic*]'. Mrs McKee explained to the Castleblayney Petty Sessions Court on 21 November 1911 that she believed that Lunney and Fleming were in collusion with her father-in-law, and that the reason why her husband had stayed so long at the house of his Protestant friends was because Joseph McKee's parents did not wish him to return to her. After considerable argument, the charges against Lunney and Fleming were withdrawn on condition that the defendants would not interfere with the plaintiff in the future.[50]

The furore surrounding this marriage continued when Bertha McKee, through her father, later took a civil action at the Ballybot Quarter Sessions in Newry courthouse on 26 January 1912 against her father-in-law for causing her grievous bodily harm. The court was told that as the couple were leaving the court after the previous hearing, they had been approached by Joseph McKee's father and invited back to the home of his brother in Mucknow Street, Castleblayney. As the three arrived at the house, Mrs McKee was refused entry and a glass door was allegedly slammed in her face. Moments later, through a window, she saw her husband being forced by his father into a yard at the rear of the premises where a horse and trap were waiting. Gaining access through a side entrance, she found her husband seated in the trap while his father held the reins. As she attempted to mount the trap, she received 'a blow with a loaded butt of a whip' from her father-in-law. Undeterred, she 'managed to get her foot on the step of the trap', only to be thrown onto the street as the defendant 'whipped the horse out of the yard'. Both father and son then sped from the scene of the assault while Bertha McKee was left in 'a state of collapse'. The court heard how, shortly afterwards, Mrs McKee, hardly surprisingly, left for Scotland for 'a change of air and scene'.[51]

Giving evidence, the defendant denied that he had assaulted his daughter-in-law, adding that he 'regarded the whole thing as a very foolish marriage'. The solicitor for Bertha McKee observed that this might be 'because your son married a Catholic girl, which, I suppose, you considered a hundred thousand times worse than anything he could do'. The plaintiff's husband then argued that he had been 'dragged into the marriage' and that he had been quite willing to go with his father on the occasion in question. When asked why he no longer loved his wife, he replied simply that he had 'got tired of her' and 'was glad to get home again'. A court reporter outlined Mr Justice Cherry's irritation at his response: 'never in his life had he heard such language from the lips of anyone purporting to be a man. He blushed for the country which produced such a man. He did not think that even in a savage country could they get such an exhibition.' Cherry awarded Bertha McKee £10 damages, with three guineas for witnesses' expenses.[52]

Clearly Joseph's McKee's father had objections to his son's marriage to a Catholic. The case also demonstrates how a mixed-marriage dispute

Historical Antecedents: Mixed-marriage disputes in Ireland

could intensify to verbal and physical attacks and could involve not only the immediate family but also the wider Catholic community. Moreover, as in the Shorten case, a conversion to Catholicism took place before the marriage, but this was no guarantee of marital bliss.

Although the following dispute begs an exploration of the circumstances under which the mixed marriage took place in the first instance, it shows how objections to the faith of one partner could be registered by insisting on religious conversion. A meeting of the Clonmel Guardians in 1910 heard how James Harkins, a retired Protestant shopkeeper married to a Catholic, was admitted to Clonmel workhouse hospital earlier that year.[53] In accordance with the relevant section of Article 34 of the Workhouse Rules, his application to be seen by a Roman Catholic priest with a view to converting to Catholicism was granted. It seems that Father Wall, the priest who later visited him, had received a letter about six weeks previously from Harkins' son explaining that his father had an incurable disease. In the letter, his son proposed that 'in the event of his turning a Roman Catholic [sic] the family would be prepared to take him home'.[54] The meeting also heard that Harkins' wife had agreed to visit her husband at the workhouse hospital, provided he converted to Catholicism.

The master of the workhouse decided to inform Canon Leslie, a Protestant clergyman, of Harkins' intentions, who in turn informed another Protestant clergyman, Rev. Mr Burke. Burke then visited Harkins and reminded him of his previous arrangements for a Protestant burial and also of his desire to 'die in the Protestant faith'. In spite of Burke's protestations, Harkins was later visited by Father Wall and then 'turned Catholic'. Unfortunately, it appears that his conversion came too late to allow him to return home:

> O'MEARA: 'Were there any of the Harkins family present during his last moments?'
> MASTER: 'His wife was.'
> HON. MRS. DE LA POER: 'Is the man dead?' (*in surprise*)
> MASTER: 'Yes; he is burying today.'
> ALD. MORRISSEY: 'He won't turn anymore.' (*laughter*)
> MR O'RYAN: 'It is a matter of obeying the dictates of his conscience.'
> MR DOWER: 'He knows as much as the best of them now.' (*laughter*)[55]

The Harkins case appears to have arisen from the fact that, in a mixed marriage, the Catholic Church insisted that the Catholic party should seek the conversion of the non-Catholic. Moreover, this 'conversion' pledge was taken by the Catholic party *for life*. Not only did Harkins' son state that if his father converted, the family would take him home, but Harkins' wife also wished that he would convert. The Catholic Church's position on converting non-Catholics in mixed marriages was clearly and unequivocally expressed by Archbishop McQuaid in a series of Lenten pastorals in the 1940s, '50s and '60s: 'The Catholic party is obliged in conscience prudently to strive for the conversion of the non-Catholic party. These guarantees are solemn pledges very gravely binding in conscience. Once given, they may not ever be disregarded or set aside.'[56]

A mixed marriage was also at the centre of a dispute over a will in County Kildare in 1953. William Carter of Kilmeague, who was 'bitterly opposed to mixed marriages', had made a will in 1940 in which he left £200 to his daughter Elizabeth Florence, with the proviso that 'if any child of his became a Roman Catholic or married a Roman Catholic they should forfeit all benefit under it'.[57] Eleven years later he made another will in which he left all his estate to Elizabeth Florence without any proviso about religion or marriage. Carter died in 1952 and his other daughter, Mrs Anna Maria Hawkins, took an action in order to establish the primacy of the will of 1940 under which she was a beneficiary on the basis that Carter had not been of sound mind when he made the second will. She also argued that because her sister was in a relationship with a Roman Catholic and intending to convert to that faith, Elizabeth Florence should lose her bequest as per the proviso of her father's first will. The court was then told that some years before her father's death, Elizabeth Florence was known to be 'keeping company' with a Roman Catholic and had been ordered by her father to 'give the man up'. Senior counsel Ernest Wood put it to Elizabeth Florence: 'You knew perfectly well from 1940 that if you contracted a mixed marriage or changed your religion, you would incur his displeasure.' The case was subsequently settled outside court and details of the settlement were not disclosed.[58] The Carter case shows how some were prepared to impose financial sanctions on their own children if they entered mixed marriages. This, of course, might have had as much to do with their desire to keep property in Protestant hands as it had to do with religious matters.

All these cases involve couples who were prepared to defy church directives and social mores and cross religious, political or cultural lines – only for the marriage to end in acrimony or to be tarnished in some way. And such was the sense of enmity towards some of these unions that society often saw fit to exercise some degree of control over them. The cases outlined here also show that the Tilson case was far from an isolated event; in fact, the circumstances of Mary and Ernest's dispute were similar in some respects to many of the cases discussed. The religious upbringing of the children was central to many of these quarrels, but this should not be allowed to obscure other reasons for dissension, such as differences in social class, politics, religious conversion, burial place and wills. Moreover, the community-led confessional antagonism seen in the Shorten and McKee cases was also evident in Ernest Tilson's home town of Oldcastle, County Meath, in the aftermath of the court cases, where one resident described the town as 'torn up the middle'.[59]

Objections to mixed marriages by family members in some of these cases also reflect Annie Barnes' disapproval of her own daughter's marriage to a Protestant. When Mary Tilson became pregnant out of wedlock in 1941, it is fair to say that most parents in that situation in mid-twentieth-century Ireland would have encouraged their daughter to marry the father of the child. It says a great deal about the entrenched nature of religious positions that Annie Barnes would have preferred her daughter to become a single mother, rather than see her marry a Protestant.

Notwithstanding these disputes, for much of the twentieth century (Northern Ireland during the Troubles excepted) Catholics and Protestants lived side by side in relative harmony – albeit in parallel or separate communities. In her ground-breaking work *Prejudice and Tolerance in Ulster: A study of neighbours and 'strangers' in a border community* (1972), Rosemary Harris offers some useful sociological lenses through which this apparent paradox can be examined. In terms of two groups co-existing, but sharing an unease when faced with one another's presence, she argues that it is necessary to look as much at individuals as communal groups:

> In dealing with contacts between Protestants and Catholics we are dealing with that type of situation, found in certain racially and ethnically divided societies, in which members of different groups have close relationships whilst remaining essentially separate ... It seems to me that to understand this apparent paradox of intermingled yet separate populations it is essential to look closely at the patterns of interaction of individuals.[60]

In the same vein, historian Ian d'Alton has argued that Catholics and Protestants 'got along reasonably well' in southern Ireland post-independence, in part because 'they were separate ... [with] no [or fewer] opportunities for intercommunal clashes'.[61] D'Alton's argument is valid, and from the disputes examined it appears that the close relationship or co-existence to which he and Harris refer is heavily dependent on members of each community remaining within their respective groups. But the cases illuminate what can happen when Protestants and Catholics leave their circles, enter personal relationships and attempt to live under one roof. The mixed marriages then expose the inter-communal fault lines, as shown by the acrimony between the couple, their family or the wider community.

All that said, mixed marriages do not always end in failure and the disputes discussed offer only a window on Catholic–Protestant relations in twentieth-century Ireland.[62] While Roy Foster has argued that there were very few instances of local confessional disputes in Ireland, and that those such as the Fethard-on-Sea boycott were 'always instanced' and 'endlessly rehearsed', this author's research indicates that they were much more common than many have previously believed.[63] Moreover, Foster's assertion that 'when they did come up, they were sensitively circumnavigated by politicians' will be challenged later in this book when examining John A. Costello's interparty government, which was in power when the Tilson case came before the courts.

CHAPTER 2

Ne Temere, the 'Promises' and the Dispensation

For Ernest Tilson and Mary Barnes to marry, they had to obtain a dispensation from the Catholic Church; for that to be granted, they had to agree to raise any children of the marriage as Catholics, before writing out the agreement in their own hands and then signing it in the presence of two witnesses. Mary applied in writing to the parish of St Mary, Haddington Road, Dublin for a dispensation, but this was refused; 'later, she made a second application, and again [it] was refused'.[1] It is noteworthy that while the Catholic Church would have held Mary guilty of the mortal sin of fornication, since she was unmarried and pregnant, this clearly was not a reason for the church to expedite a dispensation. Ernest then took the 'unusual move' of seeking an interview with the parish priest, the Most Rev. Dr Wall, and in turn Father Brendan Harley, curate at St Mary's parish, was deputed to interview him. The priest was later to recall in his affidavit to the High Court that during the interview Ernest 'pressed his case very strongly ... intimated that he was taking instructions in the Catholic Faith' and gave him 'every assurance that he would do all in his power to safeguard the religion of Miss Barnes and to raise the children of the marriage as Catholics'.[2] 'Convinced of his sincerity', the priest 'recommended that the application for the dispensation be allowed'. To this end, two weeks before his marriage and before witnesses, Father Harley and Father Cornelius Skehan, Ernest wrote out and signed a promise that he would baptise and educate any children of the marriage as Catholics: as a result, a dispensation was eventually granted in November 1941.

Many Protestants at the time of the court hearings in 1950 incorrectly associated the dispensation and the promises with the Catholic *Ne Temere* decree promulgated by Pope Pius X in 1907, which came into effect on Easter Sunday 1908. Many historians of the period have likewise misinterpreted the decree, and some others, as noted in the Introduction to this book, have improperly associated it with the Tilson case. This chapter will dispel the myths surrounding *Ne Temere*, in particular the widely repeated misinterpretation regarding the religious upbringing of children. It is argued that while the misunderstanding of the decree can be traced back to a widely publicised speech by Rev. J.A.F. Gregg in Cork in 1911, *The Irish Times* was largely responsible for misrepresentations of the decree in the aftermath of the Tilson case.

The Catholic decree *Ne Temere* had not featured during the Tilson court hearings, but it became a key driver of the Protestant animus at the time. For many, the Tilson case offered hard evidence that this infamous decree was not only a brazen encroachment on Protestant religious freedom, but was also largely responsible for the decline in Protestant numbers in the southern state since the first half of the twentieth century.[3] Much of the extensive newspaper coverage of the trial, particularly in *The Irish Times*, which then had a distinctively Protestant orientation, demonstrates an almost instinctive tendency to associate mixed marriages with the decree. Immediately after the High Court judgment of 27 July 1950, an editorial in the newspaper voiced serious misgivings about the decision and warned that 'issues of weighty and far-reaching moment have been raised by the judgment delivered by the President of the High Court in the Tilson case'.[4] Even though *Ne Temere* was not relevant to the judgment and was not mentioned during the proceedings, the headline over the editorial read solely 'Ne Temere'. In the months following the court decisions, the same newspaper was inundated with letters from readers addressing those judgments. On 17 August five letters were published under the strapline 'Ne Temere', but only one was concerned with the actual decree.[5] In a letter to the *Irish Independent*, the attorney general, Charles Casey, who, as noted, had earlier represented Mary Tilson in the Supreme Court, expressed his irritation with this tendency and directed some of his ire in humorous fashion at the Protestant editor of *The Irish Times*, R.M. Smyllie:

> After the decision of the Supreme Court in the Tilson case ... the *Irish Times* featured for many weeks the views of readers of that decision. That correspondence was very incautiously and irreverently published under the title 'Ne Temere'. The merest neophyte could have informed the Editor that the subject-matter of the Ne Temere Decree has as much to do with the Tilson case as Mr. Smyllie's golf handicap.[6]

Ne Temere has endured in Ireland as a lightning rod for Protestant anger into the twenty-first century.[7] This is remarkable, considering that the decree itself ceased to exist after 1917, when it was subsumed into the *Code of Canon Law*. Over the decades since, the decree has consistently been misinterpreted by commentators and by several historians of the period. In *A History of Ulster* (1992), Jonathan Bardon incorrectly states that 'the *Ne Temere* decree of 1907 laid down that Catholics marrying Protestants must bring up their children as Catholics', while Claire Mitchell similarly claims in her 2006 study of religious identity in Northern Ireland that the decree required the children of a mixed marriage to be brought up as Catholics.[8] In a 2001 essay on the Protestant Church's opposition to home rule, Alan Megahey likewise declares that the decree 'laid down regulations regarding the bringing up of children of any such [mixed] marriage in the Catholic faith'.[9] The misapprehension has also influenced literary criticism: in *Inventing Ireland* (1995), Declan Kiberd observes that the 'Catholic Church's *Ne Temere* decree ... forbids the children of mixed marriages to be raised as Protestants'.[10]

Since *Ne Temere* came into effect in 1908, any discussion of the decree must take account of the tempestuous campaign surrounding the third home rule bill. The greatest resistance to home rule was found in Ulster, where unionists and loyalists were prepared both to wage war against nationalists and to take on the might of the British state, so implacable was their opposition to even a limited form of self-government. A close reading of the third home rule bill, officially known as the Government of Ireland Act 1914, shows that only limited autonomy from Britain was being proposed. The dramatic and visceral responses of unionists and loyalists may seem disproportionate, but the historian Thomas Bartlett suggests that 'the very term Home Rule ... was deemed by the vast majority of Ulster Protestants to be quite simply an engine for their destruction that must be resisted at any price'.[11] F.S.L. Lyons noted in 1979 that the confrontation had its roots in conflicting views of life founded upon religion, since in Northern Ireland religion was considered a vital determinant of everything important in the human condition.[12] If *Ne Temere* appeared to pose a direct threat to religious liberty and freedom, it is hardly surprising that the decree became central to the anti-home rule discourse. The decree itself was concerned with the validity of all marriages involving Catholics, but many unionists at the time skilfully exploited it for political gain, using it as a working example of what life might be like in a state dominated by the Catholic Church.

In order to understand the *Ne Temere* decree, we must return to its forerunner, the Council of Trent's *Tametsi* decree of 1563. The primary purpose of *Tametsi* was to resolve the problem of clandestine marriages by insisting that all Catholics should marry before a priest and two witnesses. *Tametsi* was not uniformly promulgated, however; although it was speedily implemented in Spain and Portugal, in some Protestant countries it was not introduced or only on a piecemeal basis. In Ireland it was introduced in the ecclesiastical province of Tuam in 1568 but not in the province of Cashel until 1775. As a consequence, an interdenominational couple who wanted a valid marriage and who did not want to get married before a priest and two witnesses could simply get married in a province where the decree had not been promulgated. To provide some degree of uniformity and, perhaps more importantly, to avoid conflict with the civil authorities in Protestant countries, in 1740 Pope Benedict XIV ruled that in the Netherlands the presence of a Catholic priest was not required for the validity of a mixed marriage.[13] In relation to Ireland, this declaration was reaffirmed by Pius VI in 1785 and again in 1887 by Leo XIII in a reply to the archbishop of Dublin.[14]

Ne Temere was, like *Tametsi*, concerned with the *validity* of marriages involving Catholics. Foregrounding the challenges facing couples entering into mixed marriages in early-twentieth-century Ireland, Catholic writer Gerald O'Donovan offers a stinging critique of *Ne Temere* and the idea of validity in his 1914 novel *Waiting*. Here, a Catholic fire-and-brimstone preacher, Father Benignus, outlines the church's interpretation of the decree:

> You see how this beautiful Ne temere decree simplifies matters. A marriage of Catholic, say, with a Protestant in a register office, that used to be a valid marriage, though it was always damnable, *is no longer valid* ... every Catholic man married to a Protestant woman in a register office is no more married in the sight of God than the cats prowling round the streets at night.[15]

In practice, *Ne Temere* removed the exemption enjoyed by those in mixed marriages from the canonical form granted by Benedict XIV and reaffirmed the requirement set out in *Tametsi* that all marriages involving Catholics should take place before a priest and two witnesses. Extraordinarily, considering the aforementioned assertions by certain historians and other commentators, and the fact that so much energy has been expended over the issue, there is no mention in the decree of the religious upbringing of children as Catholics or as adherents of any other faith. In fact, mixed marriages are mentioned in only one paragraph:

XI. (2) The same laws are binding also on all Catholics, as above, if they contract betrothal or marriage with non-Catholics, baptised or unbaptised, – even after a dispensation has been obtained from the impediment of *mixtae religionis* or *disparitatis cultus*, – unless it may have been otherwise decreed by the Holy See for any particular place or country.[16]

Notwithstanding the various misinterpretations cited above, *Ne Temere* in imposition was clearly a blunt instrument and Protestants had just cause to be concerned. Implicit in the clause above is the requirement that a Protestant entering a mixed marriage with a Catholic must adhere to Catholic teachings. Historically, Protestant anger at the decree has been largely directed towards the issue of the religious upbringing of children; it was this paragraph that should have caused most concern, however, since it can be interpreted as the Catholic Church legislating on their behalf.

Although, as noted, *Ne Temere* ceased as a decree in its own right in 1917, it remained prominent in Protestant minds.[17] An indication of its persistent ability to rouse Protestant ire may be found in the *Church of Ireland Gazette* of 25 March 1965, nearly sixty years after the decree had been promulgated, when one writer argued that: 'The *Ne Temere* decree stands as an absolute barrier to the fellowship and the social intercourse that, in our view, must be the precursors of any kind of more formal unity.'[18]

Ne Temere had other implications that were hardly intended by its architects. Because its promulgation coincided with the campaign for the third home rule bill, it gained political traction that might otherwise have been avoided. When tensions in Belfast were running high over the prospect of self-government in 1910, Rev. William Corkey, minister of Townsend Street Presbyterian church, brought to public attention a case in which the validity of the marriage of Alexander McCann, a Catholic, to Agnes McCann, a Protestant, was called into question because it had not been celebrated in accordance with the canonical form established by *Ne Temere*. Apparently, the pressure being exerted on the couple by the local parish priest to remarry in a Catholic church caused Alexander McCann to leave the family home with his children against his wife's wishes. *The Irish Times* argued with some force that Agnes McCann had lost her home, her clothing and her children specifically because her marriage did not conform to the recently promulgated Catholic dogma.[19] Indeed, just after the Tilson court judgments in 1950, a correspondent to the *Church of Ireland Gazette* observed: '... the McCann case of forty years ago was a warning that largely went unheeded. The Tilson case is not merely a warning, but a practical demonstration that the Church of Rome is in earnest about making her canon law supreme here.'[20]

The McCann case was elevated from the domestic realm to the national political stage; indeed, as Andrew Scholes observes, 'it was not until the McCann case of November 1910 that *Ne Temere* became a prominent issue in Irish politics'.[21] J.H. Campbell, Unionist MP for the Dublin University constituency, first raised the issue in the British House of Commons in February 1911, repeating Agnes McCann's claim that she had enjoyed a happy marriage until 'a Roman Catholic priest interposed and informed her that her marriage was illegal'.[22] He also drew attention to the recently promulgated *Ne Temere* decree, and the fact that, as he understood it, the Roman Catholic Church had the right to declare illegal *any* marriage not celebrated in accordance with Catholic guidelines. Campbell concluded his contribution to the debate by affirming that the case strengthened the resolve of Protestant unionists and loyalists to retain their religious and civil freedom under an imperial parliament.[23] In the House of Lords, the earl of Donoughmore adopted a similar line of reasoning on 7 February 1911, arguing that *Ne Temere* was an attempt by the Catholic Church to assert its right to legislate for its own people. In his view, this raised the spectre of Roman Catholics not recognising civil law. Lord Donoughmore summed up the McCann case thus: '... a husband deserts his wife because the marriage is invalid, but the children are secured because the marriage is legal'.[24]

The McCann case also reignited concerns about *Ne Temere* among the leaders of the Reformed Churches, and had the effect of uniting other Protestant denominations on the issue.[25] The Presbyterian Church, of which Agnes McCann was a member, discussed the case at its general assembly in 1911, and issued a unanimous call for the withdrawal of the decree.[26] Church of Ireland bishop of Down, Charles D'Arcy, meanwhile argued that in the event of home rule being granted, the Catholic Church would be 'able to enforce laws without deference to the authority of the state'.[27] Evoking the stereotype of the servile Catholic, D'Arcy suggested that, despite the well-intentioned promises regarding marriage laws, decisions would ultimately be taken in Rome. He also claimed that while Irish unionists had no fear of church dogmas per se, their problem lay with a Roman church that 'still formally claims the power to control states, to depose princes ... to extirpate heresy'.[28]

To quell unionist fears that Irish nationalist politicians might at some point in the future fall under the influence of the Catholic hierarchy, and apprehensive that the outcry surrounding the affair might endanger home rule, British legislators amended the Government of Ireland Act to limit the powers of future Irish governments in relation to marriage law. As Thomas Bartlett has observed, the decree 'elicited that rarity from [British Prime Minister H.H.] Asquith – a concession'.[29] The amendment read:

> CLAUSE 3. – (Prohibition of Laws interfering with Religious Equality, etc.)
> 3. In the exercise of their power to make laws under this Act the Irish Parliament shall not make a law so as either directly or indirectly to establish or endow any religion, or prohibit the free exercise thereof, or give a preference, privilege, or advantage, or impose any disability or disadvantage, on account of religious belief or religious or ecclesiastical status, or make any religious belief or religious ceremony a condition of the validity of any marriage. Any law made in contravention of the restrictions imposed by this Section shall, so far as it contravenes those restrictions, be void.[30]

The impact of the decree at this particular juncture should not be underestimated since passions were running high in most parts of Ulster over the home rule campaign, and were further inflamed by publicity surrounding the McCann case. At a time when the streets of Belfast were echoing with the popular cry of 'home rule is Rome rule', this case presented Ulster unionists and loyalists with a clear opportunity to foment anger. As Desmond Bowen has argued, 'the *Ne Temere* decree put an end to the era when Irish Protestants had been content to sit back and watch the government's attempts to kill Home Rule by kindness, following the failure of the second Home Rule Bill'.[31] Moreover, the debate surrounding *Ne Temere* placed the relationship between church and state regarding matrimonial affairs firmly in the spotlight. And if the case united all Protestant denominations in condemnation, it also provides a rare example of the British state intervening to negate possible future consequences of Catholic Church dogma.[32]

So how and when did the Protestant community and the various historians and commentators come to misinterpret *Ne Temere* by connecting it to the religious upbringing of children? One thing is abundantly clear: in the years immediately after the decree's promulgation, it was deciphered as its creators had intended. Its objectors (and there were many) focused on the Catholic Church's self-proclaimed authority to question the validity of any marriage not sanctified in accordance with its own dogma, and, from the time of the decree's promulgation in 1908 up to and beyond the McCann case in 1910, they did not associate it with the religious upbringing of children.

At the general synods of the Church of Ireland in the years following the promulgation of the decree, much time and energy was devoted to the Catholic Church's supposed right to question the validity of all marriages. Delegates repeatedly invoked the spectre of a largely Catholic Irish government, under which canon law might supersede civil law and under which, by extension, all marriages not celebrated in accordance with Catholic Church dogma would become null and void. Rev. Chancellor O'Connor at the second session of the thirteenth annual synod – held one month after the decree came into effect – went so far as to speculate that, if the decree was observed to the letter, couples could choose to marry again outside of the Catholic Church, simply by stating that marriages not celebrated in accordance with *Ne Temere* were null and void. This situation, he argued, would lead people to be charged with bigamy.[33] Moreover, *Ne Temere* was thoroughly debated in the House of Commons and the House of Lords in the aftermath of the McCann case, and in both houses attention focused mainly on the absurdity of canon law disempowering civil law.

When opposition to the decree was expressed in other forms such as sermons, mass meetings and letters to national newspapers, attention was often drawn to its perceived encroachment on Protestant liberties. For instance, at a crowded meeting in the Metropolitan Hall in Dublin in February 1911, the Most Rev. Joseph Peacocke, Church of Ireland archbishop of Dublin, argued that, under canon law, a legally married couple could be accused of 'living in concubinage' with illegitimate children.[34] It is worth recalling that at that meeting none of the speakers – and there were many – made a connection between the decree and the religious upbringing of children.

A critical turning point, however, occurred on 17 March 1911 when the then rector of St Michael's, Blackrock, Cork, Rev. J.A.F. Gregg, delivered a lecture to members of the Cork Young Men's Association. Though obdurate at times, Gregg would later become a highly respected church leader and was revered by many in the Church of Ireland until his death in 1966. Daithí Ó Corráin has observed that 'he was the undisputed oracle on theological matters at home and abroad. With his natural reserve, rigid adherence to principle and firm chairmanship of general synod meetings, his stature within the Church of Ireland was immense.'[35] In his speech that night, Gregg was unsparing in his criticism of *Ne Temere*:

> Mixed marriages tend to rob us of our next generation, and we need to band ourselves together to stop the leakage ... [*Ne Temere*] is a wanton attack upon Irish unity, and can only make Protestants more irreconcilable to the idea of Home Rule than ever ... it will close up our ranks, it will enable us to see that Rome today is the same that Rome ever was, that no terms are possible with Rome, but that resistance in God's name, and in the name of conscience and liberty – resistance is the duty of us all.[36]

Where earlier critics who were fearful of the decree focused on the perceived right of the Catholic Church to bestow validity on all marriages, Gregg took his argument a step further by reasoning that the presence of a priest at a marriage ceremony between a Catholic and a Protestant was necessary purely to secure the Catholic upbringing of any children of the marriage:

> But now, since 1908, the presence [at a marriage ceremony] of a Roman Catholic priest is declared necessary. And I will tell you the reason why. Not in the least because there is any danger of rash or hasty marriages ... but because where the parish priest is not present, there may be no agreement concerning the children signed in favour of the Roman Catholic Church ... and so the presence of the priest is required, not so much that he may make a marriage of what, without him, would be no marriage, but that he may have his finger in the pie, and may bring with him those unmentioned extras which are what Rule 11 of 'Ne Temere' really aims at.[37]

Although Gregg qualified his line of reasoning by stating that 'not a word of this appears in Ne Temere', he effectively claimed that the decree was nothing more than a veiled instrument of proselytisation. Throughout his life, Gregg was consistent in his denunciations of *Ne Temere* and mixed marriages. On 10 November 1926, in an address in Dublin, he warned of *Ne Temere* and the upbringing of children as Catholics: 'It was immoral; it was traffic in human souls and some people seemed quite prepared to sell the souls of the unborn children.'[38] Nearly a quarter of a century later, at the opening of the general synod in Dublin in 1946, Gregg railed against the decree: 'I find it hard to conceive of anything spiritually more sinful ... than to make the signing away of the faith of the children yet unborn the bargaining counter, in return for which the marriage following on this trafficking in immortal souls shall be viewed as ecclesiastically valid.'[39]

It is not suggested that Gregg was solely responsible for twentieth-century misinterpretations of the decree, but he was the first respected figure to publicly and consistently make the connection between *Ne Temere* and the religious upbringing of children. It should be added that his speech in Cork was published and widely circulated in pamphlet form at the time and was then republished in the early 1950s.[40]

Notwithstanding the fact that Mary Barnes was pregnant and the couple wished to get married, the Catholic Church would have had grave theological concerns about the Tilson marriage. Canon 1060 states: 'The Church everywhere most severely forbids the contracting of marriage between two baptised persons of whom one is a Catholic whereas the other is a member of a heretical or schismatical sect.'[41] These concerns were rooted in the fact that the church regards marriage as a sacrament which, in its teaching, is an 'earthly extension of the Body of the Lord' or 'a symbol of the union between Christ and his Church'.[42] It follows that a marriage between a Catholic and a non-Catholic or a heretic would degrade, pollute or contaminate this sacred union.

Nonetheless, even if the Catholic Church strongly discouraged such unions, they did take place, but they gave rise, in theological terms, to the impediment, in the case of Mary Barnes as a *baptised* Catholic and Ernest Tilson as a *baptised* Protestant, of 'mixed religion' or '*mixta religionis*'. Canon 1061 sets out how a dispensation from this impediment could be obtained, allowing the marriage to proceed: 'The Church does not dispense from the impediment of mixed religion unless ... the non-Catholic party shall have given a guarantee to remove all danger of perversion from the Catholic party, and both parties shall have given guarantees to baptise and educate all the children in the Catholic faith alone.'[43] These guarantees or promises constituted the conditions or *cautiones* for the granting of the dispensation. They were required from Ernest Tilson as the non-Catholic party 'to remove all danger of perversion' from Mary Barnes, the Catholic party, and from both, to guarantee to 'baptise and educate all of the children in the Catholic faith and in no other'.[44]

The Catholic requirement that children of mixed marriages be raised in the Catholic faith has very long roots and is a separate issue to *Ne Temere*. Oliver P. Rafferty points out that Pope Pius VI's papal encyclical *Exsequendo Nunc* of 13 July 1782 stipulated that children of mixed marriages should be raised as Catholics; before this, Pope Benedict XIV, in his encyclical *Magnae Nobis* of 29 June 1748, stated clearly that 'children of both sexes born of [the mixed marriage] must be educated in the sanctity of the

Catholic religion'.[45] Drawing on an extensive study conducted by theologian Father Orsy, Brian O'Higgins observes: 'If Popes ever granted dispensations for mixed marriages, they have never been granted without the promise that the offspring of both sexes to be born of this marriage would be wholly educated in the Catholic religion.'[46] He emphasises the point further when he observes that 'the [Catholic] Church never positively permitted the children of mixed marriages to be brought up as non-Catholics. At best she tolerated the practice.'[47]

As we have seen, Ernest Tilson and Mary Barnes' application for a dispensation was by no means straightforward. When Mary's initial applications were refused, Ernest appears to have taken matters into his own hands when he took the unusual step of applying for a personal interview with the parish priest. Father Harley recommended that the dispensation be granted, which it duly was, and Ernest and Mary Tilson's promises to the Catholic Church followed theological prescripts to the letter; Ernest promised not to interfere with Mary's religion and both then promised to baptise and raise their children as Catholics. Their covenant took the following form:

> St. Mary's, Haddington Road, Dublin
>
> I, the undersigned, do hereby solemnly promise and engage that all the children of both sexes who may be born of my marriage with Mary Barnes shall be baptised in the Catholic Church, and shall be carefully brought up in the knowledge and practice of the Catholic religion; and I also solemnly promise and engage that I will not interfere with the religious belief of Mary Barnes, my future wife, nor with her full and perfect liberty to fulfil all her duties as a Catholic.
>
> (Sgd.) Ernest Neville Tilson,
> 12 Turner's Cottages, Ballsbridge
> 28th November 1941
>
> *Witnesses*:
> Brendan R. Harley, C.C.,
> St. Mary's, Haddington Road,
> Dublin.
> Cornelius Skehan, C.C.,
> St. Mary's, Haddington Road,
> Dublin.

> St. Mary's, Haddington Road, Dublin
>
> I, the undersigned, do hereby solemnly promise and engage that all the children of both sexes who may be born of my marriage with Ernest Tilson shall be baptised in the Catholic Church and shall be carefully brought up in the knowledge and practice of the Catholic religion.
>
> (Sgd.) Mary Josephine Barnes,
> 12 Turner's Cottages, Ballsbridge.
> 28th November 1941
>
> *Witnesses*:
> Brendan R. Harley, C.C.,
> St. Mary's, Haddington Road,
> Dublin.
> Cornelius Skehan, C.C.,
> St. Mary's, Haddington Road,
> Dublin.[48]

When Ernest Tilson and Mary Barnes signed the above documents before their marriage, they clearly entered into a prenuptial written agreement. Despite this, Ernest found himself in an awkward situation and later claimed that he experienced grave personal difficulty in agreeing to a demand from a church of which he was not a member. On the one hand, his partner was pregnant and he wanted to do the honourable thing, as outlined in his sworn affidavit to the High Court: 'I knew that my wife was going to have a child of which I was the father and we both earnestly desired to get married.'[49] But on the other, a register office marriage was not an option since neither his partner nor her family would agree to a marriage outside the Catholic Church. Gerard Hogan questions whether 'a modern court would hold a parent was bound by an ante-nuptial agreement executed in circumstances such as that of *Tilson*'s case',[50] and has argued that Ernest Tilson 'had ... little option but to give his consent to the undertaking that [the children] would be raised in the Roman Catholic faith'.[51]

The thorny question of whether Protestants had been forced to sign such agreements under duress is well ventilated in M.E. Francis' novel *Dark Rosaleen* (1917). Faced with one such agreement, the Protestant protagonist, Hector, finds himself battling the might of the Catholic Church over what he perceives to be the flagrant injustice of the condition relating to the religious upbringing of his children. That church's position is outlined when Father Casey informs Hector of his obligations under canon law: 'You will have to give the required pledges ... you'll have to promise in writing that you will never interfere with the free exercise of your wife's religion and that the children you may have will be baptised and brought up in the Catholic faith!'[52] The word of the Catholic Church, however, is final and Hector succumbs eventually to 'an enforced submission to the decrees of a Church in which he did not believe'.[53] In cloying terms, *Dark Rosaleen*'s narrator outlines Hector's position: 'Was he, Hector, to have no rights where the child was concerned? ... Was he to submit without a qualm to see his own child taught doctrines, which he condemned, and initiated into practices which he held to be idolatrous?'[54] In any event, *faute de mieux*, Ernest Tilson signed the agreement which would become a key factor of the High Court and Supreme Court hearings nine years later.

Although the Catholic decree *Ne Temere* has endured among Protestants as a point of resistance, it has also been misunderstood. A perception remains, for example, that the decree was primarily responsible for a dramatic fall in Protestant numbers in Ireland since 1922. Although Catholic regulations pertaining to mixed marriages were undoubtedly responsible for some decline in numbers, other factors, such as economic emigration, colonial retreat after independence, natural decrease and war deaths should be taken into account.[55] The issue of the religious upbringing of the Tilson children was central to the case that came before the High Court and Supreme Court. This was not a *Ne Temere* demand, but arose out of canon law, which allowed a dispensation for a mixed marriage to proceed, provided the couple promised to raise all their children as Catholics. Further, this Catholic Church demand significantly pre-dated the *Ne Temere* decree.

Ne Temere should be understood as 'a house keeping measure'[56] on the part of the Catholic Church, albeit effected in the febrile political environment of the campaign for the third home rule bill. In turn, it was expropriated by opportunistic unionists and later misrepresented by Archbishop J.A.F. Gregg. *The Irish Times*, in its coverage of the Tilson case, added fuel to the fire. Charles Townshend has best summed it up: 'The *Ne temere* decree was more significant for its political resonance than for any chilling effect it may have had on the likelihood of mixed marriage.'[57]

CHAPTER 3

The Birds' Nest

On 13 May 1950 Ernest Tilson left his parents' house in Oldcastle, County Meath, and travelled to Dublin with three of his four Catholic children, David (aged eight), Alan (six) and Paul (five). They were accompanied by Ernest's father, David. When the group arrived in Dublin, they separated; Ernest's father took the children to Mount Street and waited there, while Ernest walked to his home at 12 Turner's Cottages in Ballsbridge, with the intention of collecting his fourth and youngest child Neville (aged four) and rejoining the waiting group. He was greeted by his wife's sister Lily who had been minding the child. When he explained to her that he wished to speak to Neville, she became suspicious of his motives, aware of the bitter rancour that had developed over the past years between Ernest and her younger sister Mary. She was uncooperative and lied about the child's whereabouts, even though Neville lay sleeping in a room at the rear of the cottage. Eventually Ernest left empty-handed, while Lily, having left the child in the care of a neighbour, followed him surreptitiously along the leafy roads and canal bank of Dublin 4. She then witnessed the rendezvous between Ernest, his father and the three boys at Mount Street, and then followed the group to Grand Canal Street, where she saw Ernest handing over his three children at the door of the Protestant-run orphanage known as Mrs Smyly's Home.[1]

Born on 14 November 1814, Protestant philanthropist Ellen Smyly was the third daughter among seven children of Mathew and Mary Franks. In adolescence she was particularly touched by child poverty in Dublin and at the age of seventeen began her charity work in the city. Ellen Franks married the surgeon Josiah Smyly (who would later be a trustee of the Birds' Nest) and they had eleven children, two of whom died in infancy.[2] In 1850 she established a 'ragged school' in a rented unused forge on Harmony Row, off Grand Canal Street, where destitute children could receive a basic education.[3] The children were given a hot meal when they arrived and were then provided with 'the rudiments of education', which included 'instruction in the scriptures' and 'singing hymns and choruses'. Children often slept by the fire in the evening, received another meal, and were then turned out again onto the streets because there was no overnight accommodation to offer. Apparently, a pivotal moment occurred for Mrs Smyly when one of the children in her care, a six-year-old boy who was a regular pupil at the school, died of suffocation after creeping into a limekiln seeking shelter from the cold.[4]

By the 1880s Ellen Smyly had established an extensive network of ragged schools and homes for orphaned and destitute children,[5] and by that time was assisted in her work by her two daughters, Miss Ellen and Miss Annie Dallas Smyly.[6] Maria Luddy suggests that Smyly's motivation in founding such homes came from 'strongly held religious convictions'.[7] Together with Mrs George Whately, wife of the former Church of Ireland archbishop of Dublin, and their daughter Mrs George Wale, in 1859 Ellen Smyly founded the Birds' Nest, a new home for children, in a small cottage in Mounttown, Dún Laoghaire.[8] Work on a permanent home for the Birds' Nest on nearby York Road began shortly afterwards.

A report in the Protestant and unionist *Belfast News Letter* in 1860 suggested that, on completion, the orphanage would bring together the 'different branches of the Mission work in Kingstown [Dún Laoghaire] and would accommodate children between the ages of five and twelve. It would have a dormitory, school rooms and a playground and would make a fitting memorial to the late Mrs Wale, who had named the orphanage the 'Birds' Nest'.[9] The writer noted that the Birds' Nest currently housed thirty-four children 'but numbers more are longing to get in'.[10] The article described how the 'Inquiring Class for Roman Catholics on Monday evenings is always full, and very lively and interesting controversy is carried on there'. The article concluded with a call for donations to assist in the completion of the orphanage – the amount required was £1,500.[11] At a total cost of £4,000, the Birds' Nest was completed in 1861, boasting the motto 'God's Providence is mine Inheritance'.[12]

Numbers increased rapidly: an 1864 report in the *Daily Express*, reproduced in the *Cork Examiner*, stated that the Birds' Nest now catered for 160 children.[13] By 1909 the institution had become Mrs Smyly's largest orphanage, caring for and educating over 150 boys and girls; together with 'nine kindred homes', the Birds' Nest provided accommodation for over 500 children with an annual expenditure of £12,000.[14] The 1881 annual report of the rival Catholic St Brigid's Orphanage reported that the Birds' Nest catered for 212 'in house' and 26 'at nurse' children,[15] while the Census of Ireland 1901 records that there were 153 male and female 'inmates' aged between five and sixteen years. Most children listed were Irish, though some are shown to have come from Britain, Germany, the United States, India and Australia. *The Handbook of Dublin Charities* (1903) described the Birds' Nest as 'a home for neglected children of the very poor', which gave preference to 'children of mixed marriages and ... Roman Catholics'.[16] That said, the Censuses of Ireland 1901 and 1911 show that the 'religious profession' of all infants committed is 'Church of Ireland'.[17] In terms of their lives in the institution, the children slept in dormitories, were provided with three meals a day and attended education classes. They also enjoyed weekly excursions to places like Killiney Hill, and played sports such as football or gymnastics, but were also expected to do much of the day-to-day housework.[18]

In November 1894, however, the Dublin *Evening Herald* carried a report of a sermon delivered by a Rev. Mr Colohan on behalf of St Brigid's Orphanage, in which he had claimed that in 'the Glencree Reformatory for juvenile criminal offenders, out of 150 inmates 120 of them had graduated in Mrs Smyly's famous Birds' Nest'. He further claimed that 'an inmate of the Birds' Nest assured him that a statue of the Blessed Virgin was placed in the Birds' Nest in Kingstown, which he was asked to spit on, but he refused'.[19] Colohan's incendiary accusation reflects the oppositional relationship between the Birds' Nest and St Brigid's Orphanage: St Brigid's was established to 'protect children from the double calamity of spiritual and physical destitution' and 'admitted children considered at risk of being placed in Protestant homes'.[20] Ellen Smyly wrote to the editor of the *Evening Herald* to express her outrage, and her proposition to Colohan reflected her renowned commercial acumen:

> Father Colohan either believes or disbelieves the story; if he believes it let him appoint one or more Roman Catholic gentlemen, and we will appoint an equal number of Protestant gentlemen, and let the charges be fully investigated, and if proved to the satisfaction of these gentlemen, I shall place £100 to the credit of St Brigid's Orphanage, provided, if not proved, he shall place £100 to the credit of the Birds' Nest.[21]

Smyly died on 16 May 1901 at her home, 35 Upper Fitzwilliam Street, and was buried at Mount Jerome Cemetery. By the time of her death she had established seven homes and four day schools.[22] Her legacy continues today: Mrs Smyly's Homes remains an active charitable organisation operating the Glensilva and Racefield residential homes for young people in south County Dublin.[23]

By the late nineteenth and early twentieth centuries Dublin had become one of the most impoverished cities in Europe, with a dismal lack of state supports for the poor, and there is little doubt that, together with Mrs Smyly's Homes, the Birds' Nest made an extremely valuable contribution to society by rescuing children from terrible poverty. At the December 1883 meeting of the Kingstown Commissioners, Rev. Henry Fishe, Dublin superintendent of the Irish Church Missions, told the delegates that so many applications for admission to the orphanage had been received that they could 'fill three Birds' Nests' and that he had to 'write to the Protestants and Roman Catholics to tell them that there was no room in the Birds' Nest for the children they wanted to send'.[24]

The Birds' Nest's reputation (which remained with it until its closure in 1976) is undoubtedly rooted in its association with the Irish Church Missions, to the extent that 'Birds' Nest' became a generic name for all Protestant institutions, which were perceived as proselytising agencies.[25] Indeed, if a Catholic child was placed in a Protestant orphanage, he or she would often be described as having been 'Birds' Nested'. Or a parent of a disobedient child might warn, 'If you don't behave yourself, it's the Birds' Nest for you!' In 1852 Ellen Smyly formed an alliance with evangelical clergyman Alexander Dallas who founded the Society for Irish Church Missions to the Roman Catholics in 1849 – later shortened to 'Irish Church Missions'. The partnership between this society, which was an unashamedly proselytising organisation, and the Birds' Nest would endure up to the time when the orphanage eventually closed its doors.

Although the Irish Church Missions enjoyed considerable early success in Connemara and in the slums of Dublin, its activities – which were perceived to be a direct threat to the Catholic faith – were deeply resented by the Catholic laity and hierarchy. This animosity, which often took the form of social ostracism or direct violence, had colonial as well as cultural roots.[26] Since Catholicism was associated with dispossession and Protestantism with an alien coloniser, it followed that the society's work in Ireland, ostensibly on behalf of English Protestants, fomented sectarian tensions. Many Catholics also believed that English Protestant organisations, such as the Irish Church Missions, had exploited the Great Famine of the 1840s by offering starving Catholics food and shelter on condition that they converted to Protestantism. Despite their strenuous denials, accusations that the Irish Church Missions had offered Catholics inducements to convert continued to plague the organisation and those associated with it.

The notion of offering inducements was aired in 1863 in a letter from Father John O'Rourke, a parish priest in County Cavan, to the *Freeman's Journal*. O'Rourke described how one of his parishioners, Thomas Connor, a Catholic labourer, had placed two of his four children in the Birds' Nest after his Protestant wife had died, owing to his straitened circumstances. Two or three months later, and anxious to secure their return, he presented himself at the Birds' Nest on 'the committee day'. According to O'Rourke, the managers offered him 10s. to 'go away quietly without the children' and then increased their offer by a further 10s. if he would bring his two other children to the orphanage.[27] While this story may be exaggerated or invented, it was the Birds' Nest, rather than the Irish Church Missions, which was demonised for using unscrupulous methods to secure children. Allegations of offering inducements would continue well into the twentieth century. Michael Viney has noted that the Irish Church Missions workers have been described in the past as 'ghoulish monsters going around the slums with bags of English gold'.[28] Controversy around inducements that were linked to the Birds' Nest can even be found in James Joyce's *Ulysses* (1922) when Leopold Bloom observes that the Birds' Nest 'gave soup to children to change to protestants in the time of the potato blight'.[29] Bloom also refers to Thomas Connellan, a Catholic priest turned Protestant evangelist, commenting cryptically that 'Birds' Nest women run him', thereby suggesting that Connellan was somehow under the influence or control of Ellen Smyly, Mrs George Whately or their equally formidable daughters.

In the years that followed its establishment, amid reports of the use of more aggressive proselytising tactics by the Irish Church Missions, Catholic aversion to the Birds' Nest grew. In 1867 Frances (Fanny) Taylor, an English nurse and writer, who had converted to Catholicism from Protestantism, visited Ireland to study the work of the female religious orders to see how they 'defended the faith of the poor Catholics against proselytisers in their own land'.[30] While her description of the Birds' Nest contrasts sharply with her assessment of a nearby Catholic institution, her comments also reveal how the Protestant orphanage was already well known only six years after it opened:

> The orphanage [St Joseph's] stands in a good situation adjoining fields; there is no wall around the garden, and all is free and open, forming a strange contrast to its neighbour a quarter of a mile off, the celebrated

'Birds' Nest', whose dismal playground, shut in by high walls and locked dormitory, denote its true character – a prison for Catholic children.[31]

An 1862 report in the Catholic-orientated *Cork Examiner* promoted a similar perception of the modus operandi of the Birds' Nest:

It [the Birds' Nest] is to encourage Protestant mothers who wish to steal away the children of a dead Catholic father, for the purposes of perverting them from the faith in which he chose to have them reared ... Having secured their prey they do not devour their flesh, but they mould their minds into a uniform hypocrisy, and then they offer them as fitting sacrifices to heaven.[32]

A report in the same newspaper two years later describes the Birds' Nest in similar terms:

In the opinion of every Catholic – and of every liberal-minded Protestant – the Birds' Nest, of Dublin, is one of the most mischievous of all the proselytising agencies in the country. It is not only evil in and of itself, it is the cause of innumerable evils ... this Hawk's Nest – as the humbler classes of Dublin have aptly designated this trap – is constantly before the public, in one manner or another, but always as the bitter and malevolent assailant of the Catholic creed and Church.[33]

The December 1883 meeting of the Commissioners of Kingstown discussed a proposal that the town hall should not be used in future for proselytising purposes by the managers of the Birds' Nest. This proposal followed a letter written by the Catholic archbishop of Dublin, Cardinal Edward MacCabe, which was severely critical of the activities of the managers of the orphanage. MacCabe claimed that 'it [the Birds' Nest] was not a legitimate Protestant charity but had been established for purpose of trafficking in the souls of poor children, and that its managers were worse than African slave drivers'.[34] Continuing along similar lines, the bishop of Ferns, James Staunton, offered his jaundiced view of the Birds' Nest and its apparent modus operandi, in a letter to Archbishop McQuaid almost seventy years later:

Secrecy is the great weapon of the Birds' Nest, and the publicity which would follow ... would help kill their activities ... I think also that if the minister realised the position that Irish children are being raised by money partly contributed by foreign bigots, in the Protestant religion, to continue the British policy of increasing the number of Protestants in the country, and to provide suitable recruits for the British army, and that the policy is being continued after thirty years of Irish rule, he would do something to put an end to it for once and for all.[35]

But what was the express nature of the relationship between the Birds' Nest and the Irish Church Missions? According to Maria Luddy, 'Many of the Protestant orphanages were self-professed proselytising agencies, particularly those under the control of the Irish Church Missions. One of these, the Birds' Nest, organised by Mrs. Ellen Smyly, favoured children of mixed marriages or Catholic parentage as inmates.'[36] This statement is not entirely accurate: the Birds' Nest was not a 'self-professed proselytising agency', although that is not to say that proselytising did not take place within its walls. It is also unfair to claim that the Birds' Nest was 'under the control' of the Irish Church Missions. At a meeting in the Birds' Nest in 1909, Rev. Henry Fishe offered an explanation regarding the connection between the orphanage and his organisation: 'The Home Committee [of the Birds' Nest] gathered in the children and collected funds for their support, while the Irish Church Missions provided teachers and superintended the education.'[37] Vivienne Smyly, meanwhile, claims that 'the arrangement was that the Irish Church Missions should take charge of the educational department of the work, and that Mrs. Smyly's Homes and Schools should be responsible for the material needs'.[38] Both these interpretations accord with the view of Deirdre Bryan, who observes that, 'Although the teachers were supplied by the Irish Church Missions, the running of the homes was independently overseen by Ellen [Smyly] with assistance from committees of women.'[39]

That the Birds' Nest and the Irish Church Missions were separate organisations is also confirmed in a letter the Rev. W.L.M. Giff, superintendent of the Irish Church Missions, wrote to the trustees of the Birds' Nest after the Tilson High Court and Supreme Court hearings, asking for money. William Lee Mather Giff (later a key player in Ernest Tilson's legal case) was born in Mullingar, County Westmeath, on 1 December 1900 to John and Esther Giff (*née* Egar). John Giff was a sergeant in the Royal Irish Constabulary.[40] His son William was educated at Queen's University Belfast where he was awarded a BSc and an MSc. He was a

The Birds' Nest   57

missionary in Uganda between 1929 and 1934 before returning to Ireland, to serve in the parishes of Dowra, County Cavan, and Ballisodare, County Sligo. Giff served as superintendent to the Irish Church Missions from 1947 to 1951 and then worked in the parishes of Rathmolyon, County Meath, and Killucan, County Westmeath. He died in 1986.[41]

Giff's letter to the trustees of the Birds' Nest confirms that the orphanage and Irish Church Missions were separate entities. Enumerating the legal costs of the trial on the Protestant side, the letter also shows that these were paid for by the Irish Church Missions by way of donations from Protestants throughout Ireland. Giff's letter also confirms that when Ernest Tilson was charged with neglecting his children on 13 October 1950, Giff was accepted as bail person:[42]

> 16th October 1950
>
> F.T. Russell, Esq.
> Mrs Smyly's Homes,
> 21, Grattan Street,
> Dublin.
>
> Dear Mr Russell,
>
> I wrote to ask you if you could put before your trustees, for their consideration, the matter of the Tilson case. The proceeding in the High Court and Supreme Court here cost, in all, £700. Now, Tilson has been arrested on a charge of neglect of his children. Not only has he had to surrender his sons to be brought up as Roman Catholics, but legal pressure is being brought to bear to make him pay for the privilege. As the matter is one which vitally concerns the liberty of all Protestants in Eire [sic], we are providing his defence for this also. We have already received £485 in special gifts, but we need much more. Would your trustees consider giving us a donation?
>
> Yours sincerely,
> Irish Superintendent[43]

When High Court judge George Gavan Duffy sought details from the trustees of the Birds' Nest regarding the education of the three Tilson children, it was Giff of the Irish Church Missions who replied that the role of the Irish Church Missions in the Birds' Nest was primarily educational:

> Irish Church Missions
> 5a, Townsend Street,
> Dublin.
> 19th June, 1950
>
> I confirm that I am responsible for the curriculum as taught in the Bird's nest [sic].
>
> The religious instruction followed is that prescribed by the general synod of the Church of Ireland. The three children are being instructed, in their respective age groups, in
>
> (1) Church of Ireland Catechism and Formalities
> (2) Bible teaching in the Old and New Testament
>
> The children are also receiving instruction from the hand-book entitled 'The Hundred Texts' published by the Irish Church Missions and used in all our schools. The secular instruction imparted is that prescribed by the Ministry of Education for use in National Schools. The eldest child, David, is of normal intelligence, though perhaps just a little backward. The two younger children, Alan and Paul, are, in our opinion, well up to average.
>
> (Signed) W.L.M. Giff Superintendent[44]

That Giff was a key player in Ernest Tilson's legal battle to have his children reared and educated in the Protestant faith in the Birds' Nest is also confirmed in a letter written by Kenneth Mc Neill, assistant honorary secretary of the Worldwide Missionary Convention. In fact, Mr Mc Neill states that Giff was the 'instigator of the legal proceedings':

> WORLDWIDE MISSIONARY CONVENTION
>
> 12th September 1950
>
> Dear Sir,
>
> From the enclosed Programme you will see that the Rev. W.L.M. Giff of the Irish Church Missions is speaking on Friday night in connection with his work in the South of Ireland. Mr. Giff, who was *the instigator of the legal proceedings* now known as 'The Tilson Case', will refer to the original application to the Courts and the subsequent Appeal in

his address ... We feel sure that in light of the great publicity given to the Tilson Case and the decisions given, you would like to hear Mr. Giff for yourself. We therefore extend to you a very warm invitation to be present and may we add – the attendance is expected to be very large and representative of all sections of Church life.

> On behalf of the Committee,
> I am,
> Yours sincerely,
> Kenneth Mc Neill
> Assistant Hon. Secretary[45]

On 3 April 1950 Mary Tilson returned home from her employment at the Swastika Laundry in Ballsbridge to discover that 'all of the children, except Neville, were gone from the house'. She questioned her husband, but he would not divulge their whereabouts – other than to say that she 'would have a job finding out about them'.[46] After frantic enquiries to friends and neighbours, she went to Irishtown garda station, but the guards 'could not give ... any information'. The following day she visited a Miss Wogan of the Society for the Prevention of Cruelty to Children, but 'she could not give any assistance either'. A year earlier, on Wogan's advice, she had a District Court summons served on her husband because, allegedly, he was failing to provide financial support for her and their children. At the time she suffered a miscarriage, and also made an allegation that her husband had assaulted her. The judge in the District Court adjourned the case and urged the couple to try and reconcile their differences.[47]

Ernest 'eventually admitted' to his wife that he had 'taken the three eldest children down to his parents' [house at Oldcastle]. Given the fact that the children remained there for about six weeks, and had previously spent weekends and summer holidays there, it is odd that in her search she did not make Oldcastle her first port of call. Mary also claimed that she reported the matter to the police, but the police made no search for the children and their disappearance was not covered in any newspapers. In any event, she began making arrangements to travel to the County Meath town, but changed her plans when she learned (probably from her sister Lily) that he had subsequently removed the children from his parents' house and placed them in the Birds' Nest. When she learned this on 15 May, she immediately went to the orphanage. While the children were in Oldcastle, they were apparently told by their father that they would soon be leaving 'to stay in a really nice place in Dublin'.⁴⁸ However, when Ernest took his children from the family home and brought them to Oldcastle, he had no intention of placing them in the Birds' Nest; had he wished to do so, he could have brought them straight from Turner's Cottages to one of Mrs Smyly's Homes in either Grand Canal Street or Dún Laoghaire. So how or why did Ernest Tilson come to place his children in the Birds' Nest?

Two residents of Oldcastle, with memories of the case, have offered an explanation. Although Ernest's parents, who had been caring for the children, would later tell the courts that they were prepared to continue doing this as an alternative to the orphanage, in truth, as elderly people running their own business, they were struggling with that duty. Moreover, Ernest was still employed in Dublin Corporation and visited the County Meath town only at weekends. Around this time, he was introduced to a lady in Oldcastle by the name of Frances Russell. She was a member of the local select vestry of the Church of Ireland, was heavily involved in parish activities, and was an active proselytiser, with one notable previous success in the town. Russell was also a patron of the Tilson family tailoring business. When she became aware of their situation – probably through conversation with his parents at their premises or at a church service – she advised Ernest that she had 'a friend' who worked in a Protestant orphanage in Dublin who would care for the children.⁴⁹ That 'friend' may well have been Rev. W.L.M. Giff. A letter dated 8 June 1950 from the appropriately named secretary at the Birds' Nest, Mabel Bird, to T.G. McVeagh, solicitor for the trustees of Mrs Smyly's Homes, sheds some light on the matter: 'The case [Tilson children] came through Rev. W.L.M. Giff, who was in contact with the father.'⁵⁰ If we are to accept the explanation offered by the Oldcastle residents, it appears that a plan was hatched in Oldcastle between Ernest and Frances Russell to remove the children to a Mrs Smyly's Home to begin their Protestant education. This may also explain Ernest's contrived declaration at the door of Mrs Smyly's Home on Grand Canal Street on the day he took his sons there: 'These are my children and I want you to make them Protestants.'⁵¹

After spending two days at Mrs Smyly's Home in Grand Canal Street, David, Alan and Paul were brought by their father to the Birds' Nest on 15 May. Ernest later said that he had taken the children to the Protestant-run orphanage because 'they were not being properly looked after in Turner's Cottages' and that 'they would be better in the home than in the only home his wife could provide for them in her parents' four-roomed cottage'.⁵² For her part, Mary later argued that the Birds' Nest was a most unsuitable accommodation for her children, because, among other things, their companions there would include 'orphans, waifs and strays'.[53] Notwithstanding the promises he made to the Catholic Church, and the fact that they had been raised as Catholics, Ernest now wished for his children to be educated in the Protestant faith: 'I am a practising member of the Church of Ireland and I wish all my children to be brought up in my faith and to receive proper religious instructions in my own faith.'[54] Indeed, this squares with Alan's memory of arriving at Mrs Smyly's Home in Grand Canal Street. Ernest also stated in his affidavit that 'the Home [the Birds' Nest] is willing to keep them and ... I have agreed to pay and am paying the sum required by the Home for so doing'. He also argued that 'the said Home is a very suitable Home for the said children'.[55] His claim that he was making the required financial contribution to the Birds' Nest was not entirely accurate, however. On 20 June, just over five weeks after he left his children in the care of the Birds' Nest, Mabel Bird wrote to him at Oldcastle acknowledging receipt of payment of £3 but warning him that he was slipping into arrears. Ernest also appears to have made enquiries in regard to visiting times because Bird, in her response, advised him that he could visit his sons at any time:

> Mr. Ernest Tilson,
> 8 Chapel Street,
> Oldcastle, County Meath.
> 20th June 1950

Dear Mr. Tilson,

Thank you for your letter of 17th instant., enclosing £3 towards the support of your three little boys under our care, for which I enclose our receipt. This brings you up to the 5th instant, leaving two weeks due. It is better not to let it run on too long, which makes it harder to pay up!

You may go and see the children anytime – you will just have to risk them being out for a walk, but if you avoid the middle of the afternoon they ought to be in, unless there was any special picnic or party on; but that is not likely for some time as the Home is in quarantine for measles and whooping cough unfortunately.

Yours faithfully,
Mabel Bird[56]

Ernest and his sons did not arrive at the Birds' Nest unannounced. Bird wrote to the matron of the orphanage, Miss Holt, on 15 May, the day of their arrival:

15th May, 50

Dear Miss Holt,

These are the three Tilson boys – David, Alan and Paul – the youngest one (Neville) is staying with the Granny in the country.

Mr. Tilson is bringing them out to-day and has promised to let me have the ration books this evening. There has been no time to get medical certificates, so will you please get Dr. Wheeler to examine them. They look healthy enough.

Shall let you have copies of [admission?] forms in a day or two.

Yours sincerely,
Mabel Bird[57]

This short letter confirms that Bird had seen the children before they arrived at the Birds' Nest on 15 May – so Ernest had either brought them to the orphanage on an earlier visit, or Bird had met them in the Mrs Smyly's Home in Grand Canal Street, where he had first brought them. Bird's letter also confirms that Ernest had provided Bird with inaccurate information in regard to the whereabouts of his youngest son, Neville. As outlined earlier, Ernest had failed in his attempt to take Neville from the family home at Turner's Cottages. In fact, Neville remained in the care of his mother or her sister Lily throughout the High Court and Supreme Court hearings.

Although the secretary of Mrs Smyly's Homes and Schools, Francis T. Russell, told the High Court that Ernest had completed an admission form 'in respect of each of his *three* children',[58] in fact he completed *four* admission forms for each of his four sons, David, Alan, Paul and Neville. It had clearly been his intention to place all four in the Birds' Nest, but, as we have seen, he failed in his efforts to take his youngest son, Neville, from the family home at Turner's Cottages. The admission forms were headed 'Mrs Smyly's Homes for Necessitous Children: In connexion with Irish Church Missions: Dublin. Application for the Admission of a Child to one of these Homes'.[59] Ernest entered details of the boys' full names, their address, place of birth, attainments in education, their general health and whether they 'wet the bed at night', as well as his occupation as 'clerk'. Question 9 demanded 'Their Religion', to which Ernest entered these words: 'He

C. of I. – She R.C.'. Question 11 asked: 'Has the child any relative who is, in your opinion, in a position to contribute towards his maintenance?', which he answered: '5/- per week by father'. Question 14 asked: 'Does the father, or other legal guardian, desire for the child a Protestant education?' Ernest answered simply 'Yes'. Each form was signed by Ernest, Mabel Bird, and the Rev. W.L.M. Giff.

Under the heading on the form 'State here in full why this is considered a destitute case', Giff wrote in his own hand on each form: 'The mother has treated the husband very badly for some time, and has eventually deserted the children (it's a mixed marriage case). I think the father will serve his children faithfully.'[60] While Giff's remarks about Mary Tilson would later be vigorously contested in the High Court, the heading on this part of the form confirms that a child was supposed to be destitute in order to be admitted to the Birds' Nest. That it was not enough to state that you wished your child to be raised as a Protestant to gain entry to the orphanage accords with the fact that the Birds' Nest was primarily a caring institution, while education – or indeed proselytising – was left to the Irish Church Missions. Indeed, Mabel Bird also appears to have been under the impression that the Tilson children had been destitute. In response to a letter-writer from Clonskeagh in Dublin, she wrote: 'the information received prior to the admission of these children was that *they had no home*, and that they were being brought up as Roman Catholics against their father's wishes'.[61] All that said, Giff's comments about Mary on the admission form were at best a sleight-of-hand or at worst shamelessly deceitful and suggest that he had an ulterior motive.

In his sworn affidavit to the High Court, Francis T. Russell described what children could look forward to following admittance to the Birds' Nest. His encomium sharply contradicts many of the accusations made against the orphanage since its establishment:

> The children of Mrs. Smyly's Homes live under the most healthy conditions in bright, clean and airy buildings, fitted with modern sanitary and bathing arrangements equipped with electric light and steam heating. They receive a secular education (National School Standard) and also daily religious instruction. They participate in games and other activities, such as Girl Guides, Boys Brigade, Gymnastics, music and sewing … The best medical and dental treatment is available. Employment is found for them on reaching the leaving age. Some of the boys brought up in the Homes have entered Universities, some have risen to positions of trust in commerce.

> Everything possible is done to educate, train and fit them to earn their livelihood when they leave the Homes.

A 1952 account in *Erin's Hope* also gave an insight into life in the orphanage: '... one of the great secrets of making children happy is to keep them employed and [they] take great pride in their beautifully scrubbed floors and gleaming brasses'.[62] Another mid-twentieth-century commentator was undoubtedly gilding the lily when he observed: 'Cod-liver oil is also a standby and help for new and delicate children. It is swallowed delightedly, and the empty bottle looked at with long and disappointed faces.'[63] Russell concluded his affidavit by describing the welfare of David, Alan and Paul Tilson one month and three days after their father had admitted them to the Birds' Nest: 'All the said children have settled down and are contented and happy in the said Homes [*sic*] and the Trustees are willing to keep them in the said homes whether or not the parents or either of them contribute to their upkeep and maintenance.'[64]

Mary visited her children at the Birds' Nest on 15 May. In her sworn affidavit, which she signed two days later, she also confirmed that she had visited them on two occasions after this date. On the second occasion she claimed that a lady 'in immediate charge' would not allow her to see her children because 'no person was permitted to see any of the said children except [her] husband and his relatives'. She also told the 'person in charge' that 'the children were Roman Catholics' – to which the lady apparently replied, 'That is not my fault.'[65] This mocking retort caused some debate. The solicitor, T.G. McVeagh, later wrote to Francis T. Russell asking him to respond to an allegation that 'a member of your staff was rude to Mrs. Tilson'.[66] Russell responded and confirmed that Mary had indeed visited her children on 15 May but that when she arrived the following day she was not allowed to see them because 'she had seen them the previous day'. Russell also stated that he had spoken to the matron about Mary's visits and was reassured that she had 'been treated with the greatest kindness and courtesy and that no such remark was made'.[67] Mabel Bird offered an account of Mary's initial visits to the orphanage in a letter to the matron, Miss Holt, dated 17 May:

> Mrs. Tilson and her father have been here this morning, and I had a quiet talk with them. They were inclined to be a bit aggressive at the beginning, but calmed down, and became quite amenable. They quite understand that they cannot remove the children, but

she wants so badly to be allowed to see them. I have agreed that she should visit them once a fortnight, starting next Sunday. At first she wanted twice a week, but I pointed out that was too often, and only upsetting for everyone.

Bird then added perspicaciously, 'I shouldn't be surprised if she brought the case to court.'[68]

On 22 May, seven days after the three Tilson children were admitted to the Birds' Nest, George McGrath, the solicitor representing Mary, served a High Court of Justice order of *habeas corpus ad subjiciendum* on Ernest Tilson and the 'Trustees of Mrs. Smyly's Homes and Schools', dated 18 May 1950, 'to have before the Court the bodies of the said David Tilson, Alan Tilson, and Paul Tilson'.[69] This confirms that Mary wasted no time in seeking legal advice and initiating proceedings to retrieve her children, once she had established their whereabouts. Mabel Bird forwarded the High Court Order to T.G. McVeagh and asked him if he would instruct Mr Fitzsimons, a barrister, to act on behalf of the trustees. Notably, Bird also advised McVeagh to instruct Fitzsimons that 'our Trustees are willing to abide by the decision of the Court in the matter'.[70] McVeagh wrote to George McGrath: 'I wish to confirm as already indicated that the Trustees of Mrs. Smyly's Homes are not contesting this matter which appears to be one between the parents only.'[71]

Before the High Court hearing, McVeagh asked Bird to outline the sequence of events regarding the Tilson children. In response, she claimed that 'the case came through W.L.M. Giff' and stated that 'the mother had deserted the children and that the father had taken them down to his people in Oldcastle, but that they could not stay there'. She set out the sequence of events as follows:

15th May – Children admitted at request of father.
Mother called at the Birds' Nest that same afternoon and saw the children.
16th May – Mother called again at the Home and was refused permission to see the children as she had seen them the previous day.
17th May – Mother and Father called at the office [Smyly's Homes office], 21 Grattan Street, and she was given permission to visit the children once a fortnight.
18th May – Mother applied for a conditional order against her husband and the Trustees of the Smyly's Homes.
21st May – Mother visited the children again at the Birds' Nest.[72]

On 7 June 1950, just over three weeks after being placed in the Birds' Nest, David Tilson wrote a letter home to his mother:

> The Bird's Nest, [sic]
> 17 York Road,
> Dun Laoghaire,
> County Dublin
> 7/6/50
>
> My Dear Mammy,
>
> Thank you for the sweets and comics you sent us. Tell Neville, Alan and Paul was [sic] asking for him.
> When you are brining [sic] the things on Sunday do Not send slab toffie [sic], bring hollywood cake instead.[73]
> Tell neville we are getting on well hear [sic]
> Good by bye for now
> from David
> xxxxxxxxxxxxxxxxxxxxxxxxx
> xxxxxxxxxxxxxxxxx
> xx[74]

Alan Tilson holds clear memories of his time spent in the Birds' Nest and believes that he and his siblings were generally well cared for by their Protestant custodians. He recalls, however, that after living in Turner's Cottages with his parents, grandparents, uncle and aunts, the Birds' Nest felt 'very foreign to us and we could not settle'. He suggests that his older brother David may have been bullied by other children in the orphanage and believes that this may have contributed to the insecure and somewhat reclusive life he led in later years. Alan remembers gazing out of the arched sash window halfway up the creaky wooden staircase in the evenings and convincing himself that he could see his home at Turner's Cottages. It was some years later when he walked past the orphanage that he realised he had been looking in the wrong direction.[75] Before his death in 1997, Alan's younger brother Paul had only one memory of the Birds' Nest: his mother calling to visit him and his brothers and her having a testy argument with the lady in charge who had an ear trumpet. He remembered his mother leaving the Birds' Nest without them. And when he saw 'that she was crying, he knew that something was wrong'.[76]

CHAPTER 4

The Catholic Ethos and the Church/State Consensus

Mixed marriages in the 1940s and '50s were especially problematic for couples in Ireland because the Catholic Church was arguably at the height of its powers, deeply permeating all aspects of the lives of its laity, producing what has been described as 'an atmosphere steeped in the faith'.[1] Practice and devotion were paramount because Catholics were obliged to attend the holy sacrifice of the mass every Sunday and on holy days of obligation; they were also expected to partake in other forms of worship such as rosaries, confessions, parish missions, pilgrimages, processions, benediction, forty-hour novenas and the stations of the cross. In fact, rosaries were recited by groups of Catholic residents of both Turner's Cottages and Oldcastle in support of Mary Tilson during and after the High Court and the Supreme Court hearings.

The public displays of Catholicism in the 1950s were reinforced by displays of iconography within the household: statues of the Infant of Prague or of Our Lady, pictures of the Sacred Heart with the eternal lamp, crucifixes, St Brigid's crosses, holy water, sacred relics and rosary beads. In his novel *The Feast of Lupercal* (1958), Brian Moore draws attention to this domestic iconography to articulate the paralysing effect of the overbearing and oppressive church on the mind of his Catholic protagonist, Diarmuid Devine. Devine is a middle-class teacher at Ardcath College in Belfast who enters into a relationship with a young and breezy Protestant, Una Clarke, who has had an affair with a married man in Dublin. In keeping with Catholic teaching in 1950s Ireland, Devine sees sex as sinful, and regards Clarke's affair and her drunkenness as 'mortal sins'. His flat is adorned with holy pictures, one of which is of the 'Divine Infant of Prague'. Moore's description of Devine's clumsy sexual advance is described as 'a pilgrimage towards her', while the eyes of the Virgin and Child looked down upon him with 'reproach for human waywardness'.[2]

But the image of the brow-beaten, oppressed and thoroughly servile Catholic might be misplaced; religious practice for many during this period was deliberate, triumphalist and a badge of national identity to be worn prominently on the sleeve. As Tom Garvin has observed, 'clerical power was apparently approved of, or at least acquiesced in, by the vast majority of the population'.[3] In a similar vein, Catholicism, in post-war Ireland, was 'a marker of communal identity and a source of esteem and meaning for many ordinary people'.[4] The partaking in Palm Sunday, Holy Week or Corpus Christi processions, for instance, were often discretionary experiences and offered the laity a much-needed break from economic hardship, emigration and the drudgery of daily life. Rejecting the notion that Irish Catholics 'go to mass only out of habit', J.H. Whyte has argued that 'it seems unlikely that the habit would persist unless, to many Irishmen [and Irish women], it was something more than that'.[5] But practising religion for many Catholics was not just about going through the motions or paying lip service to a zealous hierarchy: for many, religion provided a spiritual experience, and above all else promised redemption, eternal rest and reward in Heaven. Observed against the economic stagnation of 1940s and '50s Ireland, that grand prize sounded far better than the dole queue or the boat to Britain; within this context, why wouldn't a lay person accept regulations and directions from the parish priest or bishop?

A further important context to the Tilson case is the Catholic Church/state consensus, which existed for many decades of the twentieth century. Much of the Catholic Church's power and influence derived from a partnership it enjoyed with the British government, before independence, whereby it was tasked with running significant parts of the country's health and education systems. After 1921 the fledgling government of the Free State inherited these arrangements and cemented the alliance, making the Catholic Church a 'powerful and autonomous agency'.[6] The construction of a Gaelic and Catholic identity had been a prime concern among Irish nationalists since the 1890s, and with partition and the newly independent Irish state, politicians south of the border were only too willing to develop a more Catholic ethos.

Bryan Fanning has observed that 'as good Catholics, legislators and voters were deeply committed to expressing their faith in the laws and institutions of the country'.[7] The Censorship of Films Act (1923), the Censorship of Publications Act (1929), the provisions set out in the Adoption Bill regarding parents in mixed marriages, and the banning of anything associated with artificial contraception are all examples of how state legislation could be harmonised with the teachings of the church. The influence of the church on the 1937 constitution is also evident in its articles dealing with the family and education. Along similar lines, Article 44 affirmed the 'special position' of the Catholic Church 'as the guardians of the Faith professed by the great majority of its citizens', while other faiths were simply 'recognised'.

The Catholic Church's determination to enshrine its social teaching in state legislation was sometimes akin to pushing an open door because successive Free State governments had strong Catholic leanings. The tone of political discourse at the time can be gauged by a statement by head of government W.T. Cosgrave in a debate in the Dáil on divorce in February 1925: 'I am right in saying that the majority of people in this country regard the bond of marriage as a sacramental bond, which is incapable of being dissolved. I, personally, hold that view.'[8] A more extreme instance of Cosgrave's Catholic and conservative outlook was his proposal that an upper house should be established consisting of a 'theological board which would decide whether any legislation was contrary to faith or morals, and that the pope might be assured that no laws contrary to Church teaching would be enacted'.[9] The Catholic Church's loyalty to the state, meanwhile, derived from an understanding that the government of the day would not impinge on its prerogatives in education, health and welfare. In fact, clerical power was demonstrated not by clashes between church and state but by the lack of them; as Tom Inglis has argued, 'the history of the relationship between Church and State in modern Ireland has not been characterised by struggle but rather by peaceful coexistence, each maintaining the power of the other'.[10]

The first interparty government (1948–51), led by distinguished lawyer John Aloysius Costello, merits attention because this coalition was in power when the Tilson case came before the courts. Although Cosgrave and Éamon de Valera were ardent Catholics, often keen to show their fidelity to the church – de Valera, for instance, used the celebratory and triumphalist 1932 Eucharistic Congress to enhance his credentials – Costello, and some of his government colleagues, appear to have been excessively deferential to it. In politics, 'integralism' is the principle that the Catholic faith should be the basis of public law and policy within civil society. By extension, it is fair to say that the period of this coalition was the high-water mark of integralism in Ireland since 'all sorts of forces were at work to make [it] a more totally Catholic state'.[11]

And while the relationship between this government and the church may not have been all plain sailing, there is no doubt that attempts were made during this period to establish an even more intimate association with the hierarchy than that previously enjoyed by the Cumann na nGaedheal or Fianna Fáil parties. Once in power, the interparty government 'seems to have gone out of its way to stress its Catholic allegiance. Almost its first action was to send a telegram of homage to the Pope [Pius XII] couched in terms even more emphatic than that sent by Mr De Valera in 1932':

> On the occasion of our assumption to office and of the first cabinet meeting, my colleagues and myself desire to repose at the feet of Your Holiness the assurance of our filial loyalty and our devotion to your August Person, as well as our firm resolve to be guided in all our work by the teaching of Christ, and to strive for the attainment of social order in Ireland based on Christian principles.[12]

It is hardly surprising that there were objections to such a pandering communiqué. Dermot Keogh has noted the disapproval expressed by the secretary of the Department of the Taoiseach, Maurice Moynihan, who felt that the language was inappropriate, and that a civil power should not 'repose at the feet of a Pope'.[13] Moreover, Keogh has also contended that

> this was a measure of the lack of confidence and excessive deference which the new government was to exhibit when dealing with the Catholic Church. The inter-party government's handling of church–state relations lacked the confidence of the previous Fianna Fáil government. Between 1932 and 1948, Éamon de Valera had established a critical distance between his government and the hierarchy, but the insecurity of Costello and MacBride in handling church–state affairs, in particular, led to a growing intimacy between civil and religious authorities between 1948 and 1951.[14]

Regarding personal piety or obedience to the church, Costello was not just ploughing his own furrow. The interparty government of 1948 was an incongruous collection of political groups made up of Fine Gael, Labour, Clann na Poblachta, National Labour, Clann na Talmhan and independent TDs, but it seems that religious fidelity did not recognise party boundaries. Some historians have suggested that what unified this disparate assortment was an abhorrence of de Valera and Fianna Fáil, but it might also be argued that they were united too in their obsequiousness to the Catholic Church. All the members of the cabinet were Catholics, while parliamentary secretary Brendan Corish, minister for education General Richard Mulcahy, tánaiste and minister for social welfare William Norton and minister for lands Joseph Blowick were members of a Catholic lay organisation, the Knights of Saint Columbanus (Costello was a member of the Columbians, an offshoot of the Ancient Order of Hibernians, which merged with the Knights in the 1920s).[15] The Knights of Columbanus was established in Ireland in 1915 and its principal objectives were to 'provide effective Catholic lay leadership [and] to promote Catholic social principles'.[16] Opposing the Beveridge Plan in Britain, Dr Stafford Johnson, supreme knight of the order in Ireland between 1942 and 1948, argued that 'an integrally Catholic State is the one and only solution to existing social problems'.[17]

Brendan Corish has been described as a 'deeply conservative Catholic';[18] William Norton repeatedly emphasised the alignment of his Labour Party policies with papal encyclicals;[19] General Richard Mulcahy had an 'innate Catholic conservatism',[20] while Joseph Blowick worked as a steward at Knock Shrine in County Mayo.[21] Meanwhile, Michael Keyes, who served as minister for local government after the sudden death of T.J. Murphy, had publicly hailed the Irish Christian Front 'for bringing into existence a social and economic system based on the Christian ideals of life as expressed in the papal encyclicals'.[22] For his part, James Dillon, minister for agriculture, was a long-serving member of the Ancient Order of Hibernians, eventually becoming that organisation's national president.[23] Alvin Jackson has noted that the previous Fianna Fáil government, which had been in power for sixteen years, had offered 'one or two token Protestants', such as Erskine Childers, without compromising its assertively Catholic identity;[24] it appears that Costello's interparty government, at least at cabinet level, did not offer any.

Seán MacBride was minister for external affairs in this coalition government and his party, Clann na Poblachta, apparently derived inspiration for its left-wing republican policies from papal encyclicals;[25] indeed, one of the central thrusts of MacBride's project was the alignment of Catholicism and republicanism.[26] Speaking in January 1948 at a general election campaign rally in Ballina, County Mayo, he told the large public gathering that 'Clann na Poblachta wanted to make the country Christian in reality and not Christian in name only' before adding that his party 'stood on the principles of the Papal Encyclicals and the social plan of the Bishop of Clonfert'.[27]

Nor was MacBride himself a shrinking violet when it came to professing his allegiance to the Catholic Church. A letter he wrote to Archbishop McQuaid on 30 October 1947 – the day of his election to the Dáil – shows that, in his mind, the lines between church and state were very blurred indeed: 'I hasten, as my first act, to pay my humble respects to Your Grace and place myself at Your Grace's disposal. I would always welcome advice which Your Grace would be good enough to give me and shall be at Your Grace's disposal should there be any matters upon which Your Grace feels that I could be of assistance.'[28] Diarmaid Ferriter put it more bluntly when he observed that MacBride's letter was a direct invitation to McQuaid to become involved in the legislative process in the 1940s and '50s.[29] Furthermore, it seems that it was not enough for MacBride just to repose at the feet of the pope. On a visit to Kylemore Abbey in 1948, his sycophantic tendencies were again evident when he was introduced to the abbess; apparently, he 'slid forward on one knee and gently, slowly and deferentially, bent his head to kiss the ring of office'.[30]

Costello appointed another Catholic, Cecil Lavery, as attorney general to the interparty government and he remained in that position until he was appointed a member of the Supreme Court in April 1950.[31] Costello then appointed Charles Casey as Lavery's successor, and while Lavery sat on the Supreme Court bench for Ernest Tilson's appeal, quite extraordinarily Mary Tilson was represented by Casey at the same hearing. Casey was an ardent Catholic and his resolute leanings were evident from a speech he delivered at the inaugural meeting of the Students Debating Society at the King's Inns, Dublin, which reads more like a Catholic bishop's sermon than a legal scholar's lecture to undergraduates. He also demonstrated an inclination to make Ireland a more integrally Catholic state:

> We in this State are fortunate in that we are living in a country where spiritual values are still supreme ... This country is predominantly a Catholic country. That does not mean that Parliament should penalise any other creed, but it does mean this, that Parliament cannot surely be asked to introduce legislation contrary to the teaching of that great Church ... The Catholic Church has to-day a membership of 400,000,000 in the world of those who acknowledge in full its teaching. Every member of that Church is bound to practise his Faith and to bring up his or her children in the same true Faith.[32]

The interparty government enjoyed some notable successes in public health and housebuilding, but it is possibly best remembered for the 'mother and child' controversy of 1951. The influence of the Catholic hierarchy on state matters was particularly apparent in this multi-layered controversy, and it is noteworthy that its genesis lay in the late summer of 1950, when the minister for health, Dr Noël Browne (also a Catholic), moved to reactivate the 1947 Health Act, which he had inherited from Fianna Fáil. This was also the period in which the Tilson case was being played out in the courts.[33]

Browne sought to address the high rate of infant mortality at the time by introducing a state maternity scheme which would be accessible without a means test. The Catholic Church strongly opposed the scheme for multiple reasons, but it was particularly concerned with the gynaecological care element because it did not accord with 'Catholic principles'. Early in the crisis Bishop James Staunton wrote to John A. Costello expressing the church's objections and advising him, among other things, that the scheme 'was in direct opposition to the rights of the family'.[34] Browne was summoned to Archbishop McQuaid's residence where the archbishop also made him aware of the church's concerns and assured him that Catholic social teaching meant 'Catholic moral teaching in regard to things social'.[35] For his part, Costello sought final appraisal for the scheme from the hierarchy – which was a bit like asking McQuaid to endorse an Edna O'Brien novel – while Seán MacBride felt it was politically impossible to ignore the views of the Catholic Church on the matter. Dermot Keogh notes that MacBride 'felt that the ministers, who were all Catholics, could not disregard the views of the bishops'.[36] Unsurprisingly, the hierarchy rejected the scheme and, with the exception of Browne, the entire interparty cabinet voted to drop it, deciding to prepare another scheme in conformity with Catholic social teaching.[37]

Ronan Fanning has observed that Costello was 'more aggressive in his deference to the church authorities than any of his predecessors'; in the aftermath of the controversy he unambiguously declared in the Dáil: 'I am an Irishman second; I am a Catholic first. If the Hierarchy give me any direction with regard to Catholic social teaching or Catholic moral teaching, I accept without qualification in all respects the teaching of the Hierarchy and the church to which I belong.'[38]

THE HOLY YEAR OF 1950

Ernest and Mary Tilson found themselves in the High Court and Supreme Court over custody of their children in 1950, which, as noted, had been designated a 'Holy Year' by Pope Pius XII. In fact, the unified and ebullient support of the affair by the Catholic Church, politicians and Catholic lay people goes some way to capturing the socio-political *zeitgeist* of the time. To mark the occasion of the Holy Year, the Department of Posts and Telegraphs issued a commemorative stamp featuring the bronze statue of St Peter in St Peter's Basilica in Rome. That measure was hardly a surprise since James Everett, the minister of that department, was a 'staunch Catholic traditionalist, a daily communicant and [was] on friendly terms with archbishop of Dublin, John Charles McQuaid'.[39] Special ceremonies were held in Ireland, and Irish people headed to Rome in their droves. Politicians, senior members of the hierarchy and the well-heeled travelled by scheduled and specially chartered aircraft from Dublin and Shannon airports, while most others went by ferry and then overland by train. One party of 800 pilgrims departed from Belfast port, while other pilgrimages to the Eternal City were organised by such groups as the Catholic Teachers, the Catholic Girl Guides, the Legion of Mary, the Gaelic Athletic Association and the Knights of Columbanus. There was even a pilgrimage organised exclusively for Irish-speakers.[40] The largest group of pilgrims – approximately one thousand – was led by the archbishop of Armagh, John D'Alton, and was seen off from Dún Laoghaire ferry port by Archbishop McQuaid and Seán MacBride. This group attended a ceremony in St Peter's Basilica among a crowd of 35,000 to 40,000 and, in a special audience afterwards, was blessed by Pius XII.[41] A report in the *Munster Express* provided an eyewitness account which also shows how some Irish Catholics could rejoice in their faith:

> The applause which greeted the Holy Father was a most inspiring moment, as we in the Irish section felt proud of our faith. The Holy Father extended a special welcome to the Irish pilgrims, which we greeted with prolonged applause. This was undoubtedly the crowning moment of the whole pilgrimage.[42]

At home, Ernest Tilson's employer, Dublin Corporation, unanimously passed a resolution tendering 'our filial homage and devotion to his Holiness on the occasion of the opening of the 25th Holy Year'.[43] Meanwhile, the Central Council of the GAA unanimously decided that it should be represented in Rome during Holy Year by its president and general secretary.[44] On that note, *Irish Times* columnist Myles na gCopaleen (aka Flann O'Brien) reported – with tongue in cheek – that in honour of the Holy Year, 'a general amnesty' might be offered to all GAA players who had 'been detected either playing or watching soccer'. He also declared that there was a suggestion in one GAA publication that 'one of the 1950 All-Ireland finals might be played in Rome and that *the ball should be thrown in by His Holiness the Pope himself!!!!*'[45]

Throughout the country, Holy Year crosses – some of which were illuminated – were erected in such places as Bray Head, County Wicklow; Ballybunion and Carrauntoohil, County Kerry; Kanturk, County Cork, and at Clogherhead, County Louth. In Waterford, several thousand people participated in a Holy Year pilgrimage by walking behind a 16 foot cross from the city centre to the village of Mothel, near Carrick-on-Suir.[46] And so that middle-class Catholic ladies might be properly attired in Rome 'during Holy Year celebrations', the Brown Thomas department store advertised that it had taken 'a delivery of French Black Lace Mantillas, for use during Papal Audiences'.[47]

Apart from the delights of a holiday, pilgrims who travelled to Rome in 1950 and who visited the four great patriarchal basilicas, St Peter's, St John Lateran, St Paul and St Mary Major, had the added incentive of being granted a jubilee indulgence. In Catholic Church teaching, an indulgence is 'a remission before God of the temporal punishment due to sins whose guilt has already been forgiven' or 'a way to reduce the amount of punishment one has to undergo for sins'. In his Lenten pastoral letter, bishop of Killaloe Michael Fogarty described the Holy Year jubilee indulgence more succinctly as the 'great fruit obtainable' from the journey to Rome, and reasoned that 'the more indulgences we gain, the shorter will be our suffering in Purgatory'.[48]

For his part, Archbishop McQuaid announced that some people could qualify for the special indulgence without travelling to Rome and could visit Irish churches and cathedrals instead; they included people over seventy years of age, those engaged in care for the sick and 'girls and women living ... in institutions for women'.[49] If 'fallen women' were lacking in the wherewithal to travel to the Eternal City, they could take comfort in the knowledge that they too would be afforded the opportunity to lessen their term in Purgatory.

Irish political leaders saw the Holy Year as an opportunity to deepen the special relationship between Ireland and the Holy See and were well represented in Rome. In fact, with the exception of Dr Noël Browne, all members of the cabinet of the interparty government attended.[50] At the opening ceremony in January, President Seán T. O'Kelly represented the people of Ireland while Seán MacBride represented the government. Also attending during the year was leader of Fianna Fáil, Éamon de Valera, ambassador to the Holy See, Joseph Walshe, and taoiseach, John A. Costello, who presented Pius XII with an Irish rosary.[51] Minister for justice, Seán MacEoin, attended a special ceremony,[52] as did the attorney general, Charles Casey. A memo on 'Irish Ambassador to the Holy See' headed notepaper shows that during his visit, on 15 January 1950, Costello met monsignors Giovanni Montini (the future Pope Paul VI) and Domenico Tardini, who was a long-time aide of Pope Pius XII and who was later appointed Cardinal Secretary of State by Pope John XIII. Apparently, during the meeting Tardini 'referred to the mixed-marriage situation in Ireland without defining the precise points of law or procedure to which the Holy See objected'.[53] In his 1999 biography of McQuaid, John Cooney writes that Tardini made enquiries about the Tilson case, suggesting that the Vatican had taken a special interest in it.[54] It is clear that the Vatican had a concern regarding mixed marriages in Ireland at this time and that Costello was aware of this. From an Irish perspective, the Holy Year celebrations were a huge success; the 'special relationship' with Rome was reinforced and 'all members of the inter-party government demonstrated, if demonstration were required, that Ireland was ever loyal to Rome'.[55]

Despite all this, the southern state was bi-confessional when Ernest Tilson married Mary Barnes in 1941 and remained so when their dispute came before the courts nine years later. Catholics made up 95 per cent of the population, but the overwhelming majority of the remaining 5 per cent were Protestant. After partition, the Protestant minority in the south found itself politically and culturally isolated and under threat from what it perceived to be an overbearingly Catholic state; Protestants faced the loss of their ethnic or cultural identity through assimilation with the Catholic majority and also through falling numbers.

That said, Protestant decline in Ireland had begun a lot earlier with the reform of the penal laws, the disestablishment of the Church of Ireland and the transfer of land from Protestant ascendancy to Catholic tenantry.[56] And as Daithí Ó Corráin has noted, the decline of the Protestant population in the south predated independence, with the greatest decrease in numbers occurring between the censuses of 1911 and 1926 when the population fell by more than 30 per cent.[57] The trend continued after that period, albeit at a slower pace, and can be attributed to such factors as the end of the political union between southern Ireland and Britain, and, for some Protestants, the unpalatability of the Catholic ethos of the Free State; emigration prompted by the Second World War; the departure of British army personnel and civil servants; and finally, the Catholic Church directives on mixed marriages.

In fact, the Protestant population in the Republic of Ireland fell almost five times faster than the overall population between 1946 and 1951, and by the end of the 1960s it stood at 130,000.[58]

Nevertheless, successive Free State governments were keen to retain the support of the minority, and Protestants were generally well protected in such matters as religious equality, health and education and were disproportionately represented in industry and in professions such as the law and medicine. Caleb Wood Richardson notes that although Protestants made up just 5 per cent of the population by the late 1950s, 'they still occupied 20 per cent of the administrative, executive and managerial positions in Ireland'.[59] Of course, these statistics, as Richardson also notes, do not take account of the experiences of working-class Protestants in southern Ireland like Ernest Tilson.

Deirdre Nuttall has observed that in the early independence period, the number of urban working-class Protestants 'declined dramatically and rapidly – much more quickly than the decline of rural Protestants'. In terms of how working-class Protestants were often perceived, one of her interviewees, who had lived in a tenement flat in Dublin as a child, said, 'they always taught here that Protestants were well-off … there was no such thing as poor Protestants, yet you have the Society for Distressed Protestants, and you had the Protestant Aid, all these things were set up to help Protestants who were in poverty, living in these conditions'. Another of Nuttall's interviewees described how her Protestant mother and father, the latter a member of the Orange Order, experienced 'frequent tensions' and 'fierce arguments' with Catholic neighbours in a working-class area in Dublin.[60]

Turner's Cottages was predominantly Catholic, but there is no evidence to suggest that Ernest Tilson's relations with his immediate Catholic neighbours were strained or difficult. Employed as a gardener in the Parks Department of Dublin Corporation, and earning approximately £5.00 per week, his correspondence shows that he was reasonably well educated, articulate, with an above average lexical range. Judy Tilson's description of him as a 'charming, dapper, ladies' man', who often wore a suit and tie and always carried an umbrella on his arm, is hardly consonant with the image, advanced by some, of the post-independence southern Protestant cowering in the face of intimidation or an overbearing Catholic ethos.[61]

Addressing the working-class Protestant experience of life in the Free State, Ian d'Alton has observed that 'for poorer Protestants, especially urban ones, the ghetto hardly existed and they were picked off all the easier by mixed marriages and economic emigration'.[62] In the same vein, Andrew R. Holmes and Eugenio F. Biagini have argued that working-class Protestants suffered disproportionately from the effects of *Ne Temere* because they did not have the social capital to find suitable Protestant partners and ended up either 'submitting to the decree' or remaining unmarried.[63] In any event, Ernest Tilson was introduced to his working-class Catholic wife by her father and then 'submitted to *Ne Temere*' before his marriage in 1941.

PART 2

The Tilsons and the Courts

CHAPTER 5

Paternal Supremacy and the Irish Courts

The Catholic Church and the state held conflicting positions regarding the religious upbringing of the children of a mixed marriage.[1] Civil law had long dictated that the father had an absolute right to decide on the religious upbringing and education of his children, a principle known as 'paternal supremacy', which was a relic of old English common law. In contrast, the Catholic Church insisted that children of mixed marriages should be brought up as Catholics, irrespective of the faith to which either parent belonged. By analysing previous court judgments, this chapter examines how the father, in civil law, enjoyed the sole prerogative in determining the religious upbringing of his children. It is argued, particularly in light of the Frost case judgment of 1945, that Ernest Tilson and his legal team would have been confident, if not certain, that they would win their case in the High Court. J.M. Kelly outlines the father's position up to the Tilson case in 1950:

> The principles applied in Ireland were those inherited from the old common law and appeared to be well settled. The right of the father to the custody of his child was fundamental; he also had the collateral right to control his child's education, and in particular to determine its religion; his wishes in this last respect could be enforced even after his lifetime ... so fundamental did this prerogative appear that the law would not allow the father to divest himself of it.[2]

In preparation for the High Court hearing, Tilson's legal team would have taken comfort from the fact that in all previous judgments concerning the religious upbringing of children of mixed marriages – unless there was a threat to the welfare of the children – Irish courts followed precedent. Precedent is evoked to provide consistency in the application of the laws, and two objectives are pursued: first, that the law is applied equally, so that similar cases are treated uniformly; second, and perhaps more relevant to the Tilson case, that the law becomes more predictable since one can determine in advance the legal quality of a proposed course of action.[3] Moreover, because previous decisions in cases often relied on common law, precedent has an added significance in that 'common law systems, unlike their civilian equivalents, by and large lack authoritative codes, their rules are to be found in the decisions of courts which are assigned the task of applying them'.[4] That said, the operation of the doctrine of precedent depends on the principle that inferior courts must follow the relevant prior rationales of superior courts. To do otherwise would make it difficult to assess the relative authority of competing precedents.[5] It is important to note, however, particularly in regard to the Tilson case, that the doctrine of precedent has never been an absolute constraint on judges 'because there are a variety of ways by which judges can pay lip service to the doctrine and yet not be bound by it'.[6] In other words, Mr Justice George Gavan Duffy, who would hear the Tilson case in the High Court, was not bound to follow the doctrine of precedent.

The issue of paternal supremacy is also referred to in Anne Crone's novel *Bridie Steen* (1949), which is set in the border county of Fermanagh in post-partition Northern Ireland. The novel's Catholic eponymous protagonist intends to marry William Henry, a Protestant. However, her Catholic stepmother, Rose Anne, not only spells out to Bridie the danger of marrying a Protestant, but also tacitly refers to paternal supremacy when she remarks, 'You would be mad to marry him, because no mixed marriage ever comes to good and he'd make your children Protestants.'[7] If Bridie were to follow the teaching of her own church, the children would be raised as Catholics, but under civil law, William Henry, as the father, would be legally entitled to raise any of his children in his own Protestant faith.

The Meade case came before the courts in 1870, just after the disestablishment of the Anglican Church of Ireland, which supposedly set all religious denominations in Ireland on an equal footing by placing them all in the category of voluntary non-state bodies. In 1859 Robert Meade, a Protestant, married Alice Ronayne, a Catholic.[8] Eight years later Ronayne died. A dispute soon arose over the religious upbringing of the children of the marriage who had, up to the time of their mother's death, been raised as Catholics. The sister of the deceased, Mary Ronayne, also a Catholic, took an action at the court of chancery in Dublin in order to ensure that the children would continue their Catholic upbringing and that the father be restrained from 'interfering with the religion or the religious education of the minors'.[9] The dispute evidently arose when Robert Meade formed a relationship with 'a Protestant lady who was animated by strong religious zeal' and then decided that he wished to raise his children as Protestants, appointing a Protestant governess to this end.[10] Crucially, the court heard that, before his marriage, he had promised to raise his children as Catholics when 'required to do so by the officiating clergyman' – consistent with the fact that this Catholic requirement predated *Ne Temere*.[11]

The judge, Lord O'Hagan, was well aware that paternal supremacy was enshrined in civil law, and that the wishes of the father should normally be granted, but he was also very mindful of the welfare of the children. His decision took into account the rights of the father and the question of whether a sudden change of religious faith would be in the best interests of the children. In any event, he concluded that 'the authority of the father to guide and govern the education of his child is a very sacred thing, bestowed by the almighty, and to be sustained to the uttermost by human law'. Despite the judge's assertion of paternal supremacy, his choice of words clearly invoked religious principles. As in previous cases, O'Hagan took time to interview the children and ascertained that, even though their 'Catholic convictions had been shaken' by their recent introduction to Protestantism, they now 'had learnt something of both [religions] but had confident belief in neither'. Although the children expressed a desire to continue with their Catholic upbringing, he ultimately dismissed Mary Ronayne's petition, and the children were raised in their father's Protestant religion.

The significance of the ruling lies in the fact that paternal supremacy – and, by extension, civil law – held sway, even though the children had been raised as Catholics for many of their formative years. The ruling was based primarily on the rights of the father, with the proviso that the children's welfare, if raised as Protestants, would not be compromised. With regard to the promise that Meade made to the officiating clergyman at his wedding regarding the Catholic education of the children, the judge said that, although Meade undoubtedly made this promise, 'that engagement was not of binding force in law'.

The Grey case of 1902 also upheld paternal supremacy, although circumstances were markedly different. Both Charlotte Callan and Henry Grey, who had married in 1886, were Protestants. There were six children of the marriage, three daughters and three sons. Henry Grey died intestate in 1900, and his wife, unable to provide for the upkeep of her daughters, placed them in a Protestant orphanage in Harold's Cross in Dublin. However, in November 1901, Callan entered an interfaith relationship that resulted in her conversion to Catholicism and marriage to a Catholic. Shortly after the marriage, she began to raise her sons as Catholics and decided to remove her three daughters from the Protestant orphanage where they had lived for nearly two years, and to raise them as Catholics also. The court had to decide if she was within her rights, as the only surviving parent, to change the religious upbringing of her children. Lord Chief Justice O'Brien outlined the choice to be made:

> Can a mother, who had three children by a husband who was a Protestant, and who after his death, whilst she herself was a Protestant, placed them in a Protestant orphanage where they were well cared, now that she has, on a second marriage, become a Catholic, insist on these children, all of whom are of tender years, being restored to her by writ of *habeas corpus*, when the Court to which she applies for that writ is satisfied that she intends to bring them up in a faith different from that in which their father lived and died? That is the question we have to decide.[12]

The paternal relatives of the children gave evidence to the effect that their father was a devout member of the Church of Ireland and would be incensed at the notion that his children should be raised as Catholics. They also suggested that, had Grey foreseen his wife's attempts to raise them as Catholics, 'he would have endeavoured, so far as in his power lay, to safeguard his children from any attempt to change their faith'. The management of the Protestant orphanage where the children resided also gave evidence to the effect that the children were content there and did not wish to leave.

In reaching his verdict, the judge described the case as 'painful' and noted the 'weight of the arguments in support of the mother's application – mother's love, the sacredness of the home … and the mother's rights as guardian by nature and statute'. The judge also pointed out that the mother had already 'committed a breach of marital trust' when she raised her three sons as Catholics after she had met her second husband. However, his judgment centred on whether the father had 'abdicated or forfeited his right to have the children brought up in his religion'.[13] He decided that Grey had not done so, and that 'the law, whose ministers we are, makes no hesitation: it adopts for the children the religion of the father'. The judge ordered that the children remain in the orphanage and continue with their Protestant upbringing. He also offered a defence of paternal supremacy, stating that, regardless of the merits or demerits of this principle, a court could not stand

Paternal Supremacy and the Irish Courts

accused of favouring one faith over another. The appearance of impartiality was of particular importance in a country where sectarianism was an issue:

> In every country where sectarian divisions exist, it is essential that there should be a settled and intelligible rule as to the religion of the offspring of the wedlock; and, that rule be in the abstract right or wrong, it is better that there should be some rule than none at all ... a lay tribunal does not and cannot distinguish and adjudge between the claims of the various Churches as leaders of divine truth ... but it has an objective rule – the male parent's professed religion – it can decide securely and without appearance of bias.[14]

The Frost case came before the courts in 1945, eight years after the constitution was adopted. Like the earlier cases already examined, the judgment in this case – even though it was decided after 1937 – cemented paternal supremacy over prenuptial agreements. In 1930 Charles Frost, a Protestant, had married Margaret Frost, a Catholic, in a Catholic church in Dublin.[15] Before the marriage, and in accordance with the requirements for obtaining a dispensation, Charles Frost signed an undertaking agreeing that the six children of the marriage would be brought up in the Catholic faith. The marriage was not a happy one, however, and much of the couple's discontent seems to have arisen from the fact that, although their children were baptised as Catholics, Charles Frost nonetheless insisted on raising and educating them as Protestants. Margaret Frost appears to have complied reluctantly with her husband's wishes, but the couple finally decided to separate in 1940, after ten years of marriage. As part of the separation agreement, Margaret was given custody of the three youngest children, while Charles, as Ernest Tilson would do, placed the three older children in the Birds' Nest orphanage. Margaret Frost later claimed that he had taken this decision without her consent. Shortly after the separation, she fell upon hard times and, because of her poverty, was forced to hand over the three youngest children to her husband, who in turn placed them with their siblings in the Birds' Nest. A year later Charles Frost died; his widow then set about recovering her children and raising them as Catholics, by way of an order for *habeas corpus* from the High Court.

In his will, Charles Frost directed that his children should be brought up in the Church of Ireland tradition.[16] The question before the court was whether his widow now had the right to raise the children as Catholics. The court found that the two youngest children could not yet have fixed religious views, and should therefore be returned to their mother. In its ruling, the court recognised the rights of the father, but nonetheless decided that Margaret Frost had the right, because of the ages of the younger children, to dictate their religious faith; the older children should remain in the Protestant home and continue their upbringing as Protestants.[17] With regard to the Catholic prenuptial promise, Mr Justice Cahir Davitt observed that Frost had 'given the undertaking required, observed it for a period and then refused to abide by it'.[18] Although the judge recognised that Frost had entered into a signed prenuptial agreement, he found that this had no legal basis. Instead, he based his judgment on the absolute rights of the father: the children in question should be raised in the faith of the deceased father, as Charles Frost had set out in his will.

In an effort to overturn that decision, Margaret Frost appealed to the Supreme Court, where her counsel evoked Articles 41.1 and 42.1 of the constitution. Article 41.1 states that 'The State recognises the Family as the natural primary and fundamental unit group of Society' while 42.1 decrees that 'The State acknowledges that the primary and natural educator of the child is the Family'. In other words, counsel contended that the family, comprising both parents and children, was a unit; thus, any decision regarding the education of the children should be a joint decision. Her counsel claimed that Charles Frost did not have the sole right to decide on the religious upbringing of the children.

The chief justice of the Supreme Court, Mr Justice C.J. Sullivan, disagreed. He acknowledged that severe criticism by Frost's counsel of her husband's decision to 'break the undertaking which he had signed prior to his marriage' was justified, but he also stated that it did 'not deprive him [the father] of his legal right to determine the religion of the children'. His final decision was unambiguous: '... the rule which the Courts have consistently followed in this country ... is that the father has the legal right, and when that right has been exercised by him, the children must be educated in the religion he has chosen'. Essentially, in the Frost case the Supreme Court upheld paternal supremacy, arguing that common law, inherited from British law, ensured the absolute right of the father to determine the religion of his children and that this was not unconstitutional. Regarding the signed prenuptial agreement, the court was of the opinion that since both parents agreed subsequent to the marriage that their children would be raised as Protestants, it was not necessary to consider its validity: both parents had reneged on the promise given to the Catholic Church that their children would be raised as Catholics. Notably, the Supreme Court ordered that all the children – including the two youngest, who, because of the ruling of the High Court, had earlier returned to their mother – should continue with their Protestant upbringing in 'Mrs. Smyly's Homes'.[19] This judgment shows that paternal supremacy had not been nullified in Irish civil law by the 1937 constitution; the judgment also 'caused deep resentment in Catholic circles', largely because the court had ignored Catholic 'promises'.[20]

Only seven months before the Tilson case came to the attention of the courts, Cornelius Keenan, a Catholic, who gave an address at Brompton Park in Belfast, applied to the High Court in Dublin in October 1949 to make absolute a *habeas corpus* order for the production of his children, Sarah Elizabeth aged eight and Maureen aged seven. The children had been placed in the Birds' Nest five years earlier by Keenan's wife, Sarah, a Protestant who 'became a Catholic on the day she was married'.[21] The two children had been baptised and initially raised as Catholics, but, as in the Tilson case, were educated as Protestants after being admitted to the orphanage. This was also a fractious marriage. The court heard how it had been 'unhappy, uncertain and erratic from the beginning', that 'at times the husband worked, and at times he was idle' and that 'there was much disagreement, quarrels and temporary separations'. Keenan also 'had been to prison as a result of his failure to provide maintenance for his wife and children'.[22] The upshot of these troubled circumstances saw both parents agreeing to place the children in the Birds' Nest.

Keenan now wanted to remove the children to the Catholic Sacred Heart orphanage in Drumcondra so that they might be raised as Catholics; his wife, on the other hand, wished them to remain in the Birds' Nest so that they could continue with their Protestant upbringing. The court was also told that the children had been 'healthy, happy and well cared for' for the past five years in the Birds' Nest.[23] No doubt mindful of paternal supremacy and how this had been treated by the courts in the past, Mr Justice Haugh distilled the case:

> There was only one real issue for the Court to decide. Was the father, having regard to all the circumstances, now entitled to have his children removed from the institution in which they now were – a Protestant institution – to the convent at Drumcondra, where they would have a Catholic education. The law in these matters has already been argued in the Supreme Court.[24]

After considering whether the father had forfeited his right to determine in what religion his children should be educated by reason of his personal conduct, and whether he had abdicated that right by permitting them to be educated as Protestants for the previous five years, Haugh decided that because the children had formed 'no convictions of any sort on religion' the father should have custody. The children were accordingly removed from the Birds' Nest with an undertaking from Keenan that they would be placed in the Catholic orphanage in Drumcondra. Notwithstanding the principle of paternal supremacy, the courts always maintained that the welfare of the children in these cases was paramount. However, it raises this question: if the children were happy and settled in the Birds' Nest and had no fixed religious convictions, what was the merit of removing them and placing them in a different orphanage, particularly on the application of a father with a dubious parenting record? Mr Justice Haugh's decision not only removed the children from their stable environment, it also put them at risk of being unhappy in the Catholic institution.

In Ireland and elsewhere, parallel systems of governance in church and state inevitably led to conflicts. But despite the well-documented and vigorous efforts of the church, legal authority ultimately lay with the civil power. From the Meade case in 1870 to the Keenan case in 1949, Irish courts relied on civil law and generally upheld paternal supremacy, unless there was a danger to the welfare of the children. Circumstances in the Meade and Keenan cases were similar to those in the Tilson case, in that the children of the marriage were raised as Catholics for many of their formative years. However, the courts still decided that the father had the sole right to determine the religious upbringing of his children. Furthermore, in the Meade case the promise given to the Catholic Church was deemed not to be legally binding. Circumstances in the Frost case were also similar to those in the Tilson case in that the Protestant father had entered into a prenuptial agreement in which he had promised to raise his children as Catholics, only to renege on that agreement later. And, crucially, although counsel for Margaret Frost evoked the relevant articles of the 1937 constitution, the Supreme Court still upheld the absolute right of the father. In the wake of this particular judgment, Protestants in mixed marriages or those contemplating marriage to Catholics understandably felt that they had little to fear from the same constitution. Moreover, because the courts in these cases relied on the doctrine of precedent and were unequivocal in their judgments, it is likely that Ernest Tilson and his legal team would have come to court with an air of confident expectation rather than trepidation.

CHAPTER 6

The Affidavits and the High Court Case

On 18 May 1950, just three days after Ernest Tilson placed his three sons in the Birds' Nest, an *ex parte* application was made in the High Court before Mr Justice Kevin Dixon for a conditional order of *habeas corpus* against the trustees of the orphanage on behalf of Mary Tilson.[1] The hearing was widely reported in national newspapers under headlines including 'Mother Tells How Children Were Taken' (*The Irish Times*) or 'Mother To Get Her Three Children' (*Irish Press*). Two provincial newspapers – the *Anglo-Celt* and the *Meath Chronicle* – both of which were based near Ernest Tilson's hometown of Oldcastle, also carried the story. In fact, on its front page the *Anglo-Celt* ran the misleading headline 'OLDCASTLE FATHER Ordered To Give Children To Wife'.[2]

At the hearing, only Mary Tilson's first affidavit, which she signed on 17 May 1950, was read by barrister James R. Heavey to the court; at this point Ernest had not sworn an affidavit. Mary's affidavit named as respondents her husband and the trustees of Mrs Smyly's Homes and Schools – who 'manage and control an institution known variously as the "Birds' Nest" and "Mrs. Smylie's [sic] Home" at York Road, Dún Laoghaire ... wherein young children are taught and brought up in the religious beliefs of the Church of Ireland'.

Regarding their marriage in St Mary's church, Mary described how her parents did not want her to get married other than in a Catholic church, and that she accepted their position. She suggested that Ernest was so anxious that they should marry, that he was prepared to do so in a Catholic church, and that when it looked as though a dispensation might not be forthcoming from the Catholic Church, he did not suggest that they marry in a Protestant church.

The affidavit outlined how, after their marriage, the couple lived at 12 Turner's Cottages for two years with Mary's parents before moving to a cottage at St Anne's Estate, Sybil Hill Lodge, Clontarf. Mary explained how, shortly after arriving there, her husband began to drink heavily, 'squandering his wages' and failing to provide any money for herself or her children. She felt compelled to return with her children to live in Turner's Cottages with her parents and found employment at the Swastika Laundry. This situation continued 'for some time' until it was decided, 'between herself and her husband', to 'effect a reconciliation', the result of which saw Ernest returning to Turner's Cottages, with her parents agreeing to rent a separate room to them for their 'sole use'. This arrangement ended 'some months later' when he allegedly struck her when she was pregnant, resulting in a miscarriage.

Shortly after this assault Ernest 'went away on a holiday' to his parents' house in Oldcastle, taking his third child, Paul, with him. According to Mary's affidavit, he failed to provide any financial support for his family back in Dublin. She sought advice from Miss Wogan of the Irish Society for the Protection of Cruelty to Children, which resulted in the issuing of a District Court summons in December 1949. The summons was dismissed under an undertaking that the couple would 'live together once more' and that Ernest would pay Mary £4 per week in support.[3] This agreement was later cited by Mr Justice Murnaghan and Mr Justice Black when delivering their judgments in the Supreme Court. The District Court summons was also significant in drawing in external actors to the case: correspondence between W.H. Richardson, solicitor for Ernest, and Rev. W.L.M. Giff shows how much responsibility Giff had assumed on behalf of Tilson:

W.H. Richardson, Solicitor and Land Agent,
32 Kildare Street,
Dublin

Rev. W.L.M. Giff,
5 Townsend Street,
Dublin

2nd November 1950

Ernest Tilson

Dear Mr. Giff,
I enclose a copy of the information sworn by Mrs. Tilson on which she obtained the Order for her husband's arrest. Will you please go through this carefully with Tilson and let me know how soon I could see him about it. As you know we are down for hearing again on Wednesday the 15th November at 10.30.

Yours sincerely,

Henry Richardson[4]

The Affidavits and the High Court Case

According to Mary, Ernest continued making the £4 per week maintenance payment to her from December 1949 to April 1950, when the support abruptly ended. However, on 1 April 1950 he returned home 'drunk and ordered [her] out'. When she refused, 'he used violence' to manhandle her into the hallway and she, in turn, fled with the children to her mother's area of the cottage.[5] The following day she returned from work to find that her three eldest children, David, Alan and Paul, were missing.

Regarding religious practice, Mary noted that Ernest never objected to her taking the children to Sunday mass or 'their being brought up as Roman Catholics' and that she knew 'nothing to suggest that [he] treated his religion seriously'. That said, she admitted that her children had informed her that Ernest had taken them to Church of Ireland services on two occasions. Mary also described the circumstances of her marriage to Ernest on 10 December 1941, noting that she was a member of the Catholic Church and he was 'a member of the Church of Ireland'.[6] She stated that her husband at the time of their marriage 'subscribed to a solemn promise and undertaking that all children to be born to us of our said marriage should be dutifully and faithfully nurtured and brought up in the religion of the Catholic Church'. Mary then described how she had 'always striven to bring up [her children] as good Catholics' and how 'David and Alan have been attending the Convent National Schools of St. Mary's, Haddington Road'. She claimed that 'in their present environment [the Birds' Nest]' they were 'in grave spiritual danger' because their 'religious education and training' had 'reached a stage where any attempted indoctrination or Protestant teachings' would 'be bound to cause great mental and moral upset and confusion'. It is interesting that in preparation for the High Court hearing, Mabel Bird sought information regarding the religious education of the children in the Birds' Nest on behalf of T.G. McVeagh, solicitor for Mrs Smyly's Homes, and that she wanted to know how the children were 'reacting' to their new Protestant education:

16th June, 50
re/ Tilson Children

Dear Miss Jackson,

Would you please let me have by Monday morning any information you can regarding the religious beliefs of the three Tilson boys in the Birds' Nest, and also particulars of what they are being taught at present and how they are reacting to the teaching they are now receiving.

This information is required by our solicitor, and he is anxious to have it as soon as possible.

Yours sincerely,

Mabel Bird[7]

Mary proposed in her affidavit that if her husband would commit to supporting her and the children financially, she would give up her job in the Swastika Laundry. If her husband refused to make such a commitment, she would continue in her employment and the children would be cared for by her mother and sister. Either scenario would allow her children to receive 'proper schooling ... in the principles of the Catholic religion'. When the reading of her affidavit had concluded, Mr Justice Dixon granted a conditional order of *habeas corpus* directed to Ernest and the trustees of Mrs Smyly's Homes to produce the three children David (eight) Alan (six) and Paul (five).

Two weeks later, on 3 July, Mary Tilson applied to the High Court to make that conditional order absolute. The case, which came before Mr Justice George Gavan Duffy, received widespread national newspaper coverage under such headlines as: 'Mother Claims Her Three Children' (*The Irish Times*), 'Put Children in Birds' Nest' (*Irish Press*) and 'Children's Religion: An issue in Dublin parents' dispute' (*Irish Independent*). Mary Tilson's solicitor, George McGrath, instructed Mr T.K. Liston SC and James R. Heavey. Ernest Tilson's solicitor, W.H. Richardson, instructed Mr W.I. Hamill, Mr F.G.O. Budd SC, Mr W.H. Carson SC and T.B. Hannon. The trustees of Mrs Smyly's Homes were represented by their solicitor, T.G. McVeagh, who instructed E.S. Fitzsimon. Through their lawyers, the trustees maintained a neutral position throughout the case, stating that they would abide by whatever decision the court reached.

Mary and Ernest Tilson's affidavits to the High Court were a litany of claim and counterclaim consistent with marital breakdown. In fact, Gavan Duffy described them as 'a confused mass of evidence, always hard to summarise when husband and wife fall out'.[8] That said, they offer a clear insight into the couple's domestic lives, revealing many of the reasons why the rancour occurred and intensified. Although both parties give an account of their marriage in 1941 and their own versions of the promises they made to the Catholic Church regarding the religious upbringing of their children, religion or religious difference is shown not to be the predominant cause of the dispute.

The Affidavits and the High Court Case

The first day of the hearing was almost entirely taken up with the reading of the affidavits of Mary Tilson; Ernest Tilson; Ernest's mother, Harriette Tilson; the secretary of Mrs Smyly's Homes, Francis Russell; and David Tilson's teachers, Miss Traynor and Miss Ryder. In response to his wife's first affidavit, which had been read at the earlier High Court hearing before Mr Justice Dixon, Ernest offered his version of the circumstances surrounding their marriage in 1941:

> As to the undertaking signed by me [the Catholic Church promise] and referred to in said paragraph, I say that at the time of the signing the said undertaking, my wife and her parents would not agree to our marrying otherwise than in a Roman Catholic Church, and informed me that a dispensation could not be obtained unless the said undertaking was signed. I knew that my wife was going to have a child of which I was the father and we both earnestly desired to get married.

He suggested that conditions at Turner's Cottages were cramped and uncomfortable: the couple had lived there with their four children along with her parents, her three sisters, her brother and her aunt. Ernest noted that the house had four rooms and 'a very small pantry which is not larger than 6ft. by 3ft'. To begin with, the couple had no room of their own and shared the available space with her parents and relatives. Ernest recalled that the money he gave to his wife was handed on in turn to her mother. He had also footed bills for a bed costing £21, 'a cot which cost approximately £3.10 and a tricycle which cost approximately £12'. Ernest claimed that the purchase of the tricycle for their eldest son, David, was his wife's idea, and that he had objected because he 'thought the money could have been spent more wisely'.

Ernest then described how the couple had obtained 'a Corporation house' in the Sybil Hill Lodge estate in Clontarf, where they had lived for three or four months before their second child, Alan, was born. The couple returned to Mary's parents' house at Turner's Cottages for Alan's birth, after which she refused to return to Sybil Hill Lodge. About a month later, Ernest left Turner's Cottages and moved into 'lodgings with a friend', but soon afterwards, his wife visited him there and they agreed that they would move back to Clontarf. However, the sequence of events repeated when Mary was pregnant with their third child, Paul, and moved back to Turner's Cottages for the birth, only then to refuse to return to Sybil Hill Lodge. According to Ernest, she claimed that the accommodation there 'was not good enough' and the upshot saw Ernest living there alone and later moving to lodgings elsewhere. He flatly denied his wife's allegation that he was drinking heavily and had failed to provide any financial support for her and the children. He stated that he was earning £3 15s. per week and gave her £3 from this; the remaining 15s. met his personal 'expenses, including bus fares, cigarettes and any drink [he] had and other incidentals'. He also claimed that because she was receiving £3 a week from him, there was no need for her to work: 'Every time since our marriage that my wife went out to work it was against my wishes as expressed to her.'

Some months later Ernest returned to live with his wife at Turner's Cottages, but reported that living conditions were hardly conducive to a happy marriage when 'my wife, myself, her sister and her father occupied the one bedroom'. This situation was remedied to some degree when his mother-in-law 'got permission to sub-let' a room to them. In August 1949 Ernest took the children for a holiday to his parents' home in Oldcastle; when he returned, he lived with his wife in this room for about a month. However, soon afterwards she 'went back to her parents' part of the cottage, taking the children with her and leaving me alone'. This situation, which continued for about two months, was later overstated as an act of desertion by Ernest, and indeed by Rev. W.L.M. Giff when the children were being admitted to the Birds' Nest.

Ernest admitted in his affidavit that he did not provide his wife with any financial support during this period because 'she was living apart from me and working and earning'. According to his account, it was at this point that Mary contacted Miss Wogan and 'took out the [District Court] summons referred to in ... her affidavit'. After the couple's subsequent reconciliation, he set about obtaining a new council house for the family from Dublin Corporation, but his wife warned him that, even if this application was successful, she would refuse to live with him in a new home.

Ernest denied outright that he had used physical violence against Mary and caused a miscarriage. He admitted that there had been a row on the occasion described by his wife but suggested that this had been caused by the fact that the children were spending too much time with her in his 'mother-in-law's part of the cottage'. Ernest confirmed that he took the children from the house without his wife's consent on 3 April 1950 and brought them to his parents' home in Oldcastle because 'there was nobody to look after them'. He attempted to justify his action by again insisting that he wished his wife to 'give up her work' to look after the children on a full-time basis. He also confirmed that he had placed his three sons in the

'Mrs. Smyly's Home' on Grand Canal Street on 15 May 1950 and that he also wished to place his youngest son, Neville, there 'so as to have them all together'.

Admitting that he did not inform his wife of the children's whereabouts while they were in Oldcastle, Ernest claimed that he had sent her numerous notes at the time requesting that they meet: 'I wanted to explain to her what I was going to do – namely to put the children into the said home as I felt that they were not being properly looked after in Turner's Cottages.' He recalled that he had asked for the children's ration books but 'did not get them' (this is consonant with Mabel Bird's letter to Miss Holt, described in Chapter 3). Of Mary Tilson's discovery that her children were in the Birds' Nest, Ernest simply observed that 'she found out that information for herself'.

Ernest Tilson disputed his wife's assertion that she always strove 'to bring up [her children] as good Catholics' by claiming that he never knew her 'to teach the children anything in the way of religious instruction' and that 'she took them to Mass irregularly'. His views on the religious upbringing of his children were forthright:

> I also objected to David making his first Communion and went to see Rev. Father Harley ... I did not wish my children to be brought up as Roman Catholics and my wife was well aware of this all along. I am a practising member of the Church of Ireland and wish all my children to be brought up in my own faith and to receive proper religious instruction in my faith. When my wife first started taking the elder children to Mass I objected and told my wife that I did not wish them to go to Mass and wishes [*sic*] to have them brought up as Protestants and there was constant friction between us from that time on about this question.

Ernest then outlined his reasons why he thought the children would be better off in the Birds' Nest than at Turner's Cottages: first, Mary's employment at the Swastika Laundry meant that she was not at home to mind her children and was living apart from him; second, Turner's Cottages was an unfit place to raise children because of the cramped conditions. Moreover, since Mary's family were Roman Catholic, he 'respectfully' suggested that it would not be 'possible to ensure that [his children] would be brought up in the faith of the Church of Ireland which is my earnest wish'.

In the last paragraph of his affidavit, Ernest hedged his bets: mindful of the possibility that the High Court might uphold the rule of paternal supremacy but deem the Birds' Nest an unsuitable environment in which to raise his sons, he proposed 'as an alternative' his mother's offer to care for the children, including Neville, who was not subject of these proceedings, in her 'seven-roomed house' in Oldcastle. He noted that his mother, father and unmarried sister and brother lived there and were all 'practising members of the Church of Ireland' and that 'there [was] a Protestant Church [Church of Ireland] about 300 yards away'.

In her affidavit, Ernest's mother, Harriette Tilson, supported his proposal. She stated that as 'an alternative to allowing the children ... to remain in ... Mrs. Smyly's Home' she would permit them to 'live with us'. She described how there was a large garden and an open field to the rear of the house where the children could play, and that 'they had often spent their summer holidays there ... including seven weeks this year'. She confirmed that the family had the financial resources to care for the children: her husband was self-employed and worked as a tailor earning £1 10s. 0d. a week; her thirty-six-year-old daughter Mitty worked as a seamstress in the family business and earned £4 a week; and her son Thomas, a lorry driver with the Great Northern Railway, earned £5 a week. She added that her son Ernest had 'arranged to pay me for the upkeep of the said four children'.[9]

After the affidavits had been read, Mr T.K. Liston SC, for Mary Tilson, rose to make his submissions, but W.I. Hamill intervened and stated that 'he had understood that the case was to come before the Court that day only for the purpose of having the affidavits read'. Gavan Duffy responded by saying that 'there were matters in Mr. Tilson's affidavit that his wife should have an opportunity to respond to; it was difficult for the Court, reading these affidavits, to know where the truth lay'.[10] He adjourned the case until 24 July 1950.

Mary's ambiguous response to her husband's previous affidavit was read when the court resumed. She denied the claim that her parents had been responsible for their marriage in a Catholic church, and argued that her parents had never approved of the marriage in the first place: this accords with the views of Alan and Judy Tilson, who recall that Ernest was 'never liked' and was 'despised by his mother-in-law'.[11] Mary stated that she was willing to accept her parents' standpoint in regard to her marriage but gives an impression that it was Ernest who was determined that the marriage should proceed. She was also adamant that her husband never expressed a desire to get married in any church other than a Catholic one:

> My parents strongly opposed our marriage, and I was willing to accept their decision. My husband, however, was very anxious that we should marry, and he was also anxious that we should marry in a Roman Catholic Church and according to the rites of my religion. Accordingly, we applied to the Rev. Brendan Harley, C.C. of Saint Mary's ... for the necessary permissions and dispensations to enable us to be married by him in the said Church. At no time, when it appeared that no dispensation would be granted, did the said Ernest Tilson ever suggest that we should be married otherwise than in a Roman Catholic Church and in the Roman Catholic Religion.

Mary also disagreed with her husband's account of living conditions at Turner's Cottages and Sybil Hill Lodge. She claimed that the house at Turner's Cottages had five rooms, not four, and that the room she occupied with her husband and four sons measured '18 feet by 12 feet'. She also claimed that the cottage at Sybil Hill Lodge had only two rooms and 'was always in a very bad state of repair and condition'. Moreover, since her husband had no furniture when they got married, her father had lent him 'a single bed, a wardrobe, a deal kitchen table, three chairs and a mirror'. He later sold this furniture and 'spent the proceeds'. She also suggested that Sybil Hill Lodge was 'a lonely place' situated on 'a large demesne' and recalled that when her husband had been drinking heavily, she often left the cottage late at night and 'walked along the road to meet him and waited on the road for long periods'.

Mary also disputed her husband's claim that while the couple were living at Sybil Hill Lodge he had been giving her £3 per week, alleging that Ernest would 'invariably borrow the greater part of it back ... and never repaid it so that in effect I was without money'. She also claimed that Ernest frequently spent money from her Swastika Laundry wages and seldom repaid it. While they were living apart, she claimed that 'I never got any sum larger than ten shillings from my husband.' She then contradicted her husband's assertion that he would have preferred that his wife had remained at home rather than going out to work, arguing that 'he took advantage of the situation to help himself to part of my earnings by "means" few of which he repaid'.

Mary next disputed her husband's account of his return to Turner's Cottages, suggesting that on the night in question her husband had 'appeared unexpectedly [sic]', saying that he had 'no money and nowhere to go to spend the night'. Unwilling to turn him away, Mary's father offered Ernest a bed in a room to be shared with him, Mary and one of her sisters.

Ernest did not leave the next day and was apparently content with this sleeping arrangement afterwards.

Mary then unequivocally denied her husband's charge that he never knew her 'to teach the children anything in the way of religious instruction'. The two eldest had attended convent national schools, and all the children attended mass every Sunday and on holy days of obligation. At her expense, David, the oldest, subscribed 'to two religious publications, namely *The Far East* and *The Golden Hour*'. She said that from an early age she had taught her children their morning and night prayers, the 'simpler articles of faith', the existence of God the creator, 'the fight they must wage with the devil', the Nativity of the Child Jesus and the meaning of the sacraments. She also described her mother as a 'very religious and pious woman' who subscribed to 'several Catholic religious publications' and was 'continually telling the children about good and evil, heaven and hell, the lives of the saints, the rosary and other religious matters'.

Her account of the children's religious upbringing is sometimes inconsistent and contradictory. She claimed that her husband 'never objected to any of the children attending school or Mass, nor did he object to their being brought up as Roman Catholics', adding that 'I know of nothing to suggest that my husband treats his religion seriously. Every Sunday he lies in bed until dinner time ... I can state categorically that ... he has never attended any religious service or meeting on any Sunday since we were married in the year 1941.' Later in the same affidavit, however, she mentioned that her children had sometimes attended Church of Ireland services with their father:

> The children were dressed for Mass when my husband took them out, and I am informed by them and believe, took them to a service of the Church of Ireland. On another occasion, as I was informed by them and believe, my husband waited for them outside of the Church where they were attending Mass, and, when they came out, took them to a service of the Church of Ireland.

Mary agreed that Ernest had objected to David making his First Holy Communion and that he had visited Father Harley to make him aware of this. These statements are consistent with family memories of the period – Alan recalls his father removing a Holy Communion medal from around David's neck and tossing it in the fire.[12] She also noted Ernest's objections to the presence of Catholic iconography in Turner's Cottages, recalling that there were two 'glazed pictures of sacred objects on the walls' in their room and that on one occasion when her husband had returned to live with her, he 'passed some vaguely slighting remark' to the effect that 'the likeness was imaginary as there were no photographs in the time of our Lord'. After one visit from Ernest's parents, Mary recalled that 'the pictures had been taken down and stacked in the hall'.

Mary clearly saw no future with her husband and in her conclusion to this affidavit she emphasises the importance of the religious upbringing of her children:

> I am determined that he shall not live with me or my children. I am convinced that a man so devoid of honour and sense of moral obligation as to violate his voluntary and most sacred undertaking as to the children's upbringing, and so callous and indifferent to their moral and spiritual welfare as to forsake their religious balance and undo the careful training of years by forcibly commencing their training as Protestants is not a man who ought to be permitted to live with me and have any close control over our family.

Ernest denied all the charges his wife had made against him in her affidavit. On the circumstances of their marriage, he repeated his claim that his wife was prepared to get married in a Protestant church in 1941 but that 'her parents would not allow her to be married other than in her own Church ... under the circumstances, I had no option but to be married in a Roman Catholic Church ... it was absolutely incorrect to say that I was anxious to be married in that Church'. Regarding his wife's allegations of physical violence, he stated that he had just returned from 'holidays in Oldcastle' and that she had told him that he 'had a cheek to come back. She then hit me with her shoe. I was in bed at the time and pushed her away.'

Ernest questioned his wife's claim that she was responsible for raising the children as devout Catholics, arguing that it was 'untrue to say ... that the children went to Mass as mentioned by her'. He also argued: 'I say most emphatically that they only went there periodically ... I say I never knew my wife to teach the children their prayers ... in fact I never knew her to teach them anything.' He also disputed her claim that she regularly attended Mass: 'I never knew her to say any prayers herself and during the time we were at Sybil Hill Lodge she never went to Mass.' He repeated his claim that he 'was constantly objecting to the children going to Roman Catholic Schools and to Mass and being brought up in the Roman Catholic faith', reiterated his objections to David making his First Holy Communion and mentioned his visit to Father Harley to express those protestations.

Catherine Ryder, teacher of the infants class at St Bridget's school on Haddington Road, provided an affidavit for the High Court in which she described David's Catholic education: how she had prepared him for his First Confession and First Communion and taught him 'the greatness of the Sacrament of Communion'.[13] Francis Traynor, David's teacher at St Mary's national school on Haddington Road, also provided a supporting affidavit claiming that the school was 'specially distinguished at the [annual] Religious Knowledge Examination' and that if 'any section of the school ... were not of a very high standard in the knowledge of Christian Doctrine, the reward [sic] would not have been made'.[14]

Opening his submissions on behalf of Mary Tilson, Liston said that the 'governing consideration' was the welfare of the children and that she was ready and willing for them to return to Turner's Cottages where they had been raised. He argued that these were 'more natural surroundings for them than to have them placed in an institution'. Liston observed that Ernest was also clearly determined to place his youngest son, Neville, in the Birds' Nest since on 3 May he had attempted to remove Neville from the family home and bring him to the institution. He added that 'this was not the attitude of a father who was really anxious for the future welfare of his children'. Liston then turned to Ernest's promise to the Catholic Church at the time of his marriage regarding the religious upbringing of his children, arguing that the undertaking was binding because in the absence of that undertaking the marriage would never have taken place. He then described how Ernest had made two applications to the bishop for a dispensation – both of which were refused – before going personally to Father Harley and telling him that he was taking instruction in the Catholic faith with a view to converting. Liston noted that Ernest 'now denied that he made that statement'. At this point Mr Justice Gavan Duffy intervened, indicating at an early stage the direction in which he was leaning: 'The Courts both in Ireland and in Britain have consistently refused to give effect to such undertakings [the Catholic Church prenuptial agreements] but the question arises as to what the position is now under the present constitution which has created a different jurisdiction from the old and created a new jurisprudence.'[15]

Liston did not allow this opportunity to pass and pursued the theme of the constitution and paternal supremacy, which the judge had just raised. He stated that since the constitution had come into effect, it 'never appeared to have been decided as to whether the promise given before marriage to have the children brought up as Catholics was binding'. Reinforcing the point, he continued: 'The father having given that promise could no longer rely on his position simply as father and say he could determine the religion in which his children were to be brought up.' The senior counsel apparently wished to make sure that this crucial issue was firmly implanted in the judge's mind. Replying for Ernest Tilson, Carson countered that the passing of the constitution did not 'in any way affect the law as it stood before 1937'. He then focused on Mary and her 'point blank refusal to live with her husband', quoting directly from her affidavit:

> On account of my husband's habits of drinking to excess and quarrelling with me I am always afraid that he will give scandal to the children by drunken conduct in their presence as has happened many times when they were very small, and for this reason I always had misgivings about our living together. Now, however, on account of his action in taking the children away and putting them in the 'Birds' Nest' I am determined that he shall not live with me or them.[16]

Carson added that he thought Mary had 'an unusual attitude', prompting Gavan Duffy to ask, 'Do you think [Ernest's] attitude was unusual?' Carson agreed that it was, but then changed tack. He argued that 'there was not the slightest corroboration from anyone in the house in Turner's Cottages where Mrs. Tilson resided or from anyone outside the family of any of the allegations which Mrs. Tilson made against her husband'. He then turned his attention to living conditions at Turner's Cottages 'where there was very little family life'. Gavan Duffy, however, was unconvinced and, in a further tacit admission of his sympathies, asked: 'What was there to justify this terrible action of taking the children away suddenly?'

Carson then turned his attention to the potentially more solid ground of paternal supremacy, arguing that the father was entitled to determine the 'education of his children, religious and otherwise'. He said that the offer made by Ernest's parents – to raise the children as Protestants at their home in Oldcastle – was genuine, noting that they 'were comfortably circumstanced with an income of about ten guineas per week', in contrast with 'Mrs Tilson's parents, who never disclosed how much they were earning or gave the Court any idea of their income'. Although they sought to pursue the case on the basis of paternal supremacy, Ernest's legal team also emphasised that, from the point of view of the children's welfare, the alternative accommodation at Oldcastle was secure and of a higher standard.

Carson resumed the following day by arguing that there was no dispute as to how the law stood before the enactment of the 1937 constitution. He further submitted that 'if the law was to be changed, it would have to be changed by something explicit'. He continued:

> The fact that the children had been living with their mother at Turner's Cottages had been relied on by counsel for Mrs. Tilson as a very strong factor in the determination of this case. [Mr T.K. Liston SC] seemed to wipe aside the protection that could be afforded not alone by the parents but also in the Home [the Birds' Nest], in which he admits that they were being well cared for, and, in more than one instance, these Homes had been brought favourably before the notice of the Court.[17]

Suggesting that 'in this case there were two issues: who was to have custody of the children, and in what religion they were to be brought up', Carson argued that it was unjust for a father to be expected to support, maintain and provide for his children if he was not also given custody of them. He again raised the prospect of alternative accommodation at Ernest's parents' home in Oldcastle and pointed out that the parents, brother and sister had attended every day of the Court hearings and were 'anxious and willing to have custody of the children ... they were anxious that the children should be brought up as Protestants and being Protestants themselves were prepared to have them brought up as such'.

Gavan Duffy intervened, asking about 'the question of acquiescence'.[18] Carson replied that this did not arise in this case 'as the children would not have formed any definite religious opinions'. Focusing on David, he argued that 'from the time the eldest boy was going to take his First Communion the father did not acquiesce and told Father Harley that he objected to it'.[19] Somewhat incongruously, Carson added that when Ernest was giving 'this woman £4 a week she went out to work, though the husband objected to it, apparently to get some money for herself, so that she could enjoy herself'. He concluded his defence by asking 'the Court to hold that the father was entitled to the custody of the children and that he was entitled to bring them up in his own religion if he so thought fit, and that the conditional order be discharged'. Gavan Duffy said that he would like to see David, and it was arranged that the boy would attend to be interviewed by the judge. He described their meeting to the court:

I have seen David. I was considerably impressed by the evidence from his two teachers, showing that he has a good mother. Miss Ryder who taught him for two years until the end of June, 1949, deposed that he is exceptionally clean in his habits and attended school most regularly; while Miss Traynor, who taught him from July, 1949, until March, 1950, found him to be a well-cared-for child and always exceptionally neat and clean. Those are notable tributes to the child's upbringing ... He is happy in the 'Birds' Nest'; the boys have been allowed to see their mother and little Neville there every Sunday. He used to enjoy a holiday at Oldcastle and would like to live there, but he likes Turner's Cottages better ... he used to go to confession once a month and remembers his Catholic prayers. He is taught a different catechism now; he volunteered no preference and I found him too young to question on the two creeds; he gave me an extremely childish version of one of St. Patrick's exploits. I think he is attached to both his parents. The boys seem to have been treated kindly at the 'Birds' Nest' and at Oldcastle as well as at home.[20]

As the case was being heard in the High Court, Mary received numerous letters of support from people throughout Ireland, most of which came from mothers.[21] One wrote to her in July and made a strong argument for the powers of the rosary and Our Lady; she also suggested that the Catholic Church would help 'behind the scenes'. This is an unwitting allusion to the fact that Mary Tilson undoubtedly had support for her legal case from the Catholic Church:

> Lisgrey,
> Athboy,
> County Meath.
>
> July 50
>
> Dear Mrs Tilson,
>
> I feel I must write to you. I have watched your great and brave struggle to get back your dear children with prayer and interest.
> You see, I'm from Oldcastle too and I feel the horror you must be going through, but with God's help you will succeed. Now what I want you to do – go to the priest that married you & ask him to help you, go also to the Bishop – he will not fail you. And they will give you the best of advice and *behind backs they will do a lot more*. For you

now don't fail [*sic*] <u>Just put your whole trust in God's Blessed Mother</u> [letter-writer's emphasis]. Say a full rosary every day and offer it to her as a mother, and ask her to get your children home safe to you. You will find everything will come right. The Blessed Virgin is the most powerful Saint you can pray too [*sic*] & she never fails you. Indeed I too am asking her to help you. Be of good heart & remember to have the Rosary with your children every evening. It is a sore trial for you but God will bless you, you have your pluck and courage & your little darlings too.

I say from my heart, God bless you all.
I remain,

Yours faithfully,
(Mrs.) Brigid Meade[22]

Another mother wrote to her around the same time:

Holy Year
July 1950

Dear Mrs Tilson,

Stick to your guns and place your trust in Our Blessed Lady. May God bless your Husband and Children always.

P.S. Say the Thirty Days Prayer.
Hope we shall meet soon.
An Irish Mother[23]

Another wrote:

Dear Mrs Tilson,

I am watching your case with interest. You are a great woman. Only wish I was as plucky years ago ... I tell you to pray to Our Lady. She has granted all souls very great favours.

I am praying for you.

Cáit[24]

On the day that Gavan Duffy delivered judgment, another mother wrote to Mary Tilson from County Kildare:

> Newbridge,
> County Kildare.
> 27.7.50
>
> Dear Madam,
>
> I have been sending my little silent prayers to the Sacred Heart of Jesus, for your dear children to be restored to you. And I feel that my little prayers have been heard. Please get your three Darlings to say a prayer for me. May God Bless you and them.
> From a mother of three boys.
>
> (Mrs) M. Kennedy[25]

Gavan Duffy delivered judgment on 27 July. The hearing was attended by Ernest's parents, brother and sister and Barnes family members, and also by Rev. W.L.M. Giff and clerics from both churches.

CHAPTER 7

George Gavan Duffy

Mr Justice George Gavan Duffy, who presided at the High Court hearing, had a reputation as an outstanding constitutional lawyer and made a significant contribution to the drafting of the 1937 constitution.[1] A devoted and passionate Catholic, he was steeped in the nationalist tradition. Born in 1882 in Rock Ferry in Cheshire, England, he was the eldest son of Charles Gavan Duffy, a founding member of the Young Ireland movement, which supported non-sectarian education and advocated cultural nationalism, and who was later the editor of *The Nation* newspaper. His son's later preoccupation with *habeas corpus* may be traced to Charles Gavan Duffy's arrest in 1848 for alleged insurrectionary plans, after which the British authorities took the extreme measure of suspending *habeas corpus* proceedings as a means of suppressing the political clubs that the Young Irelanders had sought to establish in various parts of the country.[2] Both Gavan Duffy's brothers joined the priesthood, while his sister Louise was also strongly Catholic and nationalist. An Irish language enthusiast, a Gaelic revivalist and secretary of Cumann na mBan, Louise was present in the GPO during the 1916 Rising. In 1907 Gavan Duffy married Margaret Sullivan, who co-founded the Catholic Social Welfare Bureau with Archbishop McQuaid in 1942. The bureau focused on overseeing the religious and moral welfare of emigrants; Gavan Duffy and Margaret's only daughter, Máire, would later become a director.[3]

Along with 1916 rebel Joseph Plunkett, Gavan Duffy received much of his education at Stonyhurst College, a Catholic public school in Lancashire run by the Jesuit order, and subsequently took a three-year course in philosophy instead of attending university.[4] He qualified as a solicitor in London in 1906. After his marriage, Gavan Duffy was active in London Irish nationalist politics and, as an active member of the Irish Club, forged links with Sinn Féin. As a result, he corresponded with Bulmer Hobson, Countess Markievicz, P.S. O'Hegarty and Arthur Griffith and regularly attended Sinn Féin executive meetings and general political meetings in Ireland.

Gavan Duffy practised as a solicitor in London between 1906 and 1916, and in due course became a partner in the firm Munton, Morris,

King, Gavan Duffy & Co. He came to prominence when he represented Roger Casement in 1916 after Casement had been arrested and charged with treason. Roy Foster observes that 'the circumstances of [Casement's] return to Ireland and capture, the campaign for a reprieve and the bravery with which he met his terrible death by the hangman's noose all added to the mystique'.[5] It is hardly surprising that Gavan Duffy's association with Casement added to his pre-eminence in legal and Irish nationalist circles.

Casement had travelled to Germany in late 1914 in an attempt to secure arms for the Irish revolutionaries and to recruit an Irish brigade from among more than 2,000 Irish prisoners of war being held in prison camps there. He was arrested after he was put ashore by a German U-boat on Banna Strand, County Kerry. In April 1916 Gavan Duffy was at his holiday home – a leased coastguard station in Glenvar, County Donegal – when news of Casement's arrest reached him. He wasted no time in returning to London to prepare the defence. Owing to the febrile atmosphere in Britain regarding the 1916 insurrectionists, Gavan Duffy had some difficulty securing a barrister to accept the brief for the defence: Sir John Simon refused, as did Gordon Hewart and Tim Healy. Thomas Artemus Jones, J.H. Morgan, Michael Francis Doyle and Gavan Duffy's brother-in-law A.M. Sullivan, however, eventually accepted the brief.

Despite their efforts, Casement was convicted of treason on the basis that his actions were classified as criminal even if they were committed, as allegedly, 'beyond the king's realm'. Gavan Duffy's determined attempts to have the judgment overturned were unsuccessful, and it fell to him after Casement's execution to identify the dead man's remains. Although he was adamant that the body should be interred in consecrated ground outside London's Pentonville Prison, where Casement had been incarcerated, Gavan Duffy was referred to the Capital Punishments Amendments Act 1886, which specified burial within the prison, and Casement was laid to rest there. To add insult to injury, as one of the executors named in Casement's will, Gavan Duffy requested that he be given all of Casement's personal effects (including his infamous 'Black Diaries') but he was handed only a few trivial items by the British authorities.[6]

Gerard Hogan suggests that 'the Casement trial seems to have affected [Gavan Duffy] deeply, for he afterwards moved to Ireland'.[7] As a devout Catholic, he may also have been touched by the fact that Casement, a Protestant, had been received into the Catholic Church just before his death, or by the fact that Casement's death was dignified and, perhaps, even Christ-like. In his witness statement, Gavan Duffy detailed how the priest attending Casement observed that 'he talked freely of his death and was looking forward to his confession. It was like the last hours of some glorious martyr.'[8] The trial had certainly come at a professional and financial cost for Gavan Duffy: his partners in his law firm had advised him that if he persisted in Casement's defence, he would have to leave.[9] True to their word, his name was removed from the plate outside the practice's office door, impelling the former partner to move to Dublin where he was called to the bar by the King's Inns in 1917.

Gavan Duffy became deeply involved in Irish political life and in December 1918 he was elected Sinn Féin MP for South County Dublin in the Westminster election. Sinn Féin was determined to establish a republic and a constituent assembly, Dáil Éireann, and when the assembly first met in Dublin's Mansion House on 28 January 1919, Gavan Duffy read the Declaration of Independence in French.[10] In October 1921 Éamon de Valera appointed Gavan Duffy as one of the Irish plenipotentiaries to negotiate the Anglo-Irish Treaty with the British government. This decision was undoubtedly influenced by Gavan Duffy's strong analytical skills and legal mastery, even though de Valera would later refer to him and another plenipotentiary, Éamon Duggan, as 'legal padding'. Negotiations were tense and in the latter stages Gavan Duffy showed his disposition to use injudicious language: 'Our difficulty is to come into the empire, looking at all that has happened in the past.' 'That ends it,' cried Austin Chamberlain, jumping to his feet, and at once the negotiations were momentarily broken off. As F.S.L. Lyons has observed, Gavan Duffy's words were 'honest, but hardly politic'.[11] Opinion in Ireland was sharply divided over the treaty, which led to the Civil War of 1922–23. As a signatory and a staunch nationalist, Gavan Duffy had his own reservations about the document. On 21 December 1921 he told the Dáil how he had signed the treaty *faute de mieux*:

> I am going to recommend this Treaty to you very reluctantly, but very sincerely, because I see no alternative ... I do not love this Treaty now any more than I loved it when I signed it ... It is necessary before you reject the Treaty to go further than that and to produce to the people of Ireland a rational alternative. My heart is with those who are against the Treaty, but my reason is against them, because I can see no rational alternative.[12]

The provisional government appointed Gavan Duffy as minister for external affairs in January 1922. Although his tenure was short-lived, he showed his judicial independence when he resigned in July 1922 in protest at the government's abolition of the Dáil Courts, following an order of Mr Justice Diarmuid Crowley of the Dáil Supreme Court directing the release of George Oliver Plunkett, who had been held along with other republican prisoners following the outbreak of the Civil War.[13]

Beyond politics and the law, Gavan Duffy was particularly active in Catholic circles and was a founding member of the Catholic lay organisation An Ríoghacht (The League of the Kingship of Christ), which had been the inspiration of the Jesuit priest Father Edward Cahill SJ.[14] Cahill served as professor of social science and sociology at Milltown Park in Dublin from 1924, publishing tendentiously entitled works including *Freemasonry and the Anti-Christian Movement* (1929) and *The Framework of a Christian State: An introduction to social science* (1932), as well as articles on Christian sociology in *The Irish Monthly* entitled 'Ireland's Perils' (1930), 'Ireland as a Catholic Nation' (1938) and 'Freemasonry' (1944).[15] Like many Catholic Church figures at the time, Cahill was concerned about the threat of liberalism, communism and Jewry to Catholicism and was particularly apprehensive of the power of Freemasonry.[16] Neil R. Davison observes that 'while anti-Freemasonry was generally reinforced by the anti-Semitism of the 1890s, during the ensuing years in Dublin, Edward Cahill SJ rose to the forefront of an anti-Mason/anti-Jewish movement in Ireland'.[17]

Gavan Duffy and Cahill were comfortable bedfellows: both were dedicated Catholics, both were eager to embed Catholic social principles in Irish public life and both equated nationalism with Catholicism. Indeed, when Cahill died on 16 July 1941 his funeral was attended by Gavan Duffy and his son Colm.[18] Inspired by Pope Pius XI's 1925 encyclical *Quas Primas* instituting the Feast of Christ the King, in 1926 Cahill conceived the idea of 'forming an organisation for the purpose of putting into practice in Ireland the teachings of the Encyclical'.[19] Maurice Curtis has suggested more bluntly that 'An Ríoghacht was an elitist movement devoted to advancing Catholic social principles amongst those in influential positions in Irish public life'.[20] The constitution of An Ríoghacht set out its aims:

(a) Propagate among Irish Catholics a better knowledge of catholic social principles.
(b) To strive for effective recognition of these principles in Irish public life.
(c) To promote and foster catholic social action.[21]

In 1950 J. Waldron, a founding and long-serving member of the league, described its methods and achievements:

> By propaganda and other means An Ríoghacht influenced legislation on censorship, criminal law, etc., and it gave strong support to the constitution of 1937 in so far as Catholic social principles were involved ... Not least among the achievements of An Ríoghacht has been the training of some hundreds of men and women who have carried into their various spheres in public life a sound knowledge of Catholic social principles. Such persons are to be found in the Dáil and the Seanad, in the Judiciary, the professions and the Civil Service.[22]

The *Irish Independent* reported that at 'the first general meeting of ... *An Ríoghacht* in 1926, the first Ard Chomhairle was elected as follows: M.J. Lennon B.L. ... Rev. E. Cahill SJ ... and G. Gavan Duffy B.L.'.[23] Lennon was a prominent judge, and other well-connected members of the league included Dan Breen, Fianna Fáil politician and War of Independence Volunteer; politician and historian Sir Joseph Glynn; Maurice Moynihan, senior civil servant and co-author of the 1937 constitution; economist Berthon Waters, who later served as an advisor to Seán MacBride; and Professor Michael Tierney, politician, academic and president of University College Dublin from 1947 to 1964. Gavan Duffy was a member for many years: the *Evening Herald* reported in April 1937 that he presided over an An Ríoghacht meeting where Rev. J. Canavan SJ warned that 'Ireland was deficient in laymen sufficiently educated, sufficiently brave to defend Catholic doctrine in the public arena'.[24] The constitution of An Ríoghacht prescribed the functions of its members and it is possible that these expectations influenced Gavan Duffy's thinking when ruling in the Tilson case:

> *Hereunder is the Constitution of An Ríoghacht*
> Article (V) (1): It shall be the duty of all members to advocate and promote Catholic principles as occasion offers in the exercise of their vocational duties, in their trade or professional organisations and in their ordinary social relations.[25]

The central branch of An Ríoghacht was established at 39 North Great George's Street in Dublin on 28 November 1926, followed by the foundation of a Sacred Heart branch, which was confined to women, and branches in Harrington Street and Ely Place. Other branches were established in cities and provincial towns such as Cork, Limerick, Waterford, Mullingar and Nenagh. The organisation boasted hundreds of members, who were encouraged to study papal encyclicals, commentaries and other 'recognised textbooks' and to attend lectures delivered by such people as Cahill. Catholic writers such as Hilaire Belloc, Father Owen Dudley, Arnold Lunn and Christopher Hollis also gave presentations. Members who completed an An Ríoghacht course of study sat an annual examination.[26]

Mischievously characterised by the writer Seán O'Faoláin as 'Miraculous Meddlers', many similar Catholic lay organisations were founded during the Free State years, such as Maria Duce, the Legion of Mary and the Knights of Columbanus. They drew inspiration from the European Catholic social movement as an example of what could be achieved by organised Catholic lay groups[27] and were also inspired by the calls to action in early twentieth-century encyclicals by Pope Pius X and Pope Pius XI. Some have argued that An Ríoghacht was a forerunner for the avowedly right-wing, anti-communist and anti-Semitic Maria Duce group, founded by Father Denis Fahey, a member of the Holy Ghost order.[28] Enda Delaney has observed that Fahey's understanding of Freemasonry was based largely on the writings of Cahill and that he frequently referred his readers to Cahill's work *Freemasonry and the Anti-Christian Movement*, which he thought was 'an excellent discussion of the subject'; clearly this admiration was mutual, with Cahill acknowledging Fahey's help in censuring Freemasonry.[29]

After the partition of Ireland in 1922 many believed that the southern state required a distinctive political and cultural identity and, in turn, the regime chose a nationalist, Catholic and conservative path. By extension, many clerics and lay Catholics believed that a robust lay social movement would help to promote this distinctive Catholic ethos. Terence Brown has noted that the Catholic lay organisations 'were determined that Irish life in the independent state should bear a frankly Catholic complexion and that Catholic power should assert itself unambiguously in social and economic terms as it had been unable to do in the past'.[30]

An Ríoghacht was determined to wield its influence across a range of public spheres, including the drafting of the 1937 constitution, the relevant articles of which would later have a direct bearing on the High Court and Supreme Court rulings in the Tilson case. Under the guidance of Cahill, it formed a Jesuit committee tasked with drafting proposals and made numerous submissions to the taoiseach, Éamon de Valera. The committee's suggestions dealt with such issues as the dangers posed to Ireland by foreign economic and cultural influence, as well as marriage, the family and education. Held in Dublin on 1 November 1936, An Ríoghacht's twelfth *ard fheis* appeared to align and identify the proposed constitution with papal encyclicals, natural law and the nation of Ireland:

> The Fheis expressed the hope that the proposed constitution would be in accordance with the Christian principles and ideals contained in the Papal Encyclicals, and directed attention to the fact that not only were those principles and ideals implicit in the Catholic faith held by the vast majority of our people, but they were also based on the Natural Law, and *could not be repugnant to the true interests of any section of the nation.*[31]

Although Catholic Church influence on the drafting of the 1937 constitution has been occasionally exaggerated and misrepresented, An Ríoghacht clearly had an influence on matters concerning the family and education; it is also generally accepted that Cahill was responsible for the wording 'special position of the Catholic Church' in Article 44.1.2. An Ríoghacht also expressed concerns over other issues that later would be of relevance to the judgment delivered by Gavan Duffy in the Tilson case. The group feared that the constitution did not address the Catholic view on the question of mixed marriages.[32] As discussed in earlier chapters, if a Catholic married a Protestant in a register office or in a Protestant church, that marriage was regarded as invalid by the Catholic Church, but the state considered the same marriage to be valid. An Ríoghacht unambiguously argued that since the Catholic Church enjoyed a 'special position' in the constitution, the state should have regard for the marriage laws of the church. Although the organisation's submission on marriage was closer to wishful thinking than reality, Gavan Duffy would later speculate, when delivering judgment in the Tilson case, whether or not the special position of the Catholic Church in the constitution would allow him 'to take judicial notice of canon law'. An Ríoghacht's submission read:

> Seeing that the Catholic Church has its own marriage laws, the state shall, after agreement with the Holy See, bring its marriage law into conformity with Canon Law when one or both parties to a marriage are members of the Catholic Church ... Canons 1012 to 1143 inclusive, of the code of Canon Law, is hereby incorporated into the constitution and given the force of civil law.[33]

An Ríoghacht also expressed concerns with the draft article on the family and, in particular, with Article 41.3.1, which dealt with marriage. In its submission in relation to 3.2, which stated that 'no law shall be enacted providing for the dissolution of marriage', An Ríoghacht advised de Valera that the article should be worded so as 'not to preclude legislation which experience may show to be necessary'.[34] At first glance this submission suggests that An Ríoghacht had adopted a liberal position on divorce. Conversely, the organisation had in mind a situation where the Catholic Church annulled a marriage for reasons such as non-consummation and this led to a conflict between canon and civil law. An Ríoghacht was determined that the state would formally recognise the Catholic Church's marriage laws in the constitution.

An Ríoghacht had deep concerns in relation to the preamble to Article 45,[35] which declared: 'The principles of social policy set forth in this Article are intended for the general guidance of the Oireachtas. The application of those principles in the making of laws shall be the care of the Oireachtas exclusively and shall not be cognisable by any court under any of the provisions of this constitution.'

Maurice Curtis observes that An Ríoghacht took particular issue with the wording 'and shall not be ...' since it supposedly weakened 'the strength of the sections which followed'.[36] The organisation feared that the wording 'deprived them of all due sanction' and in consequence it might prove impossible to obtain a future ruling that a law in violation of the sections which followed in Article 45 was unconstitutional. An Ríoghacht saw the preamble to Article 45 as undermining 'the endeavours of Catholic organisations and their striving for social justice'.[37] Gerard Hogan notes that 'Gavan Duffy was one of the limited number of persons with whom de Valera consulted extensively over the drafting of the new constitution, and many of his suggestions were taken on board by the drafting committee'.[38] In fact, the language of the preamble to Article 45 in the finished document closely follows a draft suggested by Gavan Duffy.[39] Although Gavan Duffy made observations on sixteen or so proposed articles on the first circulated draft,[40] it is clear that in regard to the preamble to Article 45, the line between his suggestions and those of An Ríoghacht had become very blurred indeed.

De Valera did not accept many submissions promoting the interests of the Catholic Church, but An Ríoghacht was nevertheless satisfied with the outcome of the provisions set out in the draft constitution. A front-page report in the *Irish Press* stated:

> The various provisions in the Draft Constitution have been welcomed by the Ard Chomhairle of An Ríoghacht ... from which we have received the following communication: *AN RÍOGHACHT*. Since one of the aims of An Ríoghacht is to strive for the effective recognition of Catholic social principles in Irish public life, the Ard Chomhairle desire to express satisfaction at the noteworthy manner in which basic Catholic principles are recognised in the Draft Constitution now published. Especially do we rejoice at the noble preamble. *We recognise that the articles dealing with personal rights, the family, education, private property and religion are in general accord with Catholic teaching, and we applaud the emphasis placed on the family as the fundamental unit of society.*[41]

Gavan Duffy was appointed a judge of the High Court on 21 December 1936 and president of the High Court in 1946. Hogan suggests that Gavan Duffy was a 'huge admirer of the 1937 constitution and was one of the first to see the enhanced possibilities for judicial review afforded by it ... he gave leading judgments in almost every branch of law, but it was in the realm of constitutional law that he made his most notable contribution'.[42]

Two particular judgments show George Gavan Duffy's judicial independence and refusal to sidestep controversial decisions. In the *State (Burke)* v. *Lennon* (1940) case he held that the internment provisions in Part VI of the Offences Against the State Act 1939 were unconstitutional since they contravened the right to personal liberty in Article 40.4.1. This judgment led to a public outcry because the government was forced to release IRA prisoners in detention. Temperatures rose further when some of the released prisoners were suspected of being involved in what became known as the 'Christmas raid' on the magazine fort in the Phoenix Park in December 1939, when weapons and over one million rounds of ammunition were stolen. The government passed amended legislation, but when this was referred to the Supreme Court by President Douglas Hyde, Gavan Duffy's decision was upheld.

The *Buckley* v. *Attorney General* case of 1950 centred on the Sinn Féin Funds Act of 1947. This act identified certain pending litigation brought by Mrs Margaret Buckley on behalf of Sinn Féin to recover funds lodged in the High Court in 1924 by the trustees of the party in the aftermath of the Civil War. The dispute focused on the ownership of the funds, which were of a practical and symbolic value.[43] The 1947 act directed the High Court to reject the claim and to transfer the funds to a new board, Bord Cistí Sinn

Féin, which, in turn, would use them for charitable purposes. Gavan Duffy held that the Sinn Féin Funds Act was unconstitutional, since it required the courts to dismiss a claim without a hearing, violating the separation of powers principles contained in the constitution. His judgment was appealed but was upheld by the Supreme Court,[44] driving 'a powerful judicial coach and four through the Sinn Féin Funds Act of 1947'.[45]

Other judgments, such as *Cook v. Carroll* (1945) and *Schlegel v. Corcoran and Gross* (1942), were less inspired and suggest that Gavan Duffy struggled to maintain a separation between church and state in cases concerning religious matters. Moreover, his judgment in *Schlegel v. Corcoran and Gross*, and the language used while delivering it, shows what John Maurice Kelly has described as Gavan Duffy's 'dark side'.[46] In 1942 a case came before him in the High Court involving a dispute that had arisen between Teresa Schlegel, a Catholic, and Kevin Corcoran and Nathaniel Gross over a lease on part of her home at 7 Harrington Street, Dublin. Teresa Schlegel's husband Hanly, also a Catholic, had inherited this property from his father, a watchmaker, and ran a dental practice there for many years before his death in 1928.[47] Teresa Schlegel then assigned the goodwill of the dental practice to a Mr John Corcoran and also let to him, at the same address, three furnished rooms on the ground floor: a surgery, a waiting room and a workshop. John Corcoran agreed to use the rooms solely in connection with his dental practice and not to assign or sublet to any other party without the landlord's consent in writing. When John Corcoran died, the administrator of his estate, Kevin Corcoran, sold the dental practice to Nathaniel Gross and also assigned him the leasehold interest in 7 Harrington Street. A major disagreement arose between the parties when Teresa Schlegel objected to the assignment of the lease on the basis that Gross was Jewish, arguing that 'their principles [those of Jews] are not ours and they are anti-Christian and I could not have an anti-Christian living in the house where I live'.[48]

In his defence, Nathaniel Gross relied on the relevant article of the Landlord and Tenant Act of 1931, which specified that if a landlord was being unreasonable in refusing consent to an assignment, a court had jurisdiction to make an order dispensing with their consent and allowing the assignment to go ahead regardless.[49] Counsel for Gross would also argue that Teresa Schlegel's objections to their client as tenant breached the prohibition on religious discrimination contained in Article 44.2.3 of the constitution. In what Gerard Hogan has described as 'perhaps the most notorious decision ever given by an Irish court',[50] Gavan Duffy refused to hold that Teresa Schlegel was acting unreasonably, thereby preventing the court from dispensing with her consent. And, bizarrely, as a devotee of the 1937 constitution, he stated that he could not see how Article 44.2.3 applied to the case in hand. G.M. Golding notes that 'it may be significant that Gavan Duffy referred to Mrs Schlegel as being "Irish and a Catholic", whereas the proposed assignee he described as merely "a Jew". The case raises more than a suspicion that Gavan Duffy was of the opinion that only Irish Catholics could claim the benefits of constitutional rights.[51]

Outlandish as the judgment was, it was the language used by Gavan Duffy in its deliverance which would cause most concern. His reasoning here suggests that anti-Semitism was justifiable because the prejudice was centuries old:

> Anti-Semitism ... far from being a peculiar crotchet, is notoriously shared by a number of other citizens; and, if prejudice be the right word, the antagonism between Christian and Jew has its roots in nearly 2,000 years of history and is too prevalent as a habit of mind to be dismissed off-hand, in a country where religion matters, as the eccentric extravagance of a bigot, without regard to the actual conditions under which consent was withheld.[52]

Gavan Duffy explained in troubling detail how Teresa Schlegel would have to share her house with a Jew if her consent to the assignment of the lease was dispensed by the court:

> ... her relations with the new tenant will be far from intimate, but he will be installed in her hall floor and the contacts, already outlined, may be quite close enough materially to affect her amenities, if he is from her standpoint a most undesirable participator in the narrow shelter of her roof.[53]

The judge's reasoning was confused: he described objections to assignees of leases on racial, religious or political grounds as 'well understood, although not always meritorious' and then attempted to distinguish them from other 'nonsensical objections'. He continued:

> Take an otherwise satisfactory assignee, whom she sought to reject because she really entertained a violent dislike or superstition against his red hair, or his stutter, or his squint; there any Court would be disposed to overrule her objection as nonsense, although in fact she happened to be so peculiarly constituted that her amenities would

in some degree suffer in consequence … no one, I suppose, will deny that she might safely reject a Hottentot, for the sake of her domestic amenities, though he happened to be a civilised specimen.[54]

In 1942 the poisonous and deadly effects of anti-Semitism were of course apparent across Europe, but, as Ruth Cannon has speculated, Gavan Duffy's period of upbringing in *fin-de-siècle* France, where the prejudice was widespread, may also have influenced his views.[55] It is also possible that he was influenced by his own education at the hands of Jesuits[56] or by the anti-Semitic sentiment that pervaded the racialised Gaelic nationalism that emerged in the 1880s, as shown by the outbursts of Arthur Griffith, the founder of Sinn Féin who led the Irish delegation at the 1921 Anglo-Irish Treaty talks. He may also have been influenced by Edward Cahill, who was likewise deeply antipathetic towards Jews. But as Cannon astutely observes in regard to individuals in Ireland who were involved in anti-Semitic incidents at the time, 'by exaggerating the prevalence of anti-Semitism, and indeed regarding it as a natural and acceptable part of society, Gavan Duffy J. was, unknowingly or otherwise, assisting these individuals'.[57]

Gavan Duffy's ruling in *Cook* v. *Carroll* in 1945 was also controversial. This case concerned a girl from Ballybunion, County Kerry, who in 1944 became pregnant by a local man. When the man heard that paternity was being attributed to him, he visited Rev. W.J. Behan, the local parish priest, who sent his car to bring the expectant mother to the parochial house. At the meeting, which was attended by the girl and the man, Rev. Behan attempted 'to avert a public scandal in the interests of his flock' by either convincing the girl to withdraw the charge or by persuading the man to make amends for the wrong done to her. The meeting ended inconclusively and the girl's mother later sought damages on behalf of her daughter in the Circuit Court at Listowel. Behan refused to give evidence, claiming privilege regarding the conversation, which took place between the three parties at the parochial house. He was fined £10 for contempt of court and the plaintiff's action was dismissed.

The girl's mother appealed to the High Court, where the case was heard by Gavan Duffy. Once again, Behan refused to give evidence while the judge took evidence from the plaintiff and the defendant. Coining the term 'sacerdotal privilege', Gavan Duffy set the tone for his judgment when he described a priest in Ireland as 'the spiritual father of his people and his traditional devotion to his people through generations has won for him … the prerogative of an extraordinary moral authority'.

He cited cases where the seal of the confessional had been respected in the courts of England and Wales before the Reformation and before the Norman conquest, and referred to *Wheeler* v. *Le Marchant* (1881) where 'communications made to a priest in the confessional ... are not protected'. Although he claimed to base his judgment on 'four leading canons' of 'Wigmore's monumental work on the Anglo-American System of Evidence' and on the notion that 'four conditions' contained therein were present in the current case, he obfuscated his reasoning by apparently relying on the 1937 constitution and its Catholic facets or dimensions. Prefiguring the Tilson case in the High Court, he took a sideswipe at English law 'on this topic', describing it as 'warped', and those 'zealous magistrates who were trying to administer it in a spirit foreign to a Catholic people'. Those magistrates, he argued, should have conceded a 'special exception for Ireland' because 'the Catholic Church was too strong in this country'. Again, with evocations of what would arise during his hearing of the Tilson case, the judge appeared to be relying on Article 44 of the constitution when he said:

> I have to determine the issue raised in this case on principle and in conformity with the constitution of Ireland. That constitution in express terms recognises the special position of the Holy Catholic Apostolic and Roman Church as the guardians of the Faith professed by the great majority of the citizens ... in a state where nine out of every ten citizens to-day are Catholics and on a matter closely touching the religious outlook of the people, it would be intolerable that the common law, as expounded after the Reformation in a Protestant land, should be taken to bind a nation which persistently repudiated the Reformation as heresy.[58]

Ruling that the parish priest of Ballybunion committed no contempt of the High Court, Gavan Duffy's judgment privileged private conversations between priests and their parishioners, which take place in the context of their pastoral work.[59] G.M. Golding, however, draws attention to extrajudicial comments by Mr Justice Kenny and Mr Justice O'Keefe in 1976. Kenny argued that 'Gavan Duffy took the opportunity to display very militant Catholicism. I do not regard the case as being an authority on anything', while O'Keefe observed that 'it was illogical to allow the two parties to give evidence, that is, to waive privilege, and still hold the priest to be privileged'.[60]

Gavan Duffy is regarded by many in legal circles as an outstanding judge and is best remembered for his dealings with constitutional matters. The case now before him in the High Court would turn on the question of whether the constitution of 1937 had the effect of rendering prenuptial agreements effective in law. Would his Catholic background, practices, or membership of An Ríoghacht colour his judgment?

CHAPTER 8

The High Court Judgment

On the day Gavan Duffy delivered his judgment, Rev. W.L.M. Giff wrote to a Miss E. Martin of the Irish Church Missions in London and informed her that 'I am just about to go to the High Court, where judgment is to be given this morning on a case of ours which will be extremely important, not only for us, but for the whole of Protestantism in Eire [sic]'.[1]

Before dealing with Gavan Duffy's address, which lasted for ninety minutes, there are two aspects of the case that merit attention. The first concerns Mary Tilson's age. Gavan Duffy described her as 'a Catholic girl, sixteen years old' at the time of her marriage in 1941.[2] Mr Justice James Murnaghan, in his opening remarks at the Supreme Court Appeal a week later, similarly described her as 'aged between 15 and 16 years at that date'.[3] Mary's birth certificate shows that she was born on 4 August 1923, however, which means that she was aged eighteen when she was married on 10 December 1941. Both Gavan Duffy and Murnaghan were mistaken, but if the ages provided by them were correct, this would mean that Mary had been below the age of consent when she became pregnant in 1941, and under section 2.1 of the Criminal Law Amendment Act, 1935 Ernest would have been guilty of the misdemeanour of 'carnally [knowing] any girl who is over the age of 15 and under the age of 17'.[4] The offence carried a prison sentence of up to five years and no fewer than three.

The judges' misapprehensions presumably derive from the affidavit sworn by Mary on 11 July 1950, in which she states, 'I am aged twenty-four years now',[5] despite the fact that she was less than a month short of her twenty-seventh birthday. It is unclear why she provided an incorrect age. True, some people forget their ages from time to time, but it is hardly likely that a person in their mid-twenties would do so, and by such a margin. Did Ernest also believe that she was below the age of consent when she became pregnant in 1941, and might this explain his urgency to marry? We know that Father Harley stated in his affidavit that Ernest 'pressed his case very strongly' when being interviewed for the marriage dispensation. Equally, Mary, in her affidavit, claimed that Ernest 'was very anxious that we should marry'.

Or, when preparing for her High Court case, did someone prompt Mary to provide an incorrect age to implant the notion of a naive and innocent Catholic girl being taken advantage of by an older, guileful Protestant man? The judges and lawyers on both sides demonstrated scrupulous attention to detail – as shown by Mr Justice Lavery in the Supreme Court when he asked why Ernest had entered incorrect birthdays for his children on the Birds' Nest admission forms – so it is surprising that nobody saw fit to draw attention to the age Mary had provided.

Another notable aspect of the High Court case is the fact that it was heard before only one judge, when cases in the High Court can be heard before three. As president of the High Court, it was Gavan Duffy's prerogative to make that decision. Since that court's ruling was likely to depend on an interpretation of the relevant articles of the 1937 constitution and, by extension, was likely to have far-reaching implications, it is strange that Gavan Duffy decided to hear the case as the sole judge. Clearly aware of this, he offered an explanation in his opening remarks:

> I should certainly have convened a Court of three judges, *had it been practicable to do so*, for a case of this kind, especially as this appears to be the first case to raise directly for decision a far-reaching issue, that is, the juristic value under the constitution of an ante-nuptial agreement for the children's religion, made by the parties to a 'mixed marriage'.[6]

It is plausible that there was an extreme urgency to the case, since it involved three children who had been placed in an orphanage without their mother's consent. It is also plausible that there was a shortage of judges because of summer holidays. But it is also possible that Gavan Duffy took a personal interest in the case, recognised the opportunity to make a decision of lasting significance, and did not want other judges interfering with this plan. His explanation was clearly inadequate because it depended on the nebulous phrase 'had it been practicable to do so'. Given the nature of the issues at hand, it would have been appropriate for the judge to spell out the reasons why he chose to hear the case alone.

In any event, the tone of the hearing was established in Gavan Duffy's opening remarks, when he observed that Ernest had married Mary Barnes 'very properly, because she was expecting a baby'.[7] He then described in some detail the couple's living arrangements at Turner's Cottages and Sybil Hill Lodge, and suggested that 'there have been faults on both sides'. The judge also observed that Ernest 'plainly resents [Mary's] close association with her parents, while his wife twice refused to live with him elsewhere'.

He then turned to what he called 'the present dispute', identifying its genesis as 1 April 1950, when Ernest apparently returned home drunk and his wife sought refuge with the children in her parents' area of the house. Gavan Duffy specified that Ernest had denied this charge, saying that his wife had a habit of keeping the children with her mother, and when he remonstrated, she brought only the three eldest boys back, leaving Neville behind. The following day, Sunday, according to her account, he spent away from Turner's Cottages while she stayed at home with the four boys. The judge described how Ernest had denied this version of events, arguing that he had, in fact, stayed at home and cared for the children and put them to bed, while his wife spent the day with her parents in their rooms. Gavan Duffy excoriated Carson's arguments on behalf of his client:

> It is typical of this kind of dispute that Mr. Carson in his vigorous argument for the husband, far from apologising for his methods, indignantly denounces the wife because she is now resolved that he shall not live with her and the boys after his abreption [snatching away] of the boys, which I am about to describe, from their home, and their putting away in the 'very suitable' academy of his choice, there to learn a new religion. Her statement, if indiscreet, was the honest and understandable cry of an anguished mother.[8]

In highly partial terms the judge described how Ernest 'suddenly and silently' removed the three eldest boys from their home on 3 April while his wife was at work, taking them first to his parents' house at Oldcastle, and then to a children's home 'designed for necessitous children'. Of Mary's return home to find that her children had vanished, Gavan Duffy commented: 'One can imagine the mother's state of mind'; he described Ernest's decision to remove the children as a 'drastic course of action' and observed that 'the grievance is more understandable than the measures he took to correct it'.

Turning to Mary's affidavit, the judge suggested that the reconciliation the District Court had sought to effect between the couple the previous December had 'gravely embittered' the father's feelings towards the mother and observed that 'nothing else explains (though nothing can condone) his monstrous behaviour towards his wife in removing her children surreptitiously and concealing their whereabouts'.

Gavan Duffy dealt next with the three application forms completed by Ernest for his three sons' admission to the Birds' Nest, taking grave exception to the remarks made by Rev. W.L.M. Giff on each of the forms, which read: 'The mother has treated the husband very badly for some time, and has eventually deserted the children (it's a mixed marriage case). I think the father will serve his children faithfully.'[9] Gavan Duffy was adamant that Ernest had lied so that his sons could be admitted to the Birds' Nest:

> I make all possible allowances for a husband who has to live (as I infer that he thought he had to live) in an unfriendly atmosphere and for his annoyance with his wife, if he had or believed that he had just cause for it; but I find no excuse for the husband who commits her children and his to a paupers' asylum upon a deliberately false allegation that their mother had deserted them.[10]

The judge implied that Ernest had never taken the Catholic prenuptial agreement seriously, remarking that this 'does not give him any pause'. Although the judge acknowledged that the house at Turner's Cottages was 'badly congested', he was dismissive of Ernest Tilson's proposal that his children could reside at his parents' house in Oldcastle: 'I do not forget that they were lodged in the "Birds' Nest" after spending six weeks at Oldcastle.' Gavan Duffy was distinctly unimpressed with Ernest's version of events and his failure to offer a credible explanation for his actions:

> I find that upon the whole of the father's evidence the outstanding fact still remains without adequate explanation; despite his reconciliation of last December, he has now himself uprooted his own family. That was a really dreadful measure to take, and his precipitate recourse to it required the most serious and convincing reasons to justify. I do not find them in his affidavits. The secrecy of the seclusion of the boys in Mrs Smyly's Home also called for a reasonable explanation that Mr. Tilson could not advance.

The judge then turned to Mary Tilson's answering affidavit suggesting that she had given 'a satisfactory account of the children's Catholic upbringing' as corroborated by the affidavits of David's two schoolteachers. By contrast, Gavan Duffy openly questioned Ernest's assertions regarding his wife's remiss attitude to observance, noting that she paid subscriptions to two Catholic magazines for David and that her husband had never objected to the children's Catholic upbringing until David was about to make his First Communion. Gavan Duffy then observed that 'the marriage could not have been celebrated without the dispensation, which would have been refused had the fulfilment of the promises been in doubt'. He suggested that Ernest had shed 'no further light' on why he had placed his sons in the Birds' Nest, other than claiming 'that he felt they were not being properly looked after at Turner's Cottages' and concluded his evaluation of Ernest's affidavits by stating that 'I think his main ground is her "avowed intention ... to bring them up as Roman Catholics contrary to my wishes" (in his first affidavit), if she obtains their custody'.

By this point Gavan Duffy's contempt for Ernest's actions was obvious, but in law he was confronted with two issues: the common law rule of paternal supremacy, on which Ernest and his legal team were undoubtedly pinning their hopes, and the issue of the enforceability of the prenuptial agreement. Addressing paternal supremacy with reference to the Frost case, which had come before the Irish Supreme Court after the adoption of the constitution in 1937, the judge stated that 'a father's extensive rights (including posthumous authority) over his children are well settled', acknowledging that common law and precedent dictated the right of the father to control his children's education and religion.

When dealing with the prenuptial agreement, Gavan Duffy turned to the Browne mixed-marriage case of 1852, which concerned a nine-year-old girl whose Catholic father and Protestant mother were both deceased. The father had apparently made a verbal agreement before his marriage that any children should be raised as Protestants, but a master in chancery refused to give effect to this agreement because 'an agreement made in consideration of marriage is not enforceable ... it is merely oral'.[11] The case was appealed and Mr Justice Cusack Smith upheld the judgment on the basis of the agreement's lack of binding force and that any attempt to enforce it would be 'detrimental to public policy'.[12] As Gerard Hogan has observed, 'the judicial interpretation of paternal supremacy in turn led the courts to hold that an ante-nuptial agreement was unenforceable as a matter of law, principally because the enforcement of any such agreement would be at variance with the public policy objective underlying the paternal supremacy rule'.[13] Gavan Duffy also cited the similar case of *Hill* v. *Hill* (1862), where 'again the agreement alleged was not proved', before turning to the Meade case of 1870 (addressed in Chapter 5). He argued that Meade demonstrated that 'an ante-nuptial agreement, though solemn and openly avowed, that the children should be Catholics "was not a binding force in law"'.[14] The judge summed up by declaring that 'having delved into case law, I discern there no clear principle to justify the doctrine that a father is free to repudiate his ante-nuptial agreement'. On the basis that the tradition of paternal supremacy was acknowledged and that prenuptial agreements were unenforceable in law, Gavan Duffy made clear that he would be relying on the 1937 constitution, stating that 'the parties of this unhappy dispute are Irish citizens, domiciled in Ireland and the consequences of their difference have to be determined in light of the constitution of Ireland'. Addressing this, Gerard Hogan writes that:

> Even if the rule of paternal supremacy had survived the constitution and even if the ante-nuptial agreement was not binding in law, the plain facts of *Tilson* were that the husband had clearly estopped himself by his conduct in permitting the children to be reared as Roman Catholics ... while Gavan Duffy clearly recognised that this case could be disposed of on this basis, he clearly wished to haul into deeper constitutional waters.[15]

When Ernest allowed his children to be baptised in a Catholic church and then raised as Catholics for a considerable number of years, he forfeited his right to determine their religious upbringing or education. Gavan Duffy could have ruled on the case simply by relying on Ernest's estoppel and avoiding the constitution altogether, but instead he turned to the 1937 document to underpin the judgment he was about to deliver. His delivery was strongly redolent of an An Ríoghacht manifesto:

> I come to the Irish constitution. We are a people of deep religious convictions. Accordingly, our fundamental law establishes a Christian constitution; the indifferentism of our decadent era is utterly rejected by us. The Irish code makes a new departure from time-honoured precedents which are not ours and gives us a polity conceived in a spirit and couched in a language unfamiliar to the jurisprudence which dominated the United Kingdom of Great Britain and Ireland.[16]

Gavan Duffy then quoted directly from the constitution's preamble: "'In the Name of the Most Holy Trinity from Whom is all authority and to Whom, as our final end, all actions both of men and States must be referred'", observing that this 'explicitly acknowledges the supremacy of the moral law founded on Christian doctrine. In the same spirit, the Charter proceeds to derive all powers of government, under God, from the people and concludes "*Dochum Glóire Dé agus Onóra na hÉireann*"'.[17] The phrasing 'to derive all powers of government, under God, from the people' indeed echoes the judge's own draft constitution submissions regarding the sources of civil authority.

Gavan Duffy then concentrated on the 'Fundamental Rights' section of the constitution, citing Article 41 – 'The Family', 42 – 'Education' and 44 – 'Religion' and arguing that these voiced 'the cherished convictions of a pious people who revere the Christian moral order'. He quoted directly from Article 44, in which the state both '"acknowledges that the homage of public worship is due to almighty God" and "recognises the special position of the Holy Catholic Apostolic and Roman Church as the guardian of the faith possessed by the great majority of its citizens"'.[18] From these lines, the judge concluded that 'religion holds in the constitution the place of honour which the community has always accorded to it in public opinion. The right of the Catholic Church to guard the faith of its children, the great majority, is registered in our fundamental document.'

His description of Articles 41 and 42 as 'redolent … of the great papal encyclicals *in pari materia*' echoed Edward Cahill's plan of 'putting into practice in Ireland the teachings of the Encyclical' and An Ríoghacht's aim of embedding Catholic social principles in public life. The judge noted that in Article 41 'the State "recognises the family as the natural primary and fundamental group of society [and] guarantees to protect the Family" and is pledged "to guard with special care the institution of Marriage, on which the Family is founded, and to protect it against attack"'. Quoting the constitution's prohibition on divorce, whereby '"no law shall be enacted providing for the grant of dissolution of marriage"', he argued that 'Article 42 breathes the same spirit'. He then read the entire wording of Article 42.1: '"The State acknowledges that the primary and natural educator of the child is the Family and guarantees to respect the inalienable right and duty of parents to provide, according to their means, for the religious and moral, intellectual, physical and social education of their children."'

Gavan Duffy's Catholic and nationalist beliefs were evident from his verbose emphasis on the social and religious significance of these articles and his attempts to use them to authenticate Ireland as an independent and sovereign nation. As a Catholic, a nationalist, a long-term member of An Ríoghacht and a contributor to the drafting of the constitution, it was as though he now felt duty-bound to put these principles into practice:

> The strong language of these articles arrests attention. It must have been chosen of set purpose, because the grave subject-matter demanded that Ireland to-day should define her position in unequivocal terms. Thus,

for religion, for marriage, for the family and the children, we have laid our own foundations. Much of the resultant polity is both remote from British precedent and alien to the English way of life, and, when the powerful torch of transmarine legal authority is flashed across our path to show us the way we should go, that disconformity may point decisively another way.

The judge then addressed the prenuptial agreements that Ernest and Mary were obliged to sign, and which were crucial to the case. Before reading the wordings of both agreements to the court, he linked them to the relevant articles in the constitution, which dealt with the home and the family. His interpretation asserted the supremacy of these articles over common law:

> The cardinal position ascribed to the family by our fundamental law is profoundly significant; the home is our pivot of our plan of life. The confused philosophy of law bequeathed to us by the nineteenth century is superseded by articles which exalt the family by proclaiming and adopting in the text of the constitution itself the Christian conception of the place of the family in society and in the State; hence an ante-nuptial agreement, made to be effective within the family sphere and to reinforce in its vital religious role within that indispensable moral institution … has a claim to the most serious consideration in our Courts.

Leaving aside the supposed Christian import of the prenuptial agreements, Gavan Duffy argued that the making of the two documents was concurrent and reciprocal, and therefore constituted one transaction. This was because each party had made their promise on the understanding that 'the other was making his or her promise and for the immediate and common purpose of being enabled through the two promises to marry in the Catholic Church'. This had come at a price for Ernest, the non-Catholic party; although he could not stand charged 'of any abandonment of duty' by signing the agreement, he lost the power he would have enjoyed under the old tradition of paternal supremacy. He was willing to pay that price to secure his marriage, while Mary was satisfied with the promise that enabled her to marry him. Gavan Duffy's dissection of the prenuptial agreements in this way suggests that he had momentarily strayed from the conviction that the case could be decided solely against the 'Christian' articles of the constitution. It is likely that he could have avoided much of the controversy that followed his ruling if he had decided the case on the basis of the narrower ground of contract law; instead, his judgment blurred the distinctions between civil and canon law.

Before addressing how the promises were made by Ernest and Mary, he said that he would have welcomed expert evidence on the 'directly relevant Canons of the Code of Canon Law' to the case. Or, he suggested, 'even the formal proof of the Code without expert evidence would have been useful'. The judge then ventured further into canonical waters: 'Perhaps the relevant Canons were part of old Common Law and are again a part of it now that no Reformation law remains to suppress their vigour ... Possibly the constitutional recognition of the special position of the Catholic Church would authorise our Courts to take judicial notice of Canon Law.' Now on dangerous ground, Gavan Duffy changed tack – a fact unacknowledged by some historians – when he added, 'I cannot decide those questions without full debate.'

The judge then came to the substance of the issue. Although he had demonstrated that prenuptial agreements had been unenforceable in the past, he stated that the two agreements signed by Mary and Ernest were in fact enforceable, because they should be seen in light of the 'Christian doctrine' of Articles 41, 42 and 44 of the constitution:

> Quite apart from Canon Law, the Doctrine of articles 41, 42 and 44 of the constitution appears to me to present the ante-nuptial agreement of the parties upon the creed to be imparted to their future children in a new setting [and] because the agreement, far from conflicting in any way with those articles, is consonant with their spirit and purpose ... The simple, clear and positive consequence of the ante-nuptial agreement, made to comply with the rule of the Catholic Church, is this – that by the express compact of the parents 1, the constitution of their particular family (which our constitution protects) is to be Catholic to the extent required by their promises, and 2, their parental authority (which our constitution protects) is to be exercised over the children of the marriage in the Catholic way to the extent required by their promises ... In my opinion, an order of the court designed to secure the fulfilment of an agreement, peremptorily required before a 'mixed marriage' by the Church whose special position in Ireland is officially recognised as the guardian of the faith of the Catholic spouse, cannot be withheld on any ground of public policy by the very State which pays that homage to that Church.

Gavan Duffy then moved on to the welfare of the three boys, which was hardly necessary since the grounds for his judgment had now become clear. That said, it should be noted that, although the father had up until now enjoyed the right to determine his children's religion and education, this privilege was always dependent on the welfare of the children. Clearly, the judge was ticking boxes. In a more demotic tone he stated that it was absolutely necessary for 'these lads' to grow up together as one family 'under their mother's wing'; he also expressed some sympathy with Ernest's account of his wife's insistence on going out to work and leaving the children in the care of her sister. He also described Mary's removal of herself and the boys to her parents' part of the house at Turner's Cottages as an action 'without just cause'.

However, the judge concluded that even if 'her conduct had wounded [Ernest]' the steps he had taken to redress his grievance 'were very desperate methods'. The three older boys 'had been snatched from their home with a callousness – indeed, with a brutality towards his wife and their mother – that gravely discredits the perpetrator'. Running through the options available to the court, the judge first ruled out the 'institutional asylum' and pronounced that their 'deportation to the Birds' Nest by an order of the Court rejecting their mother's prayer would be to make the State complete the final destruction of their home life'. The judge then addressed the house at Oldcastle as 'an alternative retreat'. Although it had 'real advantages' in that it 'promises country air and plenty of space, indoors and out', it risked 'further disturbance of the boys in the uncertainty of their acclimatisation'. Gavan Duffy also noted that this was the place from which Ernest had removed his children before taking them to the Birds' Nest; accordingly, he was 'not at all reassured as to the warmth of their welcome, if they were sent back'. Moreover, he speculated, if the children were to move to Oldcastle permanently, they would have only occasional contact with their parents.

Gavan Duffy then considered the boys' religion, which he argued could 'not be treated as a dissociated element' in their lives; apparently, their religion could not be dissociated from the constitution either. He continued to observe that 'sitting under a Christian constitution in a State publicly pledged to respect and honour religion, this Court is deeply concerned for the spiritual welfare of David, Alan, Paul and Neville which, as far as the Court of Justice can appraise it, must be my first care'. He argued there was no question of any attempt to coerce the boys into the Catholic Church since they were already members of that church and had been baptised and educated 'in harmony with the ante-nuptial agreement of the parents'.

Before his marriage, Ernest had 'apprehended no spiritual injury to his offspring in the prospect of rearing them as Catholics'; the judge suggested that he had 'now changed his mind about their creed; that is all' and in so doing had ignored the fact that 'to Catholics baptism of these boys is of transcendent importance and bears directly on their proper upbringing ... that fact was pointedly brought home to him before he married a Catholic girl'. Gavan Duffy discounted Ernest's 'unexplained change of mind' and added, 'with regret', that 'I feel pique to have been his predominant motive in removing the children and not religious sincerity'.

With this, Gavan Duffy delivered his final decision:

> In my judgment the ante-nuptial agreement of the parents crystallised the imprescriptible right of the children under the constitution to religious education and defined that right as a specific right in each of the four boys to instruction in the Roman Catholic religion, and no other, by their parents. As I view the whole of this melancholy affair, it is a calamity for both parents, a really appalling calamity for both, involving the boys; but the little boys must be rescued from that calamity as far as possible. Their father has without just cause made a determined attempt to break up their home; and he had relegated them as mock-orphans to the care of a charity, where he would have brought them up as Protestants in defiance of his holy undertaking, cognisable by this Court. They have a good mother who will fulfil the ante-nuptial agreement and continue to bring up her Catholic children as good Catholics. And their prospective general welfare, as I see it, points clearly and unmistakably to their mother's home as the best place for them. Accordingly, I hold that the mother's claim to an order of *habeas corpus* in respect of the three elder boys stands justified; the children must be restored to her. The cause shown will be disallowed and the conditional order made absolute. The husband must pay the wife's costs of, and incidental to, these proceedings.

The ruling was ground-breaking in Ireland; Gavan Duffy had dispensed with paternal supremacy, a tradition that had survived for more than a century, including the Frost case when the 1937 constitution had been in effect for eight years. The judgment itself was also notable for being non-precedential in legal terms (a point rarely acknowledged by the received histories). In a wholly different constitutional context, the New York civil courts in *Ramon* v. *Ramon* gave state backing to the same prenuptial agreement.[19]

The High Court Judgment

The American judge in that case was also of the opinion, as Gerard Hogan is regarding the Tilson case,[20] that it might be unconstitutional not to enforce a prenuptial agreement, as doing so might undermine a citizen's right to religious freedom.[21]

Gavan Duffy's ruling made the front page of *The Irish Times* and the *Irish Press* under the headlines, respectively, 'Court Upholds Mother's Claim to Three Children' and 'Mother Gets Children Back: Judge holds religious promise is binding' and was also covered on the inside pages of the *Irish Independent* ('Mother Wins Custody of Children') and the Dublin *Evening Herald* ('Mother's Claim to Children Upheld'). The *Cork Examiner* also reported on the case under the headline 'Mixed Marriage Agreement: High Court holds it binding'. Although most reports carried the same text because they were clearly provided by one reporter, they were circumspect and even-handed and quoted extensively from Gavan Duffy's address. However, the *Irish Press* chose to highlight in bold some quotations, such as: 'The right, he [Gavan Duffy] said, of the Catholic Church to guard the faith of its children, the great majority, was registered in their fundamental document, while non-Catholics were assured that their principals [sic] should be respected.'[22] Again, under the strapline 'Ne Temere', the mood of the *Irish Times* editorialist was sombre:

> Issues of weighty and far-reaching moment have been raised by the judgment delivered in Dublin on Thursday by the President of the High Court in the Tilson case ... In every country in which the Roman Catholic Church predominates, occasional clashes between civil and canon law are inevitable. Hitherto in Ireland, whenever such a conflict occurred – such cases as there have been almost exclusively matrimonial – the civil law invariably prevailed; but the President of the High Court has made it perfectly clear that, under the constitution, a totally new factor has been introduced into our national jurisprudence.[23]

In its broad-ranging report, the *Irish Catholic* did not display the same even-handedness as the national newspaper reports. Having outlined the circumstances of the case and quoting extensively from Gavan Duffy's address, the report's conclusion, although business-like, displayed smugness in observing that the state and the constitution were firmly aligned with Catholic doctrine:

> The ante-nuptial agreement in the present case took the form of separate promises by the spouses regarding the baptism and bringing-up of the children of the marriage as Catholics. Both spouses knew they had to make them before the Catholic Church would permit their marriage ... A Catholic and a Protestant who proposed to marry under the law of Ireland must contemplate a permanent union, for they knew well that the law of the Catholic Church and the law of the state combined to forbid divorce; their children would have a constitutional right to religious instruction, which the parents would be bound to provide. For the Catholic parent that teaching would have to be instruction in the Catholic Faith, and no other, but the Catholic spouse might not marry without securing the Faith of the children in the manner prescribed by the Catholic Church and, therefore, a sincere Catholic must insist on having the prenuptial agreement signed by the Protestant spouse, if relations are not to be broken off ... *The simple, clear and positive consequence of the ante-nuptial agreement was: that by the express compact of the parents, the constitution of their family was to be Catholic to the extent required by the promises; their authority was to be exercised over the children in the Catholic way.*[24]

In Northern Ireland, Gavan Duffy's judgment was covered in the *Belfast Telegraph* and the *Northern Whig*. The Protestant-leaning *Belfast News Letter*, which had published several reports of the case since it had opened in the High Court, vented its anger at the judgment under the expressive headline 'CHILDREN NOT TO BE PROTESTANTS: Dublin judge rejects father's claim: quotes constitution':

> He [the judge] had the temerity, however, to prefer a principle of public policy that would imperatively require a man to keep faith with the mother whom he had induced to wed him by his categorical engagement to respect her convictions in the supernatural domain as to her children's creed, at least when that promise was shown to have been of grave importance to her as it must be to a Roman Catholic.[25]

In Britain, the *Manchester Guardian* offered a brief but even-handed account of the outcome under the headline 'Children of Mixed Marriage: Dublin court's order'[26] while some newspapers in the United States, such as the *Gaelic American*, the *Freedom Call* (Freedom, Oklahoma), the *Representative* (Fox Lake, Wisconsin)[27] and the *Oklahoma County Register*

The High Court Judgment

(Luther, Oklahoma)[28] also covered the case. John Devoy, the Irish Fenian leader, had owned and edited both the *Gaelic American* and the *Irish Nation* (the latter, as noted earlier, had been edited for a time by Gavan Duffy's father, Charles). The *Gaelic American* was published weekly and combined commentary on news at home and abroad with historical material.[29] Under the headline 'Irish High Court Rules on Matter of Mixed Marriages', it outlined the circumstances of the case and concluded:

> An order of the Court designed to secure the fulfilment of an agreement, peremptorily required before a mixed marriage by the Catholic Church, could not be withheld on any ground of public policy by the very state which pays homage to that Church. The highest interest of the community and the state demanded that the parties, whose marriage was permanent, should be informed by the High Court of Justice that the ante-nuptial agreement upon religion was treated under the law of Ireland as a weighty factor, by no means to be displaced except by a factor of greater weight. The judge saw no such factor in the case at issue.[30]

Meanwhile the *Freedom Call* reported that:

> An important judgment dealing with the religious upbringing of the children of a Catholic-Protestant marriage has been delivered here by the president of the high court of Ireland, Justice Gavan Duffy ... He quoted the preamble to the Irish constitution stating that the initial invocation explicitly acknowledges the supremacy of the moral law founded on Christian doctrine.[31]

Acting for Ernest, W.I. Hamill asked for a 'stay of execution' for twenty-one days. Gavan Duffy, clearly aware that an appeal was likely, replied that he would postpone 'the handing over of the children' until the following Monday and suggested that 'in the meantime Mr Hamill could take whatever steps he was advised'.[32] The following day, 28 July, Ernest's lawyers duly lodged an appeal to the Supreme Court after giving an undertaking that 'notice of appeal from the order of the President [of the High Court] would be served today and, on that undertaking, the Court put a stay on the order to produce the children, until the determination of the appeal'.[33] Since it was a condition that Tilson's lawyers had to serve a short notice of appeal, the court clearly did not wish the three boys to stay in the Birds' Nest for a day longer than was absolutely necessary.

Gavan Duffy's judgment in the Tilson case betrayed the absence of a clear distinction between church and state. In reaching his decision, it is unclear whether he relied on the relevant articles of the constitution or was unduly influenced by his own deep-rooted Catholicism and nationalism, or whether he was simply discharging his obligations as a member of An Ríoghacht as set out in Articles (I) and (V) of its constitution. It is also possible that he came under the influence of somebody else. A letter sent by Archbishop McQuaid to Cardinal Francesco Marchetti-Selvaggiani in the Vatican on 4 September 1950, just four weeks after the Supreme Court appeal, may shed some light on this question. Marchetti-Selvaggiani participated in the enclave of 1939 that elected Pope Pius XII and was secretary of the Congregation for the Propagation of Faith, dean of the College of Cardinals and secretary of the Holy Office. It is fair to say that he was the most senior figure in the Vatican after the Holy See.

Enclosing a copy of the Tilson judgment, McQuaid wrote that 'in the case of Tilson vs Tilson, the President of the High Court (who is ex officio a member of the Supreme Court) gave judgment in favour of the Catholic mother against the Protestant father who had broken the prenuptial guarantees and placed his four children in a Protestant orphanage'. McQuaid then went on to describe how he had previously agreed a 'commission' with Rome 'to have the British law, with which the Republic has lived, effectively changed in favour of the prescriptions of the Church'. He also outlined how he 'approached [the 'commission'] with great secrecy'; 'consulted ... with only one colleague in the Hierarchy' and 'consulted for long with two members of the Judiciary whom [he] could trust'. The archbishop of Dublin also described how he 'spoke several times [about the 'commission'] with the Head of the Government [John A. Costello], whom [he] found very sympathetic', before declaring that he had 'waited for a favourable opportunity'. He stated that the 'opportunity came with the Tilson case'.[34] Clearly, McQuaid's letter was not a bolt out of the blue for Marchetti-Selvaggiani who, in turn, was gracious in his response: 'I thank you Your Most Reverend Excellency and I sincerely congratulate You, whose vigilant prudence and assiduous effort have achieved such a positive result.'[35]

McQuaid's letter and the cardinal's response contain strong echoes of another letter which Irish ambassador to the Holy See, Joseph Walshe, apparently sent to the Dublin archbishop after judgment was delivered in the High Court: 'I can echo your Grace's expression of relief at the Gavan Duffy decision – and I am above all delighted that it was brought about by your patient and consistent work.'[36] Notwithstanding McQuaid's disclosures, or his possible involvement in the Tilson case's legal process, it was now up to the Supreme Court to decide on the custody of the children and, by extension, their religious upbringing. It was also an opportunity for that court to put some distance between church and state.

CHAPTER 9

The Supreme Court Appeal

The Supreme Court appeal opened on Monday, 31 July 1950 before the chief justice, Conor Maguire, Mr Justice James Murnaghan, Mr Justice John O'Byrne, Mr Justice William Black and Mr Justice Cecil Lavery. Mr Justice William Bullick Black was the only Protestant on the bench; the other four judges were Catholics. In fact, Black had been active in Sinn Féin and later Fianna Fáil, and was the running mate of Seán McEntee in the Dublin Township constituency in the June 1938 general election.[1] Ernest Tilson was represented by R.G.L. Leonard KC, E.C. Micks SC and W.I. Hamill, all of whom were instructed by the solicitor W.H. Richardson. Mary Tilson was represented by the attorney general, Charles Casey, T.K. Liston SC and J.R. Heavey; her barristers were instructed by George C. McGrath.

The grounds for Ernest's appeal were that the order of the High Court had been made without due regard to the welfare of the children, to the wishes of the father, to the right of the father to determine in what religion the children should be brought up, or to the impossibility of the mother, if given custody of the children, to bring them up in the faith of the Church of Ireland in accordance with the wishes of the father; that the finding of the High Court that the welfare of the children required that they should be given into the custody and control of their mother had been against the evidence and the weight of evidence, and was contrary to law and to the accepted principles of law and the equitable jurisdiction of the court; and that the discretion of the High Court in finding that the welfare of the children required that they should be given to the mother, and, in making the absolute order, had not been exercised correctly in accordance with the legal principles applicable.

In other words, Ernest's lawyers argued that Mr Justice Gavan Duffy had erred in making absolute Mr Justice Kevin Dixon's conditional order of *habeas corpus ad subjiciendum*.

His team also argued that George Gavan Duffy had misdirected himself in law by failing to apply the principles accepted by the Supreme Court in the Frost case of 1945, and by ascribing to the Tilsons' prenuptial agreement a force and validity not justified by law and contrary to the constitution, and in particular to Articles 41, 42 and 44 which concerned the family, education and religion.[2]

Gerard Hogan notes that 'the first question which the Supreme Court was required to confront was whether the paternal supremacy rule was inconsistent with Article 42.1'.[3] Crucial to the case, this article declares that: 'The State acknowledges that the primary and natural educator of the child is the Family and guarantees to respect the inalienable right and duty of parents to provide, according to their means, for the religious and moral, intellectual, physical and social education of their children.' In his opening remarks on the first day of the appeal, R.G.L. Leonard for Ernest addressed the prenuptial agreement, arguing that:

> The validity, in law, of a prenuptial agreement between two people in a mixed marriage would arise … between a Protestant man and a Catholic woman where he had given an undertaking that any children of the marriage would be brought up in the Catholic faith. The principle of law was the same whether the undertaking was given by a member of the Church of Ireland agreeing to raise his children as Roman Catholics or a member of the Catholic Church agreeing that his children should be brought up in the tenets of the Church of Ireland. The question was a question of law, how far any person giving such an undertaking was justified in not abiding by it, and whether it was binding or not.[4]

Leonard also added that whatever other objections his client had to his children being raised in Turner's Cottages, one was that he did not wish his children to be raised as Roman Catholics but in his own Church of Ireland faith.[5] At this point Rev. W.L.M. Giff's written observations on the Birds' Nest admissions forms came in for scrutiny. The court was aware that children had to be destitute to be admitted to the orphanage, but since the children were clearly not destitute, it raised the issue of proselytism. Mr Justice Lavery intervened, observing 'that is not what he told Mr. Giff. He told him the children were destitute because the mother had deserted them.' In reply, Leonard said that it was evident from Mary's affidavit that she did not wish to live with her husband and she denied that he had suggested that she had abandoned the three boys. Mr Justice Murnaghan asked 'if it was not Mr Giff's reason for having the matter investigated to find out whether or not they were destitute'. Leonard said that he thought Giff's handwritten endorsements on the back of the three admission forms derived from third-party information. While Leonard did not know whether the matter had been investigated or not, he thought the main grounds for Ernest Tilson's request for custody were that he wished his children to be 'brought up in the faith of the Church of Ireland'. Leonard added that 'there was no question of proselytising on either side in this case; it was purely a case in which there was a difference between the father and the mother'.[6]

Leonard turned back to the prenuptial agreement and argued that this was not enforceable in law; it was 'purely a matter for Ernest Tilson's conscience whether or not he fulfilled that promise'. 'What the Court had to consider in every case,' he continued, 'was what was best for the children. It would not be for the welfare of the children if there had been acquiescence for so long as to give them an opportunity of forming such settled opinions as would result, after a change, in the alteration of outlook.' He continued:

> The only law that the Court was administering was the law of the State, and that law says that a marriage can be validly performed by a minister of any religion or by a civil registrar. The view held by the Courts was that a man had no rights to sign away the future faith of his children without having regard to what his future outlook might be ... As to Canon law, it was a foreign law binding the members of the Roman Catholic Church just as the domestic law of other Churches bound the members of those Churches, but it was the law of the state which was to be administered by the Courts.

Implicitly dismissing Gavan Duffy's speculation in the High Court case that the state might take cognisance of canon law, Leonard stated that that notion was contrary to the constitution's recognition of other religions. Mr Justice O'Byrne asked him if there was any evidence of Ernest having changed his mind. Leonard claimed that his client had always wanted to raise his children in the Church of Ireland faith. O'Byrne then proposed that there were two possible ways in which one could look at the promise: first, that it was given conscientiously and that Ernest had intended to honour it, but had changed his mind; or, second, that he made the promise fraudulently, with no intention of keeping it. Leonard replied that he would be sorry to think that his client had entered into the promise on the basis of fraud and said that he did not believe that this was the case. He argued that the promise was 'a matter between [Tilson] and his God ... it was a matter for his own conscience'. A subsequent exchange reveals the direction in which the court was beginning to lean:

MR JUSTICE LAVERY: 'What about his wife? The woman whom he married – the woman who is to bear him children – has she no rights in this matter?'

Leonard replied by saying that the President of the High Court had said that the signing of this agreement was an abrogation of the father's rights.

MR JUSTICE MURNAGHAN: 'It is not the father's rights. The constitution puts it in the parents' rights, parents in the plural.'

Leonard agreed that it was the parents' rights, but that, between the parents, it would be the father who would have the right.

MR JUSTICE O'BYRNE: 'Before 1937 the mother had no rights regarding the religious education of her children. It was the father who had the right in these matters, but had the constitution of 1937 changed that?'

Leonard submitted that the insertion of 'parents' in the plural did not change the law.

MR JUSTICE MURNAGHAN: 'The point may arise that the parents have agreed. Can one parent alter the agreement?'

Unsurprisingly, Leonard replied that one parent could alter the agreement.[7]

The following day, 1 August, Leonard continued his submission, focusing initially on the spiritual welfare of the children. Although in common law the father had the right to decide their religious upbringing, this was always subject to the welfare of those children. Leonard argued that 'the spiritual welfare of the children undoubtedly was part of their welfare which was not going to be disregarded'. 'It was recognised,' he continued, 'that where they had children so indoctrinated in the tenets of a particular Church that any changes would result in alteration of an outlook, it was their welfare that they should be left in that religion whose tenets they had come to receive and accept.' Qualifying this line of reasoning with reference to the constitution, Leonard argued that the court could not support the notion that the acceptance of the tenets of one church rather than another would 'injure the spiritual welfare of the child', unless 'the Article of the constitution which referred to the special position of the Roman Catholic Church had altered that position', a qualification that echoed Gavan Duffy's suggestion that the court might take cognisance of canon law.[8]

Proposing that if Ernest and Mary could 'come together and establish' a home, the 'children would have both father and mother', Leonard submitted that neither parent in the case had rendered themselves unfit to have custody of the children – 'unless it was suggested that refusal to fulfil a promise would be necessary to render the father unfit to have custody of his children or before it could be held that he had abdicated his right'. He added that in a case where a person had a right to custody, that person could not sign that right away *in futuro*. Leonard argued that the court could not hold that it would be injurious to the welfare of the children, who had not formed any definite religious opinions, should they be brought up as either Catholics or Protestants. Addressing the notion that Ernest may have estopped himself by allowing his children to be baptised and raised as Catholics, Leonard argued that 'a man did not abdicate his right of determining in which faith his children should be brought up by having his child baptised in one particular faith'; he would abdicate his right only when he allowed a child sufficient time 'to form its mind in the mould of that faith'. Leonard was clearly basing his line of reasoning on the fact that David Tilson, at eight years old, had only a rudimentary understanding of his Catholic faith.

Relying on the tradition of paternal supremacy and the judgment in the Frost case, Leonard summed up his argument on behalf of his client: 'The right of the father as against the mother, which was settled law, was not affected by the constitution, and that the Supreme Court had decided that in another case, and was bound by that decision.' He pointed out that it had never occurred to him that 'the constitution was a copper-fastened document governing every aspect of human relations, [and] unless something could be found in the constitution inconsistent with the existing law, the existing law would continue to be the law of the state'. Mr Justice Black interjected with the observation that

> it seemed a very plausible view that the constitution did not confer any new right or duty on parents, but recognised an existing duty on parents to provide, according to their means, for the religious and moral training of their children. That would mean there was an already existing duty of right, independent of the constitution.

Black would later elaborate in some detail on this matter. Sensing that he might have found an ally on the bench, Leonard continued:

> The law could not recognise the domestic legislation of any church. Notwithstanding the special position of the church of the majority, the constitution definitely stated that its provisions were not to be

made discriminatory between one and another. How could there be anything in the constitution to make inappropriate the law, acted upon for so many years, that agreements made before marriage were not binding for always and that the Courts would not enforce them against the wishes of one of the parties.[9]

Leonard turned next to George Gavan Duffy:

> The President of the High Court [held] that where there was an agreement before marriage that the children should be brought up in a particular religious belief, effect must be given to that undertaking. Such an undertaking, however, could not be binding; it was the right and duty of the father to change his mind when he so decided, and effect must be given to the father's wishes.[10]

Although Leonard dismissed the notion that the court might recognise canon law, stating that precedent dictated that prenuptial agreements were unenforceable, his submission on behalf of Ernest was primarily based on paternal supremacy. He argued that Ernest's right to determine the religious upbringing of his children extended to him changing his mind. This was supported by previous court judgments, and the 1937 constitution had done nothing to alter that right. Leonard was emphatic that the spiritual welfare of the children (the point on which paternal supremacy might depend) had not been compromised because the three boys were too young to have fixed religious beliefs or convictions.

On the third day of the hearing, the attorney general, Charles Casey, appeared for Mary Tilson. Casey was born on 2 January 1895 in Dublin and was educated at the Christian Brothers' O'Connell School, Castleknock College and the King's Inns. After qualifying as a barrister, he joined the legal staff of the Free State army and was called to the bar in 1923, where he built up a substantial practice in civil and criminal law. One of the most high-profile cases he was involved in was the Sinn Féin Funds case in 1947, presided over by Gavan Duffy and discussed in an earlier chapter, in which he appeared for the plaintiff with John A. Costello and Seán MacBride. He was appointed attorney general in April 1950 and a High Court judge in June 1951. As outlined in Chapter 4, Casey was a particularly devout Catholic who favoured an integrally Catholic state. Unusually for an attorney general, he acted as spokesman for the government on its decision not to introduce adoption legislation, explicitly declaring that the state should harmonise its legislation with the teaching of the Catholic Church on salvation and arguing that legal adoption would facilitate proselytism.[11]

It was highly unusual for an attorney general to appear in person in court; although it was not uncommon before independence, the practice had effectively been abandoned after the formation of the Free State. It is worth noting that the main functions of the attorney general are to act as legal adviser to the government and to represent the state in legal proceedings. J.P. Casey questions why John A. Costello, the taoiseach at the time, did not intervene to prevent Casey's appearance, arguing that 'the case gave rise to considerable controversy about the implications of Article 44 of the constitution, and it was hardly desirable for the Attorney General to have been – unnecessarily – involved in this'.[12] Archbishop McQuaid's letter to Cardinal Francesco Marchetti-Selvaggiani is again of relevance here, since it suggests that the archbishop had the ear of the attorney general before or during the court hearings. After describing to the cardinal how 'the opportunity came with the Tilson case', McQuaid added, 'I was given the greatest assistance by the chief law officer of the Republic, the Attorney General.'[13] Having lost their High Court case and listened to a judgment delivered in the language of a sworn Catholic, to then be confronted with Charles Casey in the Supreme Court, Ernest's legal team could have been forgiven for thinking that they were in a battle not just against a working-class woman from Turner's Cottages, but against the might of Catholic Ireland.

In a letter to a W. Navan in Bangor, County Down, Rev. W.L.M. Giff certainly suggested that Mary Tilson's legal team and their patrons had been determined to do whatever was necessary to win the case:

> ... thank you too for your very kind reference to the Tilson case. I need scarcely tell you that it has been a time of great anxiety to me. Not that I am afraid to see it through, but that any step I might have taken would have been detrimental to the prestige of Protestantism in Ireland. *When one was fighting people who were prepared to throw in anything*, it was hard to keep one's hands clean, and any slip I might have made would have reflected on the whole of our Protestant cause.[14]

Casey opened proceedings for Mary Tilson by stressing the 'great importance' of the case, 'not only to the parties before the Court and those who had contracted mixed marriages but to those who might be contemplating entering into such a marriage'.[15] Although he placed most emphasis on the articles dealing with fundamental rights in the constitution, such as family, education and religion, as attorney general he was sailing particularly close to the wind when he stated that the Catholic Church claimed to be the One True Church:

> Marriage in Ireland was a permanent union of both spouses, and naturally it was of great importance that the parties to a marriage should know their exact legal position as would be decided by that Court. The mother was a Catholic and the claims of her Church were bound up with her position before that Court. The Catholic Church claimed to be the One True Church, and one of its strictest obligations was that Catholic parents should bring up their children in the faith of that Church. The Catholic Church made regulations governing the Sacrament of marriage, one being that it would not allow a Catholic to marry a non-Catholic unless certain guarantees were given ... the guarantee given by the non-Catholic was two-fold – a guarantee for the children, and a guarantee for the wife and mother. The guarantee formed the basis on which the contract of marriage was entered into, and the guarantee had been accepted in this case by the wife as a solemn promise to be fulfilled by the husband.[16]

Casey argued that if the 'framers of the constitution' had it in mind to endow one parent more than another with a particular right, 'it would have been a simple matter to have stated that'. It followed that if the parents had equal rights under the constitution, 'the constitution preserved them'; or 'if they had no such rights beforehand, the constitution gave them those rights'. Casey pointed out that this was the first time 'a marriage guarantee, where the marriage had taken place after the constitution, had come before the Court for consideration'.[17] He asserted that since the state protected marriage in the constitution 'with special care', it gave 'the right in conscience for Mrs. Tilson in the practice of her religion to do what she was compelled to do by her Church and Mr. Tilson had guaranteed that right under his own hand'. It followed that the only way in which the state could now protect Mary's rights through the courts was by seeing that Ernest honoured the agreement he had signed. Further, the articles dealing with fundamental rights, 'when read as a whole, compelled Mr. Tilson to honour his obligations'.

At this point Black intervened, noting that, under the constitution, a woman had a right to bring up her children in the Catholic faith, as Casey had said. However, asked Black, 'did the constitution give the husband any right; if he were a Jew or a Mohammedan did it give him the same right as the wife who was a Catholic?' Casey replied that it all depended on the religion; he might not be bound to bring up his children in that religion:

> MR JUSTICE BLACK: 'Suppose he is a member of the Church of Ireland; do you think he does not consider that he is bound to bring up his children in that religion?'
> ATTORNEY GENERAL: 'I am sure he does, provided he is conscientious about his religion, but if he was conscientious about his religion, he would not sign an undertaking of that nature.'
> MR JUSTICE BLACK: 'Supposing he thinks he is bound, and his wife thinks she is bound, how can you reconcile them?'
> ATTORNEY GENERAL: 'He has signed an undertaking, and no Catholic can marry a Protestant in a Catholic Church without that undertaking.'[18]

The following day *The Irish Times* published a letter from George Irvine in Terenure, Dublin. Irvine, a Protestant, was a Gaelic scholar, a member of the Irish Republican Brotherhood (IRB), a veteran of the 1916 Rising and an important republican voice in the Church of Ireland.[19] By 1950 he had become disenchanted with the lack of secularism in independent Ireland and frequently wrote along such lines to the press. In this instance, he took issue with Charles Casey's use of the term 'non-Catholic' in court, the use of which not only underlined the fact that the southern state was overwhelmingly Catholic, but also suggested that Protestants there were regarded as 'other':

> Sir,
>
> The Attorney General, when laying down the law for other citizens, should be careful to keep within the law himself, both in letter and in spirit.
>
> In the Declaration of Independence of 1916 and in the constitution, which was framed on the Declaration, the Republic acknowledges the rights of all religious communities, and in paragraph 4 of the Declaration, expressly uses the phrase: - 'Cherish all the children of the nation equally.'
>
> Therefore, citizens of the Republic, when speaking in their public capacity, as representing the Republic ... should not give offence to any of those religious communities, no matter what their private opinions may be.

The use of the term 'non-Catholic', when referring to any Christian community or members of it, is a public insult to the community in question, as the Attorney General used it in his speech on the Tilson case. – Yours etc.,

G. Irvine[20]

On 4 August, the final day of the Supreme Court hearing, T.K. Liston appeared for Mary. Since he highlighted the religious nature of the 1937 constitution, Liston's argument was consonant with that of Gavan Duffy of the High Court. He observed that 'the President of the High Court was well justified in his observations in his judgment ... the ante-nuptial agreement upon religion was treated under the law of Ireland as a weighty factor, by no means to be displaced except by a factor of greater weight, and that he [Gavan Duffy] discerned no such factor in the present case'.[21]

Referring to paternal supremacy, Black pointed out to Liston that in the past where a principle had been settled and accepted by the legal profession, a final court of appeal would not overturn it. He asked if there was any precedent for such a court to ignore 'a doctrine which had been laid down for 100 years and [had] never [been] questioned apart from the constitution'. Black wanted to know if the age-old tradition of paternal supremacy should be ignored in favour of 'the constitution and the constitution alone'; Liston's response bore all the hallmarks of Gavan Duffy's views and beliefs:

> If ... the articles of the constitution relating to religion, marriage and the family and the education of children were to be of any efficacy at all, the Court would give effect to them by upholding the promise made in this case ... if the State recognised the Roman Catholic Church as the guardian of the faith of the majority and to secure the progeny of its own members would be brought up in that faith, then, having regard to the constitution, the State ought to give recognition to the way in which the faith would be safeguarded.[22]

Black responded by arguing that the constitution also recognised the position of other churches as guardians of their particular faiths. Although Liston agreed with this assertion, he maintained that the constitution was fundamentally religious in construction and articulation:

> One could put religion in the background and say that the father could make his children anything he liked, or one could put religion

in the foreground, as was done in the constitution. The preamble to the constitution indicated that it was a Christian constitution. The constitution placed religion in the foreground. If there was a solemn agreement relating to religion, that agreement should be upheld by the Court.[23]

Clearly dissatisfied with this response and determined to examine whether the constitution discriminated against other faiths, Black asked, 'Would it be upheld if it was the question concerning a Jew? Supposing the father agreed to bring up the children in the faith of his Jewish wife, what then?'

Irritated with the line of questioning, Liston's response echoed the pronouncements of Gavan Duffy, identifying paternal supremacy with the Victorian era:

> Is it necessary, with all respect, to discuss that point in this particular case? Once you give religion the importance which it does get in the constitution, it is difficult to say that an agreement relating to religion, which both parties regard as being of importance, should be relegated to some authority which appears to be based on some Victorian concept of the position of the father.
> MR JUSTICE BLACK: 'Is the constitution discriminatory?'
> MR LISTON: 'As regards religion, this is a non-discriminatory constitution, but it is not a constitution under which you can say religion is not important.'[24]

Replying next to a question from Murnaghan, Liston emphasised the importance of religion in the constitution, explaining that if parents made an agreement relating to religion,

> it was not in harmony with the constitution to say 'We will listen to any agreement the parents may have made with regard to property etc., but we will not listen to anything you have agreed upon in relation to religion' ... in view of the importance attaching to religion in the constitution, an ante-nuptial agreement of this kind must be lifted to a high level.[25]

Leonard then interposed with the suggestion that the prenuptial agreement at the heart of the case to bring up children as Catholics was 'accidental' and should be approached as though the promise had been made by a Catholic

BIRDS' NEST—KINGSTOWN.
FOUNDED 1859.

1. The Birds' Nest Orphanage, Dún Laoghaire, County Dublin [early twentieth century].
   Image courtesy of Dun Laoghaire-Rathdown Local Studies Department

2. *(Top left)* Charles Casey, who was attorney general in 1950.
Image courtesy of St Vincent's Castleknock College, Dublin

3. John A. Costello TD *(on right)* with papal nuncio Gerald O'Hara and General Richard Mulcahy TD. Costello was 'more aggressive in his deference to the church authorities than any of his predecessors', while Mulcahy had 'an innate Catholic conservatism' (*c.* 1952).
Image courtesy of the National Library of Ireland (IND, R 0152)

4. Mr Justice George Gavan Duffy (*c.* 1950).
Image courtesy of the National Library of Ireland (VTLS 299312)

5. (*Top left*) Rev. W.L.M. Giff.
Image courtesy of The Irish Times

6. Seán MacBride *(right)* with Cecil Lavery. Lavery sat on the Supreme Court bench for the Tilson case.
Image courtesy of Ms Caitriona Lawlor

7. John Charles McQuaid, archbishop of Dublin.
Image courtesy of the Dublin Diocesan Archives

8. (*above*) *L to R*, Alan, Paul and David Tilson on summer holidays in Oldcastle, 1949.
Private collection

9. The three Tilson children leaving the Birds' Nest, accompanied by their mother and solicitor, George McGrath.
Image courtesy of the Daily Express *(Irish edition)*

10. Letter sent by David Tilson to his mother from the Birds' Nest.
Private collection

11. Reunited in London: Ernest and Mary Tilson.
Private collection

father to raise his children in the Protestant religion. Leonard said that there was nothing in the 1937 constitution that altered the right of the father to raise his children in the religion of his choice: 'Established law showed that ante-nuptial agreements were not binding. The Supreme Court in this country had been definitely of the opinion in another case that ante-nuptial agreements were not binding unless the constitution affected the position.' He suggested that a 'net issue' remained, and asked 'was there anything in the constitution of 1937 that made repugnant the decisions adopted by these courts that ante-nuptial agreements had not the effect of taking from the father his right of deciding the religion of his children?'[26]

Murnaghan probed him on his line of reasoning: 'If a husband and wife definitely agreed on a particular course of religion as a pact between them, it is your argument that the father would be able to revoke that?' Leonard, obviously aware that the welfare of the children superseded paternal supremacy, agreed: 'Yes, but there comes a point when he cannot. The moment the children have acquired settled convictions, he cannot. It would be wrong to start teaching them different tenets then.'

> MR JUSTICE MURNAGHAN: 'Supposing before the children had got such fixed ideas, would you say that if husband and wife had carried out such a course for, say, eight years, the father had a legal right to alter that?'
> MR LEONARD: 'There is the law and look at the constitution and say if there is anything there to alter that.'
> MR JUSTICE MURNAGHAN: 'Under the constitution, do you say that if husband and wife agree and carry out for eight years a particular course of religious education, is it the law that the father can revoke that?'
> MR LEONARD: 'There is nothing to prevent it, providing a certain thing has not happened. The welfare of the children must be treated as the overriding factor. One example of that is settled convictions by the children which must not be disturbed. In the constitution, there is an atmosphere of religion, but not of one particular form, except of Christianity. After that, religion is used in the sense of faith, apparently not necessarily a dogmatic faith, because among the religions specially mentioned is the Society of Friends, which believes in no dogma – they say they have no dogma.'
> CHIEF JUSTICE CONOR MAGUIRE: 'Do they believe in God?'
> MR LEONARD: 'Yes, my Lord.'

CHIEF JUSTICE CONOR MAGUIRE: 'That is a fairly substantial dogma to begin with.'
MR LEONARD: 'They disregard all details of all other denominations.'
CHIEF JUSTICE CONOR MAGUIRE: 'Are they Christians?'
MR LEONARD: 'Yes, my Lord.'
CHIEF JUSTICE CONOR MAGUIRE: 'Do they recognise the Scriptures?'
MR LEONARD: 'I think they do.'

Attention then turned to the notes on the three Birds' Nest admission forms, handwritten by Giff, which stated that Mary had deserted her children. Mr Justice Lavery chose to scrutinise the dates on the forms and pointed out that, in his affidavit, Ernest claimed that he had placed his three sons in the orphanage on 13 May 1950; his wife also understood that they were admitted on that day. Francis Russell, the secretary of Mrs Smyly's Homes, stated, by contrast, in his affidavit that the children were admitted on 15 May. Lavery queried this, asking why, if they had been admitted on 13 May, it had been two days before the forms had been filled in? He continued:

> On May 15th the forms were made out, and on it [sic] they say that the mother had deserted the children. Yet on that very day, the day on which the form says she deserted them, the mother went to the home and spoke to some person there about their religion ... The day on which she went to the home with the purpose of seeing her children was the day on which the forms were filled in, and they set out that the mother had deserted her children. That calls for an explanation.[27]

The four Birds' Nest admission forms record a date of 15 May 1950. Although Ernest's typed affidavit shows the date of admission as 13 May, this was later altered with a pen. The alteration was initialled with the letters 'W.H.' – obviously Ernest's solicitor W.H. Richardson.[28] Continuing his line of questioning regarding dates, Lavery next asked why Ernest had entered incorrect dates on the admission forms for his marriage in 1941 and for his children's birthdays. Leonard said that his client 'may be an ignorant man who would not know much about dates and probably made a mistake ... the man must have got muddled up on the dates'.

However anodyne this explanation was, Leonard's mitigation regarding the charge on the admission form that Mary had deserted her children required a considerable stretch of the imagination. The barrister argued that, according to his client, his wife had left him alone with the children for an entire day while she had stayed in her parents' part of the house. The next day, while she was elsewhere, he had to bathe and dress the children and 'prepare food for them and put them to bed'. According to Leonard this relatively brief absence constituted desertion, and impelled Ernest to remove the children from the family home at Turner's Cottages and take them to Oldcastle.

Lavery was unconvinced, plainly suspecting some form of jiggery-pokery surrounded the admission of the three boys, and suggested that more research should have been done into the three boys' circumstances before they were admitted to the home. Following this line of questioning, Chief Justice Conor Maguire asked, 'on [the] statement made by the father that the mother had completely deserted the children, had they not got the evidence of the mother calling?'[29]

> MR LEONARD: 'Mr Giff took the man's word.'
> CHIEF JUSTICE CONOR MAGUIRE: 'Was not the mother's calling to see the children evidence that that statement of the father was not correct? Why did not Mr. Giff change his report?'
> MR LEONARD: 'They had the mother leaving the father and going into another part of the house, bringing the children with her, and the father then having to look after them. The father considered that as desertion, and Rev. Mr. Giff accepted his word.'
> CHIEF JUSTICE CONOR MAGUIRE: 'I could understand that part, but, seeing that he [Giff] had evidence that the statement was wrong, could he not have investigated and changed his report instead of leaving it there?'[30]

Realising that he was making little headway in justifying the circumstances of the boys' admission to the Birds' Nest, Leonard returned to the safer ground of the father's rights, proclaiming pompously, 'It is no part of my business to make this particular goose a swan. It is no particular part of my business to make him any better than he is ... what is material in law is: did he do anything by his conduct which would abrogate his right?'[31]

Justices Murnaghan and Lavery turned next to Ernest's finances and the contributions he was supposedly prepared to make regarding his sons' stay in the Birds' Nest. Lavery questioned why Tilson 'should consent to the description of his children as destitute' when he had 'a permanent job with a comparatively good salary ... earning £5-14-0 per week' and was planning to contribute 5s. per week to the Birds' Nest for each of his three sons, making a total of 'fifteen shillings per week'. Mr Justice Murnaghan then raised the issue of Tilson's District Court summons, which had been served the previous December:

> MR JUSTICE MURNAGHAN: 'This man was summoned in December and only got the summons dismissed because he agreed to pay £4 per week.'
> MR LEONARD: 'He agreed to pay £4 a week on condition that they would all live together, a thing which his wife afterwards did not do.'
> MR JUSTICE MURNAGHAN: 'Was putting the children into the home an attempt to avoid paying the £4 a week?'

Leonard offered an unconvincing and improbable explanation:

> It might be that the man had found a place where he thought his children would be extremely well treated, and it might have appeared to him that this would be a good place to leave them, and that by doing so, he might be financially better off and be able to give more money to his wife. It was only after his wife had refused to live with him, and after she failed to turn up when he was going to get a corporation house and he had to look after the children and bring them to Oldcastle, that he decided to put them into the home.[32]

Ernest's counsel had no intention of concluding on this note, however, and returned again to the constitution, to precedent and to the prenuptial agreement:

> Did the constitution change what had been accepted as established law on the validity of the ante-nuptial agreement? What did the constitution say to the contrary? When they had principles accepted by the courts, they must definitely show what it was the constitution said, if they said that the constitution stated something to the contrary [I cannot] find anything laid down in the constitution that affected the findings of the courts that these ante-nuptial agreements were not binding. Was there anything in Article 44 [the article that referred to the 'special position' of the Catholic Church] that showed that what the courts decided was wrong? Where in the constitution is there some provision which makes this Court say that it [the prenuptial agreement] is binding?[33]

Leonard summed up by focusing on the validity of the prenuptial agreement and on the father's rights under the tradition of paternal supremacy. He argued that the 'chief question for the decision of the Court ... is whether an ante-nuptial agreement entered into by the parties to a marriage is or is not a valid agreement in law', submitting that '*prima facie* the father has the right to the custody of the children and the right to decide the religion in which they will be brought up'.[34] Liston summed up by arguing that:

> The law does not entitle the father in this case to alter the religion in which his children have hitherto been educated. Moreover, the religion in which his children have been brought up is in accordance with the appellant's ante-nuptial agreement. That agreement was endorsed by his marriage, and we submit that his course of conduct after his marriage disentitles him to change his mind at this stage as to the religion in which his children should be brought up. That contention is based on two grounds: first, the constitution gives him no such right, for the right of deciding the religion of the children is, by the constitution, vested in both parents equally and one parent alone cannot change that decision against the wishes of the other; secondly, the common law, on the facts of this case, gives him no such right.[35]

Meanwhile, Mary Tilson received a letter of support from a correspondent who was clearly confident regarding the outcome of the case. The writer advocated prayer, devotion to Our Lady, and applauded Mary's Catholic senior counsel, T.K. Liston:

> Dublin,
> Aug 3, '50
>
> Dear Madam,
>
> I read with great interest your case in the daily papers. So far, it's going in your favour, Thank God. When your children are handed over to you, do your utmost for them especially in religious matters, as you know he [Ernest Tilson] will be watching every move. So give him no chance, as you know he would like to have something against you, so don't forget to pray hard, nothing like prayer. God and his Blessed Mother will help you in every way. Mr Liston is a great Catholic gentleman and he is able to cut the others in there [*sic*]. I am enclosing a [Maria] Goretti [prayer]. I know you would like to read same. I may

come across you sometime, Please God, as the Bishop in Haddington Road is a second cousin of mine.

Yours,
E.W.

P.S. Everyone I speak to is in your favour. He [Ernest] must have thought you were a softy, but you let him know what you were – you stood up for your children's faith. God will reward you.[36]

At the conclusion of the hearing, Chief Justice Conor Maguire stated that the judgment should be given 'as soon as possible' and, true to his word, it was delivered at a special sitting of the Supreme Court on Saturday, 5 August. Mr Justice Murnaghan began by stating that the 'decision of the learned President was based on a point of law, viz., the binding force of an ante-nuptial agreement as to the religious education of the children'[37] (Gavan Duffy had supposedly based his decision on the fact that Articles 41, 42 and 44 had 'presented the ante-nuptial agreement ... in a new setting'). Murnaghan then described the circumstances of Ernest's employment and marriage, the difficulties he encountered when he applied for the dispensation, the signing of the agreement and the children born of the marriage.

The judge detailed Ernest's claims in his affidavits that he had objected at different times to his children being raised as Catholics, especially on or around the time his eldest son, David, was making his First Holy Communion; the judge also noted Mary's claim in her affidavit that this had been the first time her husband had made any objection to his children being brought up as Catholics.

Murnaghan stated that 'the point of law which was argued was whether, under the constitution, the agreement of Ernest Tilson and Mary Josephine Tilson to bring up the children as Roman Catholics had in law a binding force', before turning to paternal supremacy. He described how before 1882 women in England and Wales 'occupied in law a position of inferiority' to men in respect of property and how in 'common law the father had complete control over the children of the marriage and the wife had no voice against the wishes of her husband'. He noted that this situation had improved for women with the Married Women's Property Act 1882 and the Local Government Act of 1898; the Free State constitution of 1922 had then 'recognised the equality of women (article 14) and article 16 of the constitution gave the important rights dealt with by it to "every citizen without distinction of sex".[38] The judge added: 'In light of these facts I have to interpret the constitution adopted by the people in 1937. The constitution states fundamental principles ... when they are enshrined in the constitution, they become, and are, the fundamental law of the state.'[39]

Murnaghan then read Article 42.1 to the court before making a trenchant observation: 'Where the mother and father of children are alive, this article recognises a *joint right and duty* in them to provide for the religious education of their children. The word "parents" is in the plural and, naturally, should include both father and mother.'[40] He outlined how previous existing laws and principles were of no force in the state unless 'they derive efficacy from article 50 of the constitution'. Article 50 states that laws in force in Ireland before the 1937 constitution would continue to have force and effect as long as they were not at variance with the new document. In other words, the judge was suggesting that the principle of paternal supremacy had been threatened by the new constitution.

Murnaghan then turned to the Frost case of 1945, arguing that the court then had recognised that, in regard to Article 42, the mother as well as the father 'was a joint sharer of the right and duty'. Moreover, he contended that the 1945 court had not decided that where a prenuptial agreement had been made, the father alone could rescind it. Addressing Mr Justice C. Sullivan's ruling that agreement should be treated as non-binding based on previous cases, Murnaghan said that these cases were not based on any sound principle, or public policy, 'which was contrary to the constitution'.[41] Clearly, he did not view the prenuptial agreement before him as antithetical to the 1937 constitution:

> In my opinion the true principle under our constitution is this. The parents – father and mother – have a joint power and duty in respect of the religious education of their children. If they together make a decision and put it into practice, it is not in the power of the father – nor is it in the power of the mother – to revoke such decision against the will of the other party. Such an exercise of their power may be made after marriage when the occasion arises; but an agreement made before marriage dealing with matters which will arise during the marriage and put into force after the marriage is equally effective and of as binding force in law.[42]

Somewhat timorously, Murnaghan addressed the way in which counsel for Mary had relied primarily on Article 42, while seeking to bolster their arguments by reference to Articles 41, 44 and the preamble to the constitution:

> If the Court is able to arrive at a decision of the case upon the construction of Article 42, and Article 42.5 alone and without reference to Articles 41 and 44, nothing is to be gained by discussing these last-mentioned articles in the present case. It is right, however, to say that the Court, in arriving at its decision, is not now holding that these last-mentioned articles confer any privileged position before the law upon members of the Roman Catholic Church.[43]

Even though it was manifest at this juncture what the outcome of the Supreme Court hearing would be, Murnaghan chose to criticise Ernest's behaviour with considerable severity. He suggested that Tilson appeared to be 'if not intemperate, fond of drinking' and seemed 'to have not accepted his obligations as a husband to provide for his family'. Murnaghan noted that in December 1949 Ernest had been summoned by the District Court, only for the summons to be dismissed on the undertaking that he would pay £4 per week towards the support of his family. The judge then speculated that this might have been 'an ingenious way of relieving himself from the payment which he had been obliged to agree to'.[44] Murnaghan accused Ernest of creating 'a very unfavourable impression' when he took the children from the family home and placed them in the Birds' Nest under the artifice that their mother had deserted them. Regarding Mary's employment by the Swastika Laundry, for which she earned £3 per week, the judge stated that 'without this money I fear the family would have to do without much which they have up to the present been enjoying'.[45] His extraneous comments aside, Murnaghan concluded the delivery of his judgment as follows:

> In my opinion the appeal can be, and ought to be, decided on the point of law that in the circumstances Tilson had no justification on the ground of religious upbringing or any other ground for taking the children from the family home. In my opinion they ought to be returned to the mother to be educated by her, if not by the parents jointly, in the manner in which they had been taught pursuant to the ante-nuptial agreement.[46]

Black dissented from this judgment, however, and focused in his observations to the court on the prenuptial agreement and whether common law – in this case paternal supremacy – had been altered by the 1937 constitution. Black stated that the point of law was 'whether the prenuptial undertaking of the father of these infants to have them brought up as Catholics is enforceable in law',[47] noting Charles Casey's contention that the agreement was not enforceable, and Gavan Duffy's statement that 'the law was well settled against treating the ante-nuptial agreement as an enforceable contract'.[48] Where Casey and Gavan Duffy had made reference to 'countless decisions' to support their positions, Black noted that Murnaghan had asked whether the Supreme Court 'was bound by these decisions, seeing that they were not decisions of a final Court of appeal'.[49]

Black described the common law rule as 'an archaic law and a relic of barbarism', pronouncing 'a law which would deprive this mother of her children as an abomination'.[50] The judge was clearly no admirer of the principle of paternal supremacy, but the problem for him was how both courts had arrived at their decisions to rescind it. It was, to use his own terminology, 'a question ... of pure law'. He recalled how in the Meade case of 1870 the 'great judge and eminent Catholic' Lord O'Hagan had declared that '"The authority of the father to guide and govern the education of his child is a very sacred thing, bestowed by the Almighty."'[51] But if 'this dictatorship of the father' was a '"very sacred thing bestowed by the almighty"' then how could 'our constitution, with its intense religious invocations ... have interfered with a trust so bestowed or imposed?'[52]

But for Black, the crux of the matter lay in whether or not the constitution had altered common law. He pointed out that paternal supremacy had 'perished in England with the Guardianship of Infants Act, 1925, and our present problem is whether it has disappeared in Ireland by virtue of article 42'. The change in the law regarding paternal supremacy resulting from this act appears to have been lost on Murnaghan, who had argued in his judgment that 'the archaic law of England ... need not be a guide to the fundamental principles of a modern state'.[53] Black suggested that the constitution required alteration to indicate clearly that paternal supremacy had now ended, arguing:

> If the constitution alters the common law in the way mentioned, it must be by specific articles, and the articles which are said to have this effect have been specified as number 41 [the family], 42 [education] and 44 [religion] together with the Preamble, on all of which the President [Gavan Duffy] seems to have based his judgment. For myself, I see nothing in the Preamble or in Articles 41 or 44 that

lends the slightest countenance to the inference to which the learned President seemed to think they contributed support.[54]

Black then focused on Article 42.1 – on which Murnaghan had based his judgment – whereupon his argument grew more convincing:

> Now, if I confine myself to the words of this article and clause alone, it does not appear to me necessarily to confer any *new* right or duty upon parents at all, and so far as reported cases show, since the year 1937 I see no evidence that such an idea of the possible effect of this Article ever occurred to any judge or lawyer until the learned President promulgated it a few years ago ... I suggest the average sensible man-in-the-street would have been [of the view] that nearly forty years before our constitution of 1937, the rights and duties of parents now specified in article 42.1 existed already ... on the whole then, it would seem to me at least improbable that article 42.1 was intended to invest the mother with any different right in regard to her children's religion than she had previously, namely, a right subordinate in the last resort to the father's overriding dictatorship as recognised by the common law.[55]

Black trenchantly expressed his view that Article 42.1 did not abrogate the common law rule of paternal supremacy, drawing on the Frost case to further support his argument. He contended that in that case, there was a 'clear recognition that the common law rule is still a rule [paternal supremacy] ... and that when the parents differed as to their children's religious education, that rule was to be applied'.[56] Ostensibly, Black was of the view that both parents had a right and a duty in regard to the religious upbringing of their children, but he was careful to state that, in the event of a dispute, 'the decisive right still rested with the father'. This had been the case before the 1937 constitution, a document that contained nothing to alter the situation. Black abhorred the notion of paternal supremacy but could find nothing in the constitution that revoked it, and summed up his observations in relation to paternal supremacy by stating: 'I do not believe that the framers of the constitution ever intended [Article 42.1] to affect the common law rights of either father or mother.'[57] Black's views are supported by J.M. Kelly, who has persuasively argued that Article 42.1 was a narrow basis for the Supreme Court ruling:

> ... the very fact that the constitution did not expressly provide for such a radical change in the law was a fair indication that such a change was

not intended; and there is much to be said for Mr. Justice Black's belief that no such idea of the possible effect of the Article had ever occurred to any judge or lawyer before.[58]

Black then returned to his concern that the 1937 constitution might discriminate among people of different religions; a matter about which he had questioned Liston during the court hearing and an important subject which historians and other commentators have curiously tended to avoid. Black presented a hypothetical situation in which a Catholic man married a Protestant woman in a Protestant church, after which they both entered into an agreement to raise their children as Protestants. If the man later reneged on the agreement and took away his children to raise them as Catholics, under the current interpretation of Article 42.1 (after the Tilson court judgments) the agreement would be enforceable, and his Protestant wife would be entitled 'to get the children back on *habeas corpus*' to continue with their Protestant upbringing. Although this outcome would demonstrate that the constitution was non-discriminatory, Black was not convinced that Gavan Duffy's judgment in the High Court provided the same reassurance. He said that, whereas previously he had been satisfied that the constitution was non-discriminatory, on reading Gavan Duffy's judgment and its references to the canon law and the preamble, his 'first impression had been considerably weakened'.

Black was determined to pursue the matter and, turning to Murnaghan, quoted directly from his judgment:

> If the Court is able to arrive at a decision of the case upon the construction of article 42,1 and article 42,5 [education] alone and without reference to article 41 [the family] and article 44 [religion], nothing is to be gained by discussing these last-mentioned articles in the present case. It is right, however, to say that the Court, in arriving at its decision, is not now holding that these last-mentioned articles confer any privileged position before the law upon members of the Roman Catholic Church, and during the argument counsel for the respondent expressly disclaimed any such privileged position.[59]

Black felt that Murnaghan's statement did not sufficiently address the issue of one religion gaining privilege over another in the constitution. And since his colleague had not adequately dealt with the matter, Black took it upon himself to do so, and thereby did the state some service: 'I think it would be in the national interest, and in that of our jurisprudence, that we should here and now unequivocally declare that our constitution does not confer any such privileged position before the law upon members of any religious denomination whatsoever.'[60]

Black concluded his submission to the court by turning to Ernest who, he said, 'had coals of fire heaped upon his head'. Ernest had given the court incorrect details in regard to the birth dates of his children and his marriage, and had also made an inaccurate statement on the admission form to the Birds' Nest, wherein he accused his wife of deserting their children – although Black reasoned that he had given Leonard a possible explanation of that 'consistent with Tilson's belief at that time'. Black regarded these as 'petty reproaches', which should not be regarded as evidence to support the notion that he was insincere about bringing up his children as Protestants 'in the hope that [such an upbringing] would make them better than it had made him'. Although Black said that he 'did not think much of the man' and excoriated him for 'his vicious refusal not to tell his wife where he had taken the children', he added that he believed in 'giving even the devil his due'. Black addressed the view, held by some, that Ernest may have placed his children in the Birds' Nest simply to avoid paying the £4 a week maintenance amount agreed with the District Court, suggesting that was 'a reasonable suspicion to entertain' but added that if he [Black] was a juror, he 'would not be able to find it as a fact'. He defended the orphanage from the allegation that its managers could have made more inquiries before taking the three boys into its care, arguing that 'if a father brings his children to them, alleging that they are destitute, I should not think it upon them to turn the children away until they are able to make inquiries, with possible cruel consequences for the children ... I think the humane course is to take the children in on the father's word'.[61]

Seven years later, the Supreme Court decision in the Tilson case was reaffirmed in the High Court on another decision arising from a mixed marriage. In delivering his judgment in the May case, the president of the High Court, Mr Justice Cahir Davitt, referred to Murnaghan's earlier interpretation of Article 42.1 and decided that there was a 'joint power and duty' regarding the education of children established by the Tilson case. On that basis, he ruled that the father did not have the sole right to decide on the religious upbringing of his children.[62] The Tilson judgment brought down the curtain on paternal supremacy in Ireland, and the ruling was fully endorsed in the May case in 1957.

For his part, Archbishop McQuaid appears to have been in a celebratory mood after hearing the verdict of the Supreme Court. In his letter of 4 September to Cardinal Marchetti-Selvaggiani he claimed:

> I beg to report upon a recent and happy change in the marriage laws in the Republic of Ireland in regard to pre-nuptial guarantees in mixed marriages ... On appeal by the Protestant orphanage and Protestant father, the Supreme Court, by four votes to one, upheld the judgment of the President of the High Court. Henceforth, the law of the Republic of Ireland regards the pre-nuptial guarantees as a contract binding in civil law.[63]

McQuaid's claims were, perhaps, an inaccurate representation of the Supreme Court judgment. The decision of the judges did not change the 'marriage laws in the Republic of Ireland'; as we have seen, the Supreme Court interpreted Article 42.1 of the constitution to mean that the *parents* had 'a joint power and duty in respect of the religious education of their children'. Having come to that conclusion, it was 'a short and inevitable step' for the court to hold that the prenuptial agreement, into which Mary and Ernest Tilson entered, was binding.[64]

The archbishop might also have explained to the cardinal that the Supreme Court's ruling might, at some future date, benefit the Protestant party in a similar dispute. In other words, as the paternal supremacy rule was now defunct, a *Catholic* father in a mixed marriage would no longer have the sole prerogative when it came to determining the religious upbringing of his children. Given McQuaid's comments contained in the same letter, as outlined after Gavan Duffy delivered his judgment in the High Court, and given the fact that McQuaid had previously accepted a 'commission' from Rome to have 'British law ... effectively changed in favour of the prescriptions of the Church', did he now feel compelled to exalt or embellish the significance of the judgment when reporting to his superiors?

On hearing the outcome of the Supreme Court hearing, Mary Tilson's sister Lily went shopping and bought new clothes for the three boys while neighbours at Turner's Cottages planned a bonfire on the street to celebrate the children's homecoming. In Oldcastle those Catholics who used to gather and say rosaries for a successful outcome to the case were jubilant in the knowledge that their prayers had been answered.[65] In the Birds' Nest the three boys were taken to the top floor of the building, where a staff member opened the double doors of a large mahogany wardrobe to release an avalanche of second-hand boots. Later that afternoon the children were handed over to their mother, who was accompanied by her solicitor, George McGrath. For its part, Mrs Smyly's Homes issued a short acquittance confirming the boys removal that belied the emotion of the occasion:

Mrs. Smyly's Homes and Schools
(In connexion with the Irish Church Missions)

5th August 1950

David Richard Tilson, Alan John Tilson, and Paul Tilson have been removed from the care of Mrs. Smyly's Homes this day by the undersigned:

Signed: Mary J. Tilson _____Mother
          George McGrath _____Solicitor[66]

Alan Tilson's abiding memory of leaving the Birds' Nest is of walking out through the front door with his brothers, facing an intimidating barrage of press photographers, and realising, to his dismay, that one of the boots he had selected from the wardrobe had no tongue. He hoped that nobody would notice.

PART 3

The Aftermath

CHAPTER 10

Reaction to the Court Judgments

In his letter to Cardinal Marchetti-Selvaggiani in the immediate aftermath of the Supreme Court judgment, Archbishop McQuaid claimed victory but warned that there was still considerable work to be done. He also displayed nationalist and separatist tendencies when he expressed his fear for 'our Faith' if ever the six counties were 'federated with the Republic'. His lifelong antipathy towards and distrust of Trinity College Dublin was also manifest:

> My Lord Cardinal,
>
> ... It would be difficult to explain the magnitude of the triumph of the Supreme Court decision, in the face of English and Protestant jurisprudence in which all our lawyers and all our judges have been trained. The decision reverses the jurisprudence that has ruled this country since about 1540.
>
> It cannot be said that the victory is complete. Nor can the victory be complete, in my humble opinion, until a jurisprudence based on Catholic teaching has been instituted in the law schools of the National Universities.
>
> I fear that such a teaching can never be properly established until the National University has become not merely, as it is now, a university for Catholics, but a Catholic University: a fact which I have emphasised publicly in every Lenten Regulation issued by me since I became Archbishop.
>
> And even if the National University were to become Catholic, there will still remain the law school of Trinity College: the non-Catholic University which is, in this city and in this Republic, the focus of everything that is anti-Catholic.
>
> The danger to our Faith and to our institutions arising from Trinity College at the present moment will become intense, if ever the six counties be federated with the Republic of Ireland, for then the Catholics will have ceased to be the 94% of the population to become

only 64%, and a new strong Catholic minority [*sic*] will take its place in Parliament.

Your Eminence's humble and devoted servant in Christ,

John C. McQuaid,
Archbishop of Dublin[1]

While most people at the time viewed the result in the Supreme Court as a victory for Mary Tilson over her Protestant husband, and, by extension, the Catholic Church over the Protestant one, the archbishop also saw it in secular terms. His declaration that 'the decision reverses the jurisprudence that has ruled this country since about 1540' shows that the judgments, for him, also represented the moment when the Republic of Ireland ushered in its own jurisprudence – unsullied by British influences. Of course, given McQuaid's strong nationalist tendencies, his deep scepticism of English law and the sentiments he expressed in the High Court, that epoch would also please George Gavan Duffy.

It is also clear from McQuaid's letter, and from Marchetti-Selvaggiani's response, that a scheme had been orchestrated between Dublin and Rome to establish a jurisprudence based on Catholic teaching, but that the law school at Trinity College might prove to be a stumbling block in achieving those aims. To the cardinal, education meant *Catholic* education; and the plan by which the law of the land would reflect the law of the church was a genuine work in progress. It is also clear that McQuaid wanted him to continue with his work to 'have the British law ... changed in favour of the prescriptions of the Catholic Church':

16 December 1950

Most Excellent and Most Reverend Lord,
... As, however, your most Reverend Excellency, with the aforementioned letter, writes that the Church did not get a full victory, it is necessary that You, who so far has managed in the best way, will care in the future by working and watching, so that the firm principles of the Church on the Catholic education are respected, so that the laws of this Republic adhere to the ecclesiastical laws to the best extent.

I confirm my most devoted deference to You.

F. Card. Marchetti-Selvaggiani
Secret.[2]

Reaction to the Court Judgments 165

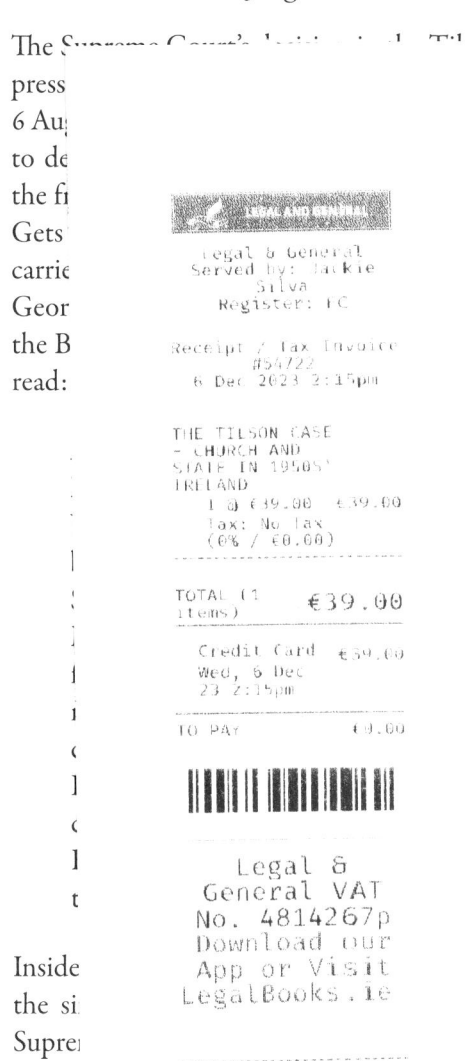

The S———— C————'s ————— ———— Til——n case was covered widely in the press ———————————————————— was delivered on a Saturday, the 6 Au———————————————————— *Sunday Independent* were able to de———————————————————— which featured prominently on the fi———————————————————— he respective headlines 'Mother Gets ———————————————————— :k Three Children'. Inside, both carrie———————————————————— sons, together with her solicitor Geor———————————————————— nerged through the front gate of the B———————————————————— page report of the *Sunday Press* read:

———————————————————— her sons, David, Alan and Paul, ———————————————————— yly's Home ('The Birds' Nest'), ———————————————————— k yesterday to take the children ———————————————————— rith an undertaking given in the ———————————————————— h Mrs. Tilson was her solicitor, ———————————————————— ained in the Home for about ———————————————————— on if she had any comment to ———————————————————— *bviously overcome with joy*. The ———————————————————— me at Turner's Cottages, Ball's ———————————————————— es arranged a big reception. The ———————————————————— their education at Haddington ———————————————————— ner vacation, under the care of

Inside ———————————————————— overage of the hearing under the si———————————————————— e-Marriage Pact Is Upheld By Supre———————————————————— hildren'. On Monday, the story receiv—— ————— ———————— on the inside pages of the main dailies, under the headlines 'Mother Wins Custody of Children' (*Irish Independent*), 'Tilson Children Appeal Dismissed' (*Irish Press*) and 'Father's Appeal Dismissed in Dublin' (*Cork Examiner*). *The Irish Times* had carried the outcome of the High Court case on its front page but relegated the story of the Supreme Court hearing to page seven, under the headline 'Appeal Dismissed in Tilson Children Case'. Its editorial summarised the facts of the 'sordid' case and concluded, as Terence Brown has observed, 'with admirable, if slightly disassociated, aplomb',[4] that 'it is difficult to avoid the impression that the philosophy underlying Irish jurisprudence is tending slowly but surely to be informed by the principles of the Roman Catholic Church. *A priori* there can be no great objection to that so long as the issue is faced squarely by everybody concerned.'[5]

Apart from minor variations in the tone of some of the headlines, the national newspaper reports of the Supreme Court hearing were relatively even-handed, including *The Irish Times*. All the reports began by offering an outline of the circumstances of the Tilson marriage, before focusing on the main points of contention that emerged during the hearing: Mr Justice Murnaghan's description of paternal supremacy as 'an archaic law of England', the relevance of the Frost case, Article 42.1 of the constitution and the question of whether 'parents' in that article referred only to the father. All the national newspapers also gave comprehensive coverage of Mr Justice Black's dissenting judgment.

The story was covered in a more partial fashion in local newspapers such as the Cork *Evening Echo*, the Dublin *Evening Herald* and the Carlow *Nationalist and Leinster Times*. A report in the *Nenagh Guardian* on 12 August speculated that the Supreme Court decision might lead to a reduction in the number of mixed marriages in Ireland:

> The legal decision may reduce the number of 'mixed' marriages in the land. The Church does not want these marriages, but always has made provision for them because of the particularly human problems involved in the relations between two people wishing to spend their lives together. All Churches may now feel bound to tell their adherents of the special requirements demanded prior to such union, and there may be an avoidance of a large sum of unhappiness.[6]

In a report on 19 August which significantly referred to a 'Catholic ruling', the *Meath Chronicle* – the newspaper of Ernest Tilson's home county – was condescending and showed little sympathy for the Protestant party in a mixed marriage:

> The question, stripped of the legal jargon by which it was confused by counsel on both sides, was whether a man, having given a solemn promise in order to attain a desired end, was legally justified, having attained the end he desired, in breaking the promise. From a Protestant point of view the Catholic ruling may seem hard, but he has his remedy – he is not compelled to marry the Catholic … the Catholic partner to a mixed marriage appreciates the condition; the Protestant party must, if reasonably intelligent, also appreciate it.[7]

Reaction to the Court Judgments

The Supreme Court ruling also received widespread coverage north of the border: perhaps surprisingly, the coverage here was generally impartial, although Black's dissenting judgment was a focal point of several reports. Some variations in tone can be discerned in headlines such as the *Belfast Telegraph*'s 'Tilson Boys to be Brought up as Roman Catholics: Eire[sic] Supreme Court dismisses father's appeal by 4-1 majority', the *Derry Journal*'s 'Children: Supreme Court says pre-marriage agreements binding' and the *Belfast News Letter*'s 'REJECTED: Mother secures custody of children'.[8] The *Londonderry Sentinel* summed up the judgment with the observation that 'The decision is of far-reaching importance in Eire [sic] as it now makes it a matter of law that ante-nuptial agreements concerning the religious education of children of mixed marriages are of a binding nature and must be upheld.'[9] The outcome was also covered in Northern regional newspapers such as the *Strabane Chronicle*, the *Fermanagh Herald* and the *Ulster Herald*.

British newspapers, including *The Times*, the *Manchester Guardian*, the *Daily Mail* and the *News Chronicle* covered the case. The *Sunday Dispatch* offered a reductionist account when it reported: 'because a £5 17s. 6d. Dublin Corporation Clerk … gave a written undertaking before he was married that his children would be reared as Roman Catholics, he lost custody of three of his sons yesterday at Dublin'.[10] Under the headline 'Mother Fights for Her Boys' Religion – Wins', the *Sunday Express* reported that 'neighbours lit a celebration bonfire last night outside Mrs. Mary Josephine Tilson's home in Ballsbridge, Dublin'.[11] Local newspapers, including the *Gloucestershire Echo*, the *Lincolnshire Echo*, the *Bradford Observer*, the *Hull Daily Mail* and the *Leicester Evening Mail*, also covered the story. *The Times* undoubtedly betrayed its own confessional and political partiality when it described Mary Tilson as a 'Roman Catholic' and reported that Ernest Tilson had placed his children in a Protestant home in 'Kingstown', even though the town's name had been changed to Dún Laoghaire in 1922. The article concluded by stating that 'Mr. Justice Black, dissenting, did not agree that the 1937 constitution overrode the Common Law in regard to the father's right.'[12] Coverage in the *Manchester Guardian* was similarly partial but more comprehensive, and described how 'a number of priests and clerics were in court when reserved judgment was given', before closing by summarising Mr Black's views: 'It seemed to [Black] at least improbable that the constitution was intended to invest the mother with any different right in regard to her children's religion than she had previously – namely a right subordinate in the last resort to the father's overriding dictatorship as recognised by common law.'[13]

The case was also covered in the United States. The *Cincinnati Catholic Telegraph Register* carried the story under the headline 'Irish Court Decision Recalls American Rulings on Offspring's Religious Training',[14] while the *Rochester Catholic Courier and Journal* ran the headline 'Irish Court Upholds Pre-Nuptial Pacts'.[15] In Wichita, Kansas, the *Catholic Advance* newspaper reported on the outcome of Ernest Tilson's Supreme Court appeal and offered a discrepant aspect to other coverage in that it noted two occasions on which American courts had upheld prenuptial agreements (this, of course, accords with the *Ramon* v. *Ramon* case): in the New York Supreme Court in 1935, Justice Meier Steinbrink ruled that a prenuptial agreement between a Jewish man and a Catholic woman, to raise his children as Catholics, was legally binding; meanwhile in Cleveland in 1949, Judge James C. Connell returned two young girls to their non-Catholic father on condition that they be raised in the Catholic faith, noting that the father had previously consented in writing to the Catholic education of his children.

Summarising the circumstances of the Tilson case, the *Catholic Advance* concluded: 'The decision of the [Irish] Supreme Court declared that an agreement that had been made by both parents concerning the education of their children could be revoked only by the consent of both parties.'[16] The report was supplied to the newspaper by the National Catholic Welfare Council (NCWC), a Catholic episcopal organisation founded in the United States in 1928 as an official voice of American bishops. Interestingly, the NCWC provided the Irish Catholic weekly *The Standard* with the same story, which was published after the Supreme Court decision on the newspaper's front page under the headline 'U.S. Courts Also Uphold Pre-Marriage Agreements'.[17] In the aftermath of the Tilson judgment, the NCWC was clearly intent on disseminating the notion that civil law had previously endorsed canon law. Further afield in Australia, the ruling was covered by the *Sydney Catholic Weekly*. Under the headline 'Ruling on Parent's Promise Upheld', the report's writer referred to Ernest Tilson as a member of the 'so-called Church of Ireland' and appeared to make a virtue of the fact that the assenting judges in the case were 'all Catholics'.[18]

If reportage in the Irish national press was even-handed and circumspect, coverage in the Protestant weekly *Church of Ireland Gazette* was notably more critical. Rev. W.L.M. Giff himself penned an erudite opinion piece for the newspaper, which was published on the front page on 11 August 1950. Ian d'Alton observes that Giff's article was an impressive piece of reasoning, intellectually demanding and rigorous, centring on the nature of Irish jurisprudence after 1937, and the discontinuity with the British common law tradition that preceded the enactment of the constitution. He quotes Burke and Locke in an erudite exposition, which must have passed over the heads of much of the readership. It is, in short, an academic sermon.[19]

Giff's column stated boldly that the Tilson 'decision, upheld by the Supreme Court, [was] the most important ruling since 1922'. Leaving aside his reliance on Burke, Locke and, indeed, Gibbon, Giff was most concerned with the possibility of an Irish government becoming unduly influenced by the Catholic Church or by the Catholic majority, a state of affairs that might lead to 'tyranny'. He also questioned whether there was 'equal liberty' for members of the Church of Ireland and 'Roman Catholics' under the 1937 constitution, and recalled that a 'leading counsel' in the court had contended that Mary Tilson would be deprived of her 'religious liberty' if she was expropriated of her right to raise her children as Catholics. Giff posed the question, 'what is to be said for the Church of Ireland husband who wishes to have his children instructed in *his* faith?'[20]

Giff argued that in 1949 Ireland 'contracted out of the Commonwealth ... but did not turn over and begin on a blank sheet [since the state had] acquired the great bulk of British jurisprudence'; that 'the warp and woof of her community life' gave people order and certainty in their daily lives, and that significant legislative change was required only 'when crisis renders it absolutely necessary'. Referring to much of the legal debate in the Tilson case, Giff did not accept that anything in the 1937 constitution abrogated the common law rule of paternal supremacy, nor was it required to do so by its authors.

He also addressed the promise that Ernest Tilson had signed up to before his marriage and, somewhat harshly, suggested that Tilson, through his 'foolish signature ... had surrendered his manhood, and had written off his unborn children to the spiritual care of a Church about which he knew next to nothing'. Giff then performed something of a volte-face by arguing that he had encountered people who were 'sincerely perplexed' before marrying under 'the provisions of *Ne Temere*', only later to discover that they had bound their children to certain Catholic beliefs and practices that were contrary to their own religion. He argued that a member of the Church of Ireland was entitled to a change of mind about the promise after making it, referring to a sermon on this matter preached by Rev. A.A. Luce four years earlier.

Giff concluded by referring to the 'evil consequences of these marriages' and addressed 'young readers' thus: 'Don't give the promise ... There are plenty of attractive girls in our Church, young man. Don't be fainthearted. You'll never know your luck. And, young woman, maybe that young man may be waiting for a little encouragement from you.' To 'middle-aged folk', meanwhile, he caustically observed that the 'Anglican tradition of liberty makes it difficult to acclimatise to the idea of a coalition between the priest and the policeman for the exclusive rights of members of one denomination' before reassuring them that if they 'inculcated' their children with 'a deep love of our Church', they would have 'no fear of the consequences of mixed marriages'.[21] The Supreme Court judgment had strengthened Giff's opposition to mixed marriages, and he displayed no desire to mend any fences between the Protestant and Catholic communities in the state.

A week later the *Church of Ireland Gazette* published another shorter commentary on the Tilson case in its 'Notes of the Week' column. The tone was sombre, and the writer was likewise pessimistic about the prospects for mixed marriages:

> It is always sad when people who have expressed for each other the affection and regard which should form the foundation of happy marriage find that they cannot live together and make a home for their children. It is sadder when they are professing Christians. This is the reason why people who cannot be one in the profession of their faith should not be married. If there is no unity at the centre, it will be hard to find it at the circumference. The recent Tilson case has added one more illustration to the folly of 'mixed' marriages.[22]

At this point Ireland's Catholic weekly newspapers *The Standard* and *The Irish Catholic*, and the ultramontane Maria Duce's monthly newspaper *Fiat*, entered the fray. A strangely woolly and ambiguous *Standard* editorial stated that 'the decision of the Supreme Court ... is of great importance to the people of this country' before recalling that in the High Court Gavan Duffy had rejected 'the contention that the undertaking signed by the husband was not binding'. The editorialist reminded readers of the Supreme Court's ruling, which stated that 'the parents had a joint power and duty in respect of the religious education of their children', then contended that 'we see no grounds' to support the assumption that the High Court and

Supreme Court 'will work in favour of the Catholic parents' and noted that the Supreme Court decision would in future decide 'a dispute between a member of the Presbyterian body and a Muslim in a mixed marriage'. Obfuscating the line between civil law and canon law, *The Standard* argued that *all* Christians in Ireland were subject to the 1937 constitution:

> It is a natural thing that Irish law should be different from English law. Law is not unchangeable although it rests on immutable principles, which are enshrined in the natural law and, for Christians, in the law of God. These principles are set out in our constitution which citizens of every denomination in this country accept and cherish.[23]

The writer also stressed that 'all our citizens should be clear that in future' prenuptial agreements would be upheld by the Irish courts, before warning against mixed marriages. The echoes of Giff's sentiments in these expressions suggest that objections of both churches to mixed marriages had been fortified in the wake of the court judgments:

> It [the court decision] should make both Protestants and Catholics, Catholics being principally affected here, hesitate to enter into mixed marriages. There is general agreement that these unions, while frequently successful, all too often end in disunion between the parents and grave harm to the spiritual life of the children ... We are well aware that many serious-minded Protestants equally object to mixed marriages, and we hope that one result of the Tilson case will be that such objections will be strengthened in the interests of parents and children alike.[24]

In *The Irish Catholic*, meanwhile, the Supreme Court ruling was covered in an even-handed front-page story headlined 'Pre-Marriage Pact an Enforceable Contract', accompanied by a photograph of Mary Tilson and her three sons leaving the Birds' Nest. The front page also featured a quotation from Mr Justice Murnaghan in bold outline: 'The archaic law of England, rapidly disintegrating under modern conditions, need not be a guide for the fundamental principles of a modern state. It is not a proper method of construing a new constitution of a modern state to make an approach in the light of legal survivals of an earlier law.'[25]

The tone of Murnaghan's comments anticipated the *Irish Catholic*'s page-two editorial on the case, which stated priggishly:

> Both parties to a mixed marriage now know that prenuptial agreements concerning the religious upbringing of their children are binding and legally enforceable in this country ... henceforth, there can be no repetition of the spectacle that has been more than once witnessed of the children of a mixed marriage being brought up as non-Catholics against their mother's wishes.[26]

Like *The Standard*, *The Irish Catholic* suggested that the significance of the Supreme Court's decision lay in its divergence from English law, and, in turn, the newspaper similarly muddled the distinction between civil law and canon law. The writer then outlined, with precision and condescension, what he saw as the differences between English and Irish law:

> The former was founded on religious indifferentism; our constitution is deliberately founded on Christian principles. The spirit and language of our constitution, recognising as it does the supremacy of the moral law founded on Christian principles, is altogether alien to the jurisprudence which dominates English law.[27]

The Irish Catholic's editorial ended on a similar note to those published in *The Standard* and the *Church of Ireland Gazette*: 'The Catholic Church has always disliked mixed marriages. So too have conscientious Protestants; but henceforth the latter will have an even greater fear of them than before.'[28] After the Supreme Court's decision, neither Catholic nor Protestant newspapers were minded to promote any form of integration between their respective communities.

Fiat's editorial – in all probability written by Rev. Edward Cahill – was very different. Its main argument was absurd, but the article provided an astute and detailed analysis of both the High Court and Supreme Court decisions. Maria Duce's *raison d'être* was its campaign to amend Article 44 of the 1937 constitution; the organisation felt that the 'special position' specified did not go far enough and favoured revision to recognise the Catholic Church as the 'One True Church'. A 1949 article in *Fiat* outlined the organisation's trenchant views:

> There is a vast difference between recognising the Catholic Church as the Church to which the great majority of Irishmen belong and recognising the Catholic Church as the One True Church. Our constitution fails completely in the all-important question of the relation of Ireland and the One True Church. It is deplorable that the

> Irish State places all religions on the same level. As far as the State is concerned the only difference between the One True Church and the 'other Churches' is a mathematical one – the number of Catholics is greater, no more. What a manifestation of National Apostasy![29]

Accordingly, following the Tilson case, *Fiat* was principally concerned to establish that the High Court and Supreme Court judgments confirmed that the 1937 constitution was non-discriminatory. The outcome of the case demonstrated the need to amend Article 44 so that in future the constitution would favour Catholics over people of other religions.

The writer conceded that the court judgments were met with 'general approval' because they accorded with 'the normal person's instinct for justice and fair dealing' before adding that 'behind the immediate outcome of the Tilson Case there lurked issues of even greater moment'. Mr Justice Gavan Duffy had recognised a legal principle in Article 42.1 (the *family* as educator) 'to justify a departure from Common Law ... which grants to the father despotic rights where the children, their education, etc. are concerned' but had then 'appealed to the Preamble, Article 41 and Article 44 as proving that the jurisprudence of Éire under the 1937 constitution was *different*'.[30] The writer admitted that the judge 'deserved credit' for recognising that 'the religious issue was vital', but suggested that he had erred in relying on the preamble of the constitution and Article 44 because these two articles 'concede in reality equal recognition to all religions, unmindful of the fact that there is only One True Religion'.

The *Fiat* writer next noted that the Supreme Court had relied on Article 42.1 without making any reference to the preamble or Article 44. By relying on Article 42.1 alone, the writer argued that the 'decision was given in Mrs. Tilson's favour *not* as a Catholic, but as a parent, enjoying ... equal rights with her husband regarding the education of her children'. The writer was adamant that the 1937 constitution was non-discriminatory:

> Catholics generally have misunderstood the implications of the *Tilson Case* decision. The decision is not discriminatory. The formal recognition by the Supreme Court of the binding nature of the prenuptial contract is excellent as far as it goes. But it does not go far enough. It does not confer any privilege on the Catholic party as distinct from the non-Catholic. *De facto* in this case the mother in whose favour the principle is operative is a Catholic. But that is purely *per accidens*. It is operative in her favour *as a parent, the equal partner to a contract, not as a Catholic.*[31]

After the Supreme Court decision, *The Irish Times* opened up its 'Letters to the Editor' page to a full-scale debate on the issue. Between late July and mid-September more than sixty letters were published under the heading 'Ne Temere', even though the decree was unrelated to the High Court or Supreme Court judgments; this clearly encouraged readers who may not have had opinions on the Tilson case to write and comment on the contentious decree. Many letters were from Protestants living in the southern state and convey a sense of increased vulnerability after the court judgment. J.W.P. from County Cork wrote, 'as a member of the Church of Ireland, living in the Republic of Ireland, I am left with a feeling of uncertainty for the future as a result of the Tilson case ... what about her husband? Is he not also entitled to equal treatment? Or does the constitution discriminate against the minority?'[32] Another Protestant correspondent, a W.M.A. Jones from the Royal School, Raphoe, County Donegal, was concerned by the decline in Protestant numbers in the Republic and by the fact that some Protestants in Ireland had difficulty in meeting a partner from within their own church:

> ... the publication of the serious fall in the number of Protestants in Eire [*sic*], coupled with the implications of the Tilson case, must have prompted more than one of your readers to wonder about the extent to which one is the cause of the other ... I learned [from a leading cleric] it was not unusual for a Protestant man, say, in a country district of Kerry, to know no one of his faith in the district with whom a marriage could be contracted. Similarly, in another district, a Protestant woman may be in the same position. Yet, neither may know of the other's existence ... There should be, among your enlightened readers, someone able and willing to make it possible for Protestants who are in areas predominantly Roman Catholic to know of each other's existence and to be able to get in touch, with a view to a possible marriage.[33]

Other correspondents used pseudonyms such as 'Irish Protestant', 'Southern Protestant', 'Proddy', 'Non-Protestant', 'Catholic', 'Irish Catholic' or 'Minority'. Although the letters published dealt with a range of related issues, the predominant theme was the promise that Ernest Tilson was obliged to sign before his marriage. This thorny issue was raised by a 'Southern Protestant':

> It [the promise] is exhorted under pressure, under the veiled threat of ostracism, social as well as spiritual, for those who resist it. The pressure is exerted at a moment when we are least capable of resistance, when our affections and loyalties are deeply pledged to another man or woman.[34]

Another letter-writer, R.B. Faulkner, drew attention to remarks supposedly made by Fianna Fáil leader Éamon de Valera at the previous week's parliamentary conference when he said that 'the signature of a man who signs his rights away with a pistol at his head has never been regarded as being morally binding on him'. The writer continued, 'but why did Mr. de Valera remain silent when the findings in the Tilson case were published ... ?'[35]

Addressing the promises sought and firmly correlating them with *Ne Temere*, a Protestant cleric, W.W.L. Rooke, wrote:

> In your leading article of yesterday you state that in all cases of mixed marriages between Roman Catholics and Protestants 'the children profess the faith of the majority'. This is untrue. In many parishes there are cases of mixed marriages where the children profess the faith of the Protestant parent. There are Roman Catholics who recognise that the *Ne Temere* decree is immoral, just as there are Protestants who have refused to be duressed into signing the 'printed form' of that decree.[36]

Letters from Catholics, on the other hand, were generally more dismissive of Protestant concerns regarding the promise. Maureen C. Ahern from Limerick wrote that 'a Protestant is absolutely and utterly free to make this promise or not to make it. Once he has made it he is honour bound to keep it.'[37]

One Catholic writer, Patrick MacCathmhaoil from Dublin, had concerns about Ernest Tilson breaking his promise:

> All my life I have had daily intercourse with Protestants, and I have formed a very high opinion of their honesty and truthfulness – therefore, it can be safely assumed that they condemn the flagrant breach of this agreement by Mr. Tilson, in which he agreed to allow his children to be brought up as Catholics. Catholics will bear me out.[38]

Along similar lines, another Catholic correspondent, 'Scrutator', addressed the commitment and the notion that it might be made under duress:

When a Roman Catholic girl says to her lover: 'I won't marry you unless you sign the *Ne Temere* undertaking' she is making a statement of the latter kind. She is quite entitled to say whom she will marry, and upon what terms she will marry him. Her suitor is free to accept her terms or to reject them. If he loves her dearly, he will be sorely tempted to accept them, but temptation is one thing, duress another.[39]

Just as the Supreme Court case was concluding, an alert 'Non-Protestant' suggested in a letter to *The Irish Times* that 'an interesting question arises in connection with the Tilson case. Both sides have briefed an imposing array of distinguished counsel. Who is going to pay the costs?'[40]

It was a pertinent question since, *ipso facto*, there was no such thing as a free legal aid scheme in Ireland in the 1950s. Both protagonists were living in modest circumstances, with Ernest earning £5 a week working in Dublin Corporation and Mary earning £3 working in the Swastika Laundry. Within three days of Mary's discovery of her children in the Birds' Nest on 15 May, both parents had assembled formidable legal teams. But who was paying them? Both Alan Tilson and Paul Tilson's widow Judy have consistently maintained that the costs of the case were underwritten by the respective churches.[41]

On 28 July, after the conclusion of the High Court case, the *Irish Press* reported that Gavan Duffy had 'directed [Ernest Tilson] to pay the costs';[42] on 7 August, the day of the Supreme Court judgment, *The Irish Times* reported that the attorney general had said that 'he would not ask for any costs'.[43] Mary may have sought no costs in the Supreme Court, but the order for High Court costs – as reported in the *Irish Press* – presumably stood, in which case Ernest would have been obliged to pay those costs and those of his legal team. If Mary's counsel was seeking no costs at all, then Ernest would have been responsible for his own costs only.[44] One thing is certain: the potential financial liabilities of Ernest or Mary's cases were substantial and were underwritten by third parties at the outset – otherwise it would have been impossible for Mary to initiate High Court proceedings and equally impossible for Ernest to defend himself there or in the Supreme Court. The identity of Mary's benefactors remains unclear, but Ernest's financial liabilities, amounting to approximately £730, were paid by individual Protestants across Ireland.

Once again, Rev. W.L.M. Giff led the charge. Correspondence between a Portadown resident, J. Templeton, and Giff during the adjournment of the High Court hearing confirms that Giff launched a fundraising campaign to cover legal costs in or around early July 1950:

> Derrymattery,
> Portadown,
> 11th July, 1950

Dear Mr. Giff,

In reply to your Special Appeal I herewith enclose cheque to the value of £4 to help you in the costs of this needy case which I sincerely trust you will be successful in holding these three children under the guidance of God.

The £4 is made up as follows: Special Prayer Meeting in Derryall Church Hall on Monday 10th July 1950 of the offering £1, Personal Gift £1 from Mr. & Mrs. J. Templeton and £2 to be treated as anonymous.

I read most of your letter at our special prayer meeting and it is possible that there might be some more that will be lead [sic] to give and if it comes in to me I will gladly send it on.

May God's richest blessing be upon the work of the Irish Church Missions under your leadership.

I remain,
Yours sincerely,

J. Templeton[45]

Two days later, Giff's reply suggests that he was not confident of a successful outcome to the case 'under present conditions':

> 13th July 50

Dear Mr. Templeton,

How very generous of you and your friends. Will you please give them my very warm thanks. We are slowly gathering together quite a little sum for this case. Already we have some £50 in hands [sic], ear-marked for it.

Of course we cannot guarantee success under present conditions in Eire [sic]. But even if we lose we shall have upheld the principles involved, and publicity is of [sic] the very essence of toleration for which Protestantism stands.

With my renewed gratitude,
Yours very sincerely,

W.L.M. Giff[46]

After the Supreme Court hearing Giff launched a new fundraising campaign by writing a letter to the *Church of Ireland Gazette* in his capacity as superintendent of the Irish Church Missions:

> Sir, – Many readers of the *Gazette* are watching the daily papers for details of the appeal in the Supreme Court against the High Court decision in the Tilson case. It would be almost impossible to exaggerate the importance of these proceedings ... We wish to assure members of the Church of Ireland that [the Irish Church Missions] has no narrow sectarian axe to grind ... We feel sure that members of the Church of Ireland will not wish us to bear the full costs of very expensive proceedings. We shall be very grateful for gifts, large and small. They will be received in the most strict confidence. We have gone forward with the case, trusting in God, and with faith in the loyalty of the people of the Church which we love.
> – Yours etc.,
>
> W.L.M. Giff,
> Irish Church Missions[47]

This was followed a week later with an appeal in the *Gazette*, again on behalf of the Irish Church Missions, requesting subscriptions to help fund the case:

> The trial will probably be considered a test case for some years to come, but, as well as being a test case, it has been a costly case, and those of our readers who feel that the Irish Church Missions have accepted a burden which could not be refused may feel constrained to send in subscriptions. We have already felt constrained.[48]

Giff's efforts did not fall on deaf ears and many cheques accordingly arrived in the post over the course of the following months. One woman wrote:

> 11 Moyne Road,
> Rathmines
> 9.10.50
>
> Dear Mr Giff,
> I wish to contribute a small sum of 10/- towards the Tilson fund.
> Enclosed also is a donation of 10/- from a friend who is interested in the Tilson case.
> Yours faithfully,
> F. Scott[49]

Giff was evidently acquainted with this donor and was gracious in his reply:

> Dear Miss Scott,
> I shall not see you this evening, so I wish to thank you very sincerely for your kindness. It is extremely good of you to give so much. When one compares your salary with the income of other donors of very considerable income, your gift is princely, and it touches me deeply. Will you please convey my grateful thanks to your friend, for whom I also enclose a receipt.
> Yours in fellowship of the service,
> W.L.M. Giff[30]

Writing from a leafy middle-class area of Belfast, a collection agent for the Irish Church Missions suggests that the total amount raised surpassed the amount of money needed to cover the legal costs:

> 20 Osborne Park,
> Belfast.
> 1 February 1951
>
> Dear Mr Giff,
> I have enclosed a note with £50 cheque from Mr. McKeown & lodged same & sent receipts to him and Miss McKeown ... I enclose amounts I have up to date not including the £20. I estimate amount to be sent in as over £800 this year to 1st April ... I hope you will escape 'the flue' [*sic*] which so many have.
> Yours sincerely,
> Chas. D. Macoun
> Thanks for the 2 'Banners' received yesterday.[51]

Giff's response confirms this, and also indicates a plan to send Ernest to Canada. Giff's out-of-character reference here to him as 'Tilson', however, rather than the more formal 'Mr Tilson' suggests he may have been losing patience with him, now that the case had been lost:

> 5th February 51.
>
> Dear Mr. Macoun,
> Thank you very much for your letter and enclosure. It is very encouraging to find that you are getting in the money so well ...
> As I make myself personally responsible for the Tilson case and for getting the money in to meet the cost, I am sure you will not mind

me writing personally to Mr. McKeown and thanking him for the £20. Actually, the case cost us £730, and now we have to send Tilson to Canada which will mean that we have little left out of the £850 ...

Yours sincerely,

W.L.M. Giff[32]

It is revealing how in his letter to McKeown, Giff argued that 'the principle of liberty' was a key driver on the Protestant side in the courtroom battle. Liberty has long been vital to Protestant identity, with Protestants seeing themselves as free and independent individuals, while at the same time viewing Catholics as being repressed under an overbearing church; Claire Mitchell observes that liberty is 'based on Protestant ideas of freedom and thought versus the perceived authoritarianism of the Catholic Church'.[33] Giff's argument, in his letter to McKeown, is clearly rooted in the notion that Ernest Tilson's liberty was being violated by the Catholic Church when it demanded that he promise to raise his children as Catholics:

T.J.P. McKeown
100 Clifton Park Avenue,
Belfast.

5th February 1951

Dear Mr. McKeown,

... I write to thank you personally for your special gift towards expenses of the Tilson case. Also, I would be very grateful if you would give my personal thanks to your friend who has contributed the other £10.

It was a sorry business, but we have no regrets whatever for having taken on the case. We stood for a principle which we believe to be absolutely essential, and which we also believe to be at the very root of the Reformation faith – the principle of liberty. Even though we cannot be said to have won, our stand is there on record, as the position of Protestantism in Eire [*sic*]. The case has cost us a lot of money, but God is still sending us in special gifts for it, and I believe that we will cover it all from the gifts without having to call on ordinary Mission funds.

With renewed thanks and all good wishes,

Yours sincerely,

W.L.M. Giff[34]

It is hardly surprising that the Tilson case fed into the febrile and sectarian debates over partition taking place in the late 1940s and early '50s. The Government of Ireland Act of 1920 had formally separated six of the nine counties of historic Ulster from the rest of Ireland;[55] introduced to avoid a possible civil war, partition accommodated unionists who were adamant that they wanted to remain part of the United Kingdom, as well as Irish nationalists who finally achieved a form of self-government in the southern state. Irish nationalists saw partition as a temporary arrangement and held deferred aspirations for an independent and sovereign reunited Ireland, encompassing all thirty-two counties. Unionists could not countenance being part of a united Ireland because they regarded their relationship with Britain as permanent. They were also determined never to live under an Irish nationalist government – particularly one that might be influenced by the Catholic Church. Unionist and loyalist rhetoric accordingly made much of the apparent influence of the church on the development of the Free State and subsequent Republic.

By 1948 Éamon de Valera's Fianna Fáil had been in power for sixteen consecutive years, but was replaced after that year's election by John A. Costello's interparty government. Partition had preoccupied de Valera for much of his time as taoiseach,[56] but it also became a fixation of the new government – particularly of the leader of Clann na Poblachta, Seán MacBride, whose desire to end partition had formed a major part of the party's election platform. In fact, Alvin Jackson has observed that 'the Costello government was associated with the most determined effort to address the issue of partition since the early 1920s'.[57] Those anti-partitionists watching were not to be disappointed, because, in power, MacBride 'duly banged the anti-partition drum'.[58] In 1949 Ireland was invited to join the North Atlantic Treaty Organisation (NATO) and MacBride, as minister for external affairs, boldly elevated the partition question centre stage at a European level by seeking 'to trade off Irish membership for a *démarche* on partition'. Dermot Keogh noted that MacBride's daring efforts might be attributed to 'the competitiveness between MacBride's Clann na Poblachta and de Valera's remobilising Fianna Fáil over partition'.[59]

If 'the evils of partition' were dominating political discourse in the southern state at this time, the issue was also of pressing concern north of the border.[60] After the British Labour Party's Westminster victory in 1945, and supporting that party's 'frayed tradition of supporting a united Ireland', a group of ten Nationalist MPs elected to the Northern Ireland Parliament at Stormont formed the Anti-Partition League (APL), which vowed to 'energise and unify nationalism within Northern Ireland and press London to reopen the partition question'.[61] The APL organised anti-partition marches and rallies in Dublin in 1948, challenging de Valera to push the British government on the question. In turn, a rally organised by the group in Derry on St Patrick's Day 1951 provocatively displayed the tricolour flag of the southern state.

Anti-partition efforts north and south of the border were set back after Taoiseach John A. Costello's solo run in Ottawa in 1948, when he announced the interparty government's intention to leave the Commonwealth and declare Ireland a republic. Westminster responded with the Ireland Act of 1949, which affirmed that 'in no event will Northern Ireland or any part thereof cease to be part … of the United Kingdom without the consent of the Parliament of Northern Ireland'.[62] An Irish government so determined to end the partition of Ireland, thereby inadvertently, through its own actions, precipitated British legislation that made the border, if anything, more permanent.

Although Costello's Ottawa declaration set in train severe new legislative hurdles for those seeking to end partition, bitter arguments between nationalists and unionists over the issue of the border continued. Just as the McCann case of 1911 in Belfast offered unionists 'hard evidence' to support the notion that 'Home Rule meant Rome Rule', in the middle of the twentieth century the Tilson case provided them with similar ammunition. At a meeting in Sandy Row in Belfast in early September 1950, Unionist MP Rev. J.G. MacManaway argued that 'the contention held by Unionists years ago that "Home Rule would be Rome Rule" had been proved to be fact by the Tilson case'.[63] The decisions of the High Court and Supreme Court, delivered in the manner that they were, were exploited to reinforce unionist opposition to a united Ireland under a Dublin government. How could a Protestant unionist live in a thirty-two-county republic if, in a dispute between a Catholic and a Protestant, the courts seemed to take the Catholic side?

Speaking at a rally in Strabane in late August 1950, another Unionist MP, Alexander Hunter, summed up the mood among unionists in the wake of the Tilson judgments when he 'misquoted' Kipling and professed to the assembled crowd: '"North was North and South was South and never the twain would meet" … What reliance can Ulster place on Costello's and MacBride's guarantees when the Supreme Court of Eire [sic] recently revealed in the Tilson case that Papacy and government are synonymous?'[64]

J. Edward Warnock, the attorney general for Northern Ireland, also entered the debate. At another meeting in Sandy Row he argued: 'If Northern Ireland was to be incorporated in the Irish Republic … we would find ourselves in a country which has a system of law, foreign to that to which we are accustomed, and subordinated to the Law of the Roman Catholic Church.'[65] This was not an unscripted contribution from Northern Ireland's chief adviser to the government on law and legal matters. At another meeting of St Anne's Unionist Association in Belfast some weeks later, Warnock referred to the Supreme Court decision in the Tilson case as

> the most serious development which [has] taken place in Eire [*sic*] for a very long time … the effect of the court's decision was that the law of the Roman Catholic Church must dominate the law of the land. This made it abundantly clear that the liberties of the Protestant people of Ulster, should they come under the jurisdiction of the Republic, would not be secure in spite of any guarantees.[66]

Like his counterpart in the southern state, Charles Casey, who represented Mary Tilson in the Supreme Court, Warnock was prepared to 'weaponise' his office when it came to the Tilson case.

Back in Dublin, after the Supreme Court hearing, Norman Porter of the National Union of Protestants wrote a series of letters to Seán MacBride, seeking a public debate on partition and 'the religious aspect of partition'. In response, MacBride conceded that the idea was 'a very good one' but stated that his preference was for 'a discussion in the public press … through the medium of a *viva voce* debate'. On 1 September Porter wrote in reply that 'we are more concerned with the religious aspect of the situation than the political'. Losing patience with MacBride's tardiness and gesturing to the Tilson case, Porter wrote again on 11 September:

> May we be permitted to ask if your Government is prepared to give the Protestant people of this island dependable guarantees for the protection and full religious liberty of Protestants? Can you clearly state whether you believe, or not, that the Canon Law of the Church of Rome should rule the 32 counties?[67]

Porter was also keeping Giff informed about the progress of his correspondence with MacBride. On NUP-headed notepaper, he wrote:

10 October, 1950

Rev. W.L.M. Giff, M.Sc.
I.C.M. Townsend Street,
Dublin, C.5

Dear Billy,

... I enclose our special edition of The Protestant which we just received late yesterday afternoon. I also enclose a copy of the latest reply from Seán MacBride.

I have requested an enquiry regarding the Tilson business and hope to let you know the result as soon as possible.

With kindest regards and every blessing.

Yours sincerely,

Norman[68]

At 6.10 p.m. on 5 August 1950, just after the Supreme Court delivered its judgment, Mary Tilson received a telegram from Senator Andy Clarkin reading: 'HEARTY CONGRATULATIONS MAY GOD BLESS YOU.'[69] Clarkin was a Catholic and had run unsuccessfully as a Fianna Fáil candidate for the Dublin South Dáil constituency at the 1944 general election. He was elected to Seanad Éireann on the administrative panel at the 1944 Seanad election and was re-elected to the Seanad at the 1948, 1951 and 1954 elections on the Industrial and Commercial Panel.

While Mary Tilson received numerous letters of support from Irish mothers across Ireland during the High Court hearing, she received many more after the Supreme Court hearing.[70] Interestingly, she does not appear to have received any letters from men about the case. Offering a perspective on the social legacy of the period, the letters were from women of a working-class background and advocated the power of prayer or the rosary and devotion to Our Lady. Tom Inglis has suggested that in the nineteenth and twentieth centuries in Ireland, a powerful alliance was forged between the Catholic Church and the Irish mother as she became the church's agent in the home, instilling in her family a pious devotion to the church and Our Lady:

> It was the mother who, from the middle of the nineteenth century, became the organisational link between the Catholic Church and the

individual. It was she who carried through the new moral and civil code from the church and school into the home ... the rosary was a time when the mother exercised her moral power and called her husband and her children to the attention of God and Our Lady. It strengthened her position as the sacred heart of the home.[71]

The letters indicate an unspoken common bond, as though the authors saw themselves as part of a sisterhood determined to promote the church's moral code. Or, as Benedict Anderson has it, 'in the mind of each [letter-writer] lived the image of their own communion'.[72]

The letters also show that the case was being followed closely by young and old in Catholic communities throughout Ireland. One letter from a correspondent in Roscrea, County Tipperary, suggests that if the outcome of the Supreme Court hearing was not announced from the pulpit, it was certainly being discussed by mass-goers in rural Ireland:

> Summerhill
> Roscrea
> 9.8.50
>
> Dear Mrs Tilson,
>
> I cannot tell you how overjoyed we all were that you got back your children. I prayed to the Sacred Heart every day, offered Masses, Communions and Rosaries on your behalf. I am sure you must have went [sic] through a dreadful time. I was afraid to open the paper myself. I couldn't speak with joy when my little boy came in from Mass with the good news. All the neighbours also prayed and were delighted, especially one little girl, Phyllis Noonan went to Mass & Communion on Sat [sic] & offered it up for you. God bless you and give you strength and courage to work for your little children. I am only a working mans [sic] wife myself with a large family.
>
> Mrs McCoy[73]

Another correspondent revealed that she had been praying for Mary throughout the High Court hearing and had recommenced prayers after Ernest had lodged his appeal to the Supreme Court:

6.8.50

Dear Mrs Tilson,

I had enclosed note ready to post to you until I saw appeal lodged. I started my prayers again and I am sure you had lots of other prayers from the loving hearts of (mothers) [sic].
<u>CONGRATULATIONS</u>
P.S. I know you will have your three darlings pray for me and mine.
God Bless

Mary[74]

After the Supreme Court ruling, Mary also received a letter from a woman who had been following the case, having returned home on holiday from the United States. She alluded to other disputes involving the religious upbringing of children, took a sideswipe at Ernest Tilson and, like other letter-writers, advocated the power of prayer:

Sun. Aug 6th, 1950

My Dear Mrs. Tilson,

Please forgive me at this time for taking the liberty of writing to you, since we are strangers, but since arriving from the U.S.A. for a holiday your case interested me very deeply regarding you and your dear children.

You know my dear you can't depend on men and these promises as there are many cases like yours, but thank God you won your case from your Husband and of course the power of prayer is great. It helped you a great deal.

I would like to write him a few lines and tell him what I think of him, if I did perhaps he would hang his head in shame, but I don't think he is worth the ink in my pen. May you be happy with your three boys, and when they grow up may they be very lucky to have such a nice Mother, as I think you are grand.

Fondly,

Miss Cath Collins,
65 Old Clare St,
Limerick City
Eire [sic].[75]

Reaction to the Court Judgments

Management at the Birds' Nest also received correspondence after the Supreme Court hearing. One letter from a female Protestant correspondent indicates a higher standard of education than some of the letters Mary received from Catholic correspondents; it is also markedly more sympathetic towards Ernest Tilson. As a benefactor of the Birds' Nest, the writer appears to have held that institution in high regard, and suggested that neither Ernest nor Mary seemed fit to raise their children. Mabel Bird's responses to her letters offer an insight into the attitude of the trustees or management of the Birds' Nest to the Supreme Court decision:

> Summerville,
> Monkstown,
> County Cork.
> Sept 21st, 50

To the Secretary of Mrs Smyly's Homes and Schools

Dear Sir,
I have been sorely tempted to write to the press, re. Tilson case, but I refrained as I don't have the full particulars of the case, nor what was or is the attitude of the Homes [sic] *Trustees*. These children may have been undesirable and the Trustees glad to be rid of them.

I am sure the general public must have been impressed with the Learned Judges of the laws and letters both ancient and modern and also by the pros and cons of the clever correspondents to the Times.

As for the breaking of the father's vow, it is easy when all is young and pleasant to make vows especially when pressure is brought. Men I have noticed in all kinds of work break their vows or promises every day of the week, or should I say, change their minds without any notice being taken of their deflections.

But through all these discussions little or nothing was said about the children and their welfare in the case, and on the face of things neither parent seemed fitted to bring up the children morally or physically – in short turning them into good citizens. The father realised his position and inability to do so and took what he thought was the best step to remedy this by placing them in the Homes where they would be cared for both morally and physically. And surely being the father had the greater authority and was free to change his mind regarding their religion. All very puzzling to understand. Childhood and their welfare is [*sic*] always an interest to me. I often think judges' wigs, while very handsome and becoming, are apt to prevent unbiased and clear thinking.

Sincerely,

Mrs. Hilda Harty[76]

The Birds' Nest had supposedly maintained a neutral position throughout the case, but Bird's reply to Harty indicates mild resentment regarding the outcome. This is apparent when she suggested that Mary was guilty of deserting her husband and children and that the 'powers that be' considered that the family would be better off in an over-crowded small cottage. She also offered a précis of paternal supremacy and the court ruling:

25th Septr. 1950

Dear Mrs. Harty,

In reply to your letter of 21st instant, we were all very sorry to have to part with the three little Tilson boys, who were very happy for the short time they were with us. They were nice children, and we should have liked to have been able to keep them and do our best for them, but the 'powers that be' considered that they would be better off living with their mother in an over-crowded small cottage. According to the father, his wife continued to leave him and the children, and refused to return.

Up to this the law has always recognised the father as the legal guardian with the prior right to decide in what religion his children should be brought up, but in the Tilson case, the ante-nuptial agreement was held to be binding, and the children were restored to their mother.

Yours sincerely,

Mabel Bird[77]

Rev. W.L.M. Giff and other like-minded Protestants were keen to ventilate their grievances after Ernest's unsuccessful Supreme Court appeal. One month after the case concluded, the Irish Church Missions placed a notice in *The Irish Times* announcing 'a public meeting' at the 'Mission Buildings' in Dublin, with Giff as the speaker. The 'subject' of the meeting was 'Ne Temere and the Constitution' but, as discussed, *Ne Temere* and the Tilson case were often conflated and it is inconceivable that Giff did not raise the case at the meeting.[78] Meanwhile, the *Church of Ireland Gazette* reported that at a meeting of the Meath Clerical Union in Drogheda on 29 August, Giff 'gave an account of the Tilson case, explaining many points that did not appear in the daily papers, and showing the father in a much more amiable light than they did'.[79] In a letter to a Herbert J. Mateer in Belfast, Giff referred to another meeting 'up North' where there were 'many people anxious to hear some particulars of the Reformed principles involved in [the Tilson case]'.[80]

At a Church of Ireland Diocesan Youth Conference in November 1950, Giff told delegates that 'the Roman Church contended … that her Canon Law was in reality the true law of every country. When Rome was in the minority, she did not press that claim; but where she had a large majority, she demanded it. That was the whole crux in the Tilson case.' He then referred to Ernest Tilson's rights under the principle of 'paternal supremacy':

> A member of the Church of Ireland wished his children to be brought up in his own faith. According to the Civil Law, he had perfect right to see that that was carried out, but under Canon Law he had to surrender them to be brought up in the faith of which he strongly disapproved.[81]

Immediately beneath the account of the Church of Ireland youth conference, and under the headline 'Home Tragedies', an *Irish Times* reporter then drew attention to Giff's cryptic remarks regarding the Tilson case:

> After making the statement quoted above, Mr Giff said that he did not want to 'throw any dirty water on our friends of the Church of Rome,' nor was he trying to be unfriendly, but the matter was very serious. If time permitted, he could tell something about the Tilson case that would show that any Church of Ireland man or woman who contemplated marriage with a Roman Catholic, either by going to Rome and surrendering his faith, or by remaining a member of the Church of Ireland, was 'the greatest fool under the sun'. He was dealing almost daily in his office with home tragedies that those marriages almost invariably brought about.[82]

Writing to Giff on 13 September 1950, Kenneth McNeill, assistant honorary secretary of the Worldwide Missionary Convention, welcomed Giff's forthcoming appearance at the convention but also proposed 'a monster meeting in Belfast … with the co-operation of the National Union of

Protestants, so that proper ventilation may be given to this great injustice'.[83] According to a front-page report in *The Irish Times*, more than one thousand people turned up at this meeting, where Giff told the assembled crowd: 'A big onslaught was being made on Protestantism in Eire [sic]... I don't think you up here half-understand our position down there.' The report then continued:

> Some people considered Dublin as representative of Eire [sic]. This was wrong; for scattered all over the country in isolation were Protestant people. Listing mixed marriages as one of the greatest problems he and his workers had met, Mr Giff said that Protestants had lost heavily in numbers in the last ten years. 'We are up against what is almost the perfect technique – the Church of Rome technique,' he declared ... Mr. Giff praised Mr. Norman Porter, Organising Secretary of the National Union of Protestants, for his great help in 'this involved work of ours'.[84]

Away from the public eye, the Rev. Pennefather of Durrus, County Cork, wrote to Giff and advised that in light of the outcome in the Tilson case, he would be bringing a resolution to the general synod on behalf of the West Cork Clerical Society, demanding that a committee should be set up as 'a means of combating all the evils latent in the Ne Temere decree'.[85] In a subsequent letter he queried the legal basis of the church document containing the promises, which couples intent on a mixed marriage were obliged to sign. Pennefather wanted to know if the document was 'in English or in Latin'; if in Latin, he wondered if it had any legal basis, since this was not a recognised language of the state. He argued that 'if this document is to be recognised in law, should it not be signed, sealed and registered with stamp affixed?'[86]

The Irish Catholic Church re-examined the question of signing 'the promises' in the wake of the High Court and Supreme Court hearings. On 10 October 1950 it was decided at a general meeting of the Irish hierarchy at Maynooth College 'to request the Faculty of Canon Law in Maynooth College to examine the forms of the guarantees now given in mixed marriages and to report as to whether, in view of the Tilson case, any change in the form of the guarantees or in the procedure in regard to mixed marriages is required in Southern or Northern Ireland'.[87] On 5 June 1951 it was reported at the bishops' conference plenary meeting that: 'After considering the Tilson case and the decree ... the Faculty of Canon Law formed the opinion that no change is required in the form of guarantees now given in mixed marriages, but that it would be desirable henceforth to make the written guarantees obligatory.'[88]

It is strange that the Faculty of Canon Law chose this moment to deem it necessary to make the 'written guarantees obligatory', since these had always been demanded in writing, a key point of contention in the Tilson case. Canon lawyer Maurice Dooley has explained that although the worldwide law of the church is the Code of Canon Law, local legislation is superimposed upon this – in this case the Maynooth Statutes of 1927, which would have been applicable to the Tilson case. Canon 1061.2 states that *as a rule* the guarantees should be required *in writing*; the Maynooth Statutes, on the other hand, stated more rigorously that the guarantees were required *in writing*. The recommendation from the Faculty of Canon Law therefore sought to make it unequivocal that the written guarantees were always required in writing, and not just *as a rule*.[89] It is undeniable that after the Tilson case the Catholic Church had little sympathy for any Protestant contemplating a mixed marriage with a Catholic and was inclined to strengthen the promises sought.

Mindful that the Tilson case might have greater significance than a dispute between a Protestant man and a Catholic woman, Pennefather suggested that the Church of Ireland should appoint somebody to promote its cause:

> We are to my way of thinking in the midst of a battle of ideologies and such questions as the Tilson case and Partition are only incidental to it. Our whole philosophy and way of life is in danger. I think one of the first requirements is to appoint a very thorough and really competent person, as what we might describe as a propaganda minister – one which would protest on every occasion to the press on which the word Catholic is improperly used, one that would see that our Bishops are properly styled and accurately reported, and who would be ready to protect our interests, to protest and to refute as occasion required.[90]

In reply, Giff commented on the form of the Catholic Church promise, agreed with Pennefather's suggestion of appointing a 'Public Relations Officer' and also criticised *The Irish Times*:

9th November 50

Dear Mr Pennefather,

... The declaration you refer to is in this country written in English ... the fact that it is under Canon Law makes it a legal document in the Church of Rome. While England holds to her present common law on the subject the thing is illigal [*sic*] there in any case ... I cannot at the moment furnish you with an exact copy of the declaration ... I actually had a copy of the Archbishop of York's statement, but in a rash moment I gave it to our Counsel in the Tilson case.

... Concerning your other suggestion, I do not know if you are aware that there is a feeling in some quarters that the Church of Ireland ought to set aside some clergyman to deal with all those problems. The title 'Public Relations Officer' has been suggested ... I do not know how long it would take to popularise the idea, but I think it is a splendid one.

It is not easy to get into the papers. Even the <u>Irish Times</u> closes down on me nowadays since my identity has become generally known. My last three letters have not been allowed to see the light of day. In yesterday's paper they just collected all the spicy bits that I had said at the Youth Conference and put them together as if I had said nothing else. It is difficult enough to keep one's hands clean in this job, without suffering contamination from the Press ...

With all good wishes,
Yours sincerely,

W.L.M. Giff[91]

On 13 December Pennefather sent Giff a copy of the resolution passed by the West Cork Clerical Society in response to the Tilson case, which read:

That this society views with alarm the implications latent in the judgment given in the 'Tilson' Case by the Supreme Court of the Republic of Ireland, and in consequence of the grave danger to our Faith and unfettered practice thereof, this society calls on all Clerical Societies of the Church of Ireland to urge the Standing Committee to enquire into the most desirable methods of combating this danger and of protecting the interests of the Church of Ireland. This society further suggests the appointment of a Public Relations Officer to express the Church of Ireland position in all such matters and to exercise vigilance when there is a possibility of the rights of the Church of Ireland being curtailed.[92]

The Most Rev. J.A.F. Gregg, archbishop of Armagh and primate of all Ireland, also voiced his concerns at the court judgments. At the opening of the Church of Ireland's general synod on 8 May 1951 he warned members about the 'serious question [which] arose after a decision in the courts of the Republic of Ireland touching a mixed marriage'.[93] He continued: 'We must create in so far as we can such a deep-rooted prejudice and such a community sense against such marriages on Roman Catholic terms that even the thoughtless will know that they constitute a grave danger to our church and should not be entered upon.'[94]

In the decades that followed, during various debates, the Tilson case became a reference point for members of both houses of the Oireachtas. In 1959, during a Court of Justice Bill debate, Senator Owen Sheehy Skeffington acknowledged that the 'judicial standard' was 'extremely high in this country' but then took aim at Mr Justice Gavan Duffy or possibly the Catholic judges of the Supreme Court when he observed: 'One could think of minor exceptions, where the standard was not quite the same – the Tilson case.'[95] In one of the 1972 Dáil debates on the fifth amendment to the constitution, which sought to remove the clause specifying the 'special position of the Catholic Church', Fine Gael TD Richard Burke cited the case and was clearly of the view that Gavan Duffy had relied very heavily on Article 44 in reaching his decision:

> I think it can be maintained that the most notable person who saw some juridical relevance in Article 44 in the history of the past 35 years was Mr. Justice Gavan Duffy. On three separate occasions Article 44 might seem to have had some slight, tangential effect on judicial decisions. But the matter was put beyond doubt by a decision of the Supreme Court in the Tilson Case.[96]

In the same vein, the Protestant senator Neville Keery of Fianna Fáil used the Tilson case to highlight the 'possible adverse effects' Article 44 might have on the Protestant minority in the southern state:

> In that case, arising from a marital situation, Judge Gavan Duffy gave a judgment which seemed to imply that Article 44 of the Constitution

gave canon law something of the same status as ordinary domestic law ... I should like to say, as someone who comes from a family with an entirely Protestant background, that that case is nevertheless a part of Protestant folklore and is cited as illustrating the possible adverse effects the special position of the Catholic Church in Article 44 might have on the Protestant community. The reference to mixed marriages in the quotation I have read and the fact that even up to the present time this is the most vexing problem as seen by the Protestant community in the development of community harmony and reconciliation in Ireland underlines how important was the feeling of apprehension aroused by the Tilson case and the effect which it has had since that time. That is one example occurring after 1937 which altered significantly Protestant views regarding Article 44.[97]

Although it was left to John A. Costello's son-in-law, Senator Alexis FitzGerald of Fine Gael, to set the record straight, he sidestepped Gavan Duffy's decision in the High Court and focused instead on the Supreme Court decision:

The Tilson case is frequently referred to as having been brought about by operation of this Article [Article 44]. This is not true. The Tilson case was not decided on the basis of Article 44. The Tilson case was decided by the Supreme Court, with Mr. Justice Black dissenting, on the basis of the rights of the parents, in the plural. The Supreme Court held that the constitutional expression of this entitled them to depart from what had been the previous law, that was that the father would determine the religion of the children.[98]

Concerns over the court decisions among Oireachtas members continued into the 1980s, however. During a 1981 Dáil debate on Constitutional and Legislative Review, Fianna Fáil TD Ciaran P. Murphy acknowledged that the 'great majority of court judgments on the Constitution transcended the confessional limitations of the Constitution', but added that there were 'one or two very Catholic interpretations of the Constitution in the so-called Tilson case and in another judgment delivered by Mr. Justice Gavan Duffy sometime in the forties'.[99]

The Supreme Court judgment generated widespread media coverage both in Ireland and in other countries. It also provoked a strong reaction from Rev. W.L.M. Giff through his writings in the *Church of Ireland*

Gazette and his 'monster' meetings; in the years that followed, other Protestant community representatives, including Archbishop J.A.F. Gregg, were also scathing in their criticisms of the judgments. The matter was also politicised in the immediate aftermath of the court cases when it reinforced opposition, among many unionists, to a united Ireland under a Dublin government, and later when parliamentarians of various hues cited it during different Dáil and Seanad debates. Indeed, it must be said that a recurring feature of those debates was criticisms of Mr Justice Gavan Duffy's decision in the High Court, rather than the all-important Supreme Court judgment. And while Mary Tilson had now to begin the onerous task of raising her four children as a single mother, she may have gained some comfort from the many letters of support she received from Catholic mothers all over Ireland.

CHAPTER 11

Reconciliation

Immediately after the Supreme Court case, Ernest Tilson sought refuge at his parents' house in Oldcastle, where, keeping a low profile, he remained for about six weeks. Things were not going well for him. He had just lost his appeal and now other matters rubbed salt in his wounds: in Dublin he was forced out of his employment in the corporation, supposedly due to victimisation by fellow employees; on 12 October he was arrested in Oldcastle on foot of a warrant charging him with neglect of his four children, and he appeared in the Dublin District Court the following day; in Oldcastle, meanwhile, many Catholic residents – encouraged by their eighty-year-old parish priest, Father O'Farrell – began boycotting the Tilson family's tailoring business.

The District Court warrant for Ernest's arrest was issued 'on information of Mrs. Mary Josephine Tilson'; when charged, he replied that 'he did not want to say anything'.[1] After his unsuccessful Supreme Court appeal, Ernest clearly had no intention of resuming the £4 per week maintenance amount due to his family, as directed by the District Court in December 1949. At the brief hearing, Mary was again represented by George McGrath and her husband by W.H. Richardson, who applied for an adjournment 'for at least a month'.[2] Following her appearance at the previous District Court hearing, Miss Wogan of the National Society for the Prevention of Cruelty to Children also gave evidence. McGrath argued that 'the case is one of urgency' and felt that 'a month's adjournment would be unreasonable' since the mother was living with relatives – her parents at Turner's Cottages – and wished to settle the matter of 'the children's support ... as quickly as possible'. The case was nevertheless adjourned until 15 November, with bail set at £50, and Rev. W.L.M. Giff accepted as independent bail person.[3] Giff offered his own views of the case in a letter to a Rev. W. Dodgson Sykes; he was in no doubt that Mary was receiving financial support for legal matters from the Catholic Church: 'he [Ernest] has had to surrender his children to Rome, and now it appears that he will have to pay for the privilege. His wife is determined to exact the last amount of anguish, and, of course, it goes without saying that she has the backing of her Church financially.'[4]

Ernest also had to deal with the boycott of his parents' business and ostracism by the citizens of Oldcastle. The court cases certainly appear to have generated huge local interest in the town, where people had queued for newspapers at a newsagent's in the morning and the evening after they had been delivered off the train. Ernest's parents, David and Harriette, and his sister Mitty did register a protest against their treatment: each Sunday for many years, the family had dressed in their best clothes and walked together along the footpath to service in the small Protestant Church, just off the square in the centre of the town. During the boycott, however, in a small but significant departure, they walked to church in the middle of the street, their heads held erect.[5] Accounts vary, but it is generally believed that the boycott eventually petered out twelve or eighteen months after the Supreme Court appeal. One local Catholic resident explained, albeit with savage irony: 'Mitty Tilson was the best seamstress in the town – if not the county. And if you had a son or a daughter making their First Communion and you wanted them dressed in the best outfit, then you went to Mitty.'[6]

Mitty passed on to her nephew's wife, Judy Tilson, stories of other forms of intimidation in Oldcastle around the time of the court cases: she described a frightening atmosphere as rosaries were said by a group of Catholics on the street outside their house; threats were made to burn her family out of their home, and, over successive nights, a man returning from the pub sang 'Faith of Our Fathers' outside their front door – a hymn that was part of 'the warp and woof of Catholic culture in those days'.[7] Judy Tilson's account is substantially corroborated by Norman Ruddock, who was a Church of Ireland rector in the diocese of Meath in the 1980s. In his memoir, *The Rambling Rector* (2005), he described how Mitty had recounted to him details of the boycott of her family, verbal abuse, the decline of her dressmaking business and her fear of Catholic antagonists as they made their way from mass.[8] A letter from Ernest to Giff dated 30 September 1950, nearly two months after the Supreme Court appeal had concluded, clearly indicates that the Tilson tailoring business remained under boycott:

> The boycott of my family is in full swing. No more work has come in from any of the R.C.s since, and my presence here does not help matters either. There is only one alternative, To [sic] quit the country as soon as possible. I feel most embarrassed living on my people and depending on them for everything, especially now since the same volume of work in not coming in and I being the cause of the trouble. I feel greatly indebted to them for their kindness.[9]

In a letter to Giff, Ernest's mother Harriette described how the parish priest of Oldcastle, Father O'Farrell, assisted by his curate, was stirring up tensions between the Catholic and Protestant communities in Oldcastle in the wake of the court cases.[10] Her letter also shows how the parish priest in Ireland at the time could act as a self-appointed moral policeman:

> 8 Chapel St.
> Oldcastle,
> 21.11.50
>
> Dear Mr. Giff,
> I wish to thank you and all concerned for the great help given to my son Ernest.
>
> The Roman Catholics in this place are making great use of their Canon Law. About a week ago, a jumble sale in aid of the local Church of Ireland table tennis club, of which Miss Russell is honorary secretary, was being held. The parish priest and his curate visited the schools the day before and warned the R.C. pupils that under no conditions were they to patronise the sale ... The night of the sale came on, and the courthouse was picquetted [sic] by Catholic action men, they warned the people outside of what the priest would do in the event of them going inside. A few walked away and others went to the sale regardless of the consequences. A very small crowd in comparison with recent sales ... We must say 'hats off' to those who defied Canon Law.
>
> Wishing you all the best,
> Yours truly,
>
> H. Tilson[11]

Regarding clerical involvement in anti-Protestant boycotts, a Rev. J. McCarthy's response to a correspondent entitled 'The Morality of "Boycotting" Non-Catholic Merchants', published in the *Irish Ecclesiastical Record* in 1953, provides some telling insights into church attitudes. A letter-writer to the journal asked: 'In the town of X where Catholics and non-Catholics are equally numerous and prosperous, Father Petrus urges his Catholic parishioners to boycott non-Catholic merchants, whether they are bigoted or not. Was he morally justified?' In legitimising his call, Father Petrus had relied heavily on canon law; canon 2316 declares that those who knowingly help, in any way, the propagation of heresy are themselves 'suspect of heresy'. Responding, McCarthy argued, somewhat ambivalently, that the boycott by Father Petrus does not, *per se*, involve any violation of strict justice. Nor does this boycott necessarily imply any injury to the common good, any violation of legal justice ... any Catholic ... has the right to abstain from dealing in any particular shop ... and may also combine with others in the use of this right of abstention.[12]

On the question of whether the boycott was morally justified, McCarthy concluded that 'the good to be achieved by the boycott must outweigh the injury done to the [boycotted] person'.[13] If we are to take the views of McCarthy as representative of those of the Catholic Church at the time, it is clear that the church condoned the boycotting of Protestant businesses – in certain circumstances. It remains unclear how the 'common good' was defined or indeed how the damage done to the injured party might be measured.

Around the time Ernest was in Oldcastle, Giff sought assistance from two figures: the aforementioned Rev. W.D. Sykes, who was principal of the Bible Churchmen's Missionary Society (BCMS) College in Bristol, England, and Norman Porter, a Baptist pastor and secretary of the National Union of Protestants (NUP) in Belfast. Giff, Sykes and Porter were comfortable bedfellows: the Irish Church Missions, the BCMS and the NUP had all been founded in England on conservative evangelical principles and were involved from time to time in battles to 'save' Catholic souls. A follower of the 'old paths', Sykes preached in a Geneva gown until his retirement; Andrew Atherstone suggests that his overlapping responsibilities as principal of BCMS and rector of St Mary-le-Port in Bristol illustrate 'the closely woven nature of the conservative evangelical network in the Church of England'.[14] Giff and Sykes were close associates: classified advertisements in *The Irish Times* in 1951 and 1953 for public meetings of the Irish Church Missions to be held at headquarters in Townsend Street list 'Rev. W.D. Sykes M.A.' as chairman of that organisation.[15] On 13 October 1950 Giff wrote to Sykes noting that: 'Continuing our telephone conversation of this morning ... Tilson had to leave his work owing to victimisation, and he has been living with friends (his own people) since the conclusion of the Supreme Court proceedings.'[16] It is likely that Giff was hoping to enlist Sykes' help in finding employment for Ernest in England or farther afield.

Like the BCMS, the NUP had been established in England around 1942 to combat perceived high church and Roman Catholic tendencies in the Church of England.[17] An advertisement placed in *The Times* by the NUP in 1944 called for the

elimination in all Churches of the Church of England all Doctrines and Practices which were rejected at the Reformation such as:
The Sacrifice of the Mass
Transubstantiation
The Adoration of the Sacrament
The Veneration of Saints and Images
Those who desire these things can lawfully obtain them elsewhere.
Readers can help the movement by becoming members of
THE NATIONAL UNION OF PROTESTANTS[18]

An Irish branch of the NUP was established in Belfast in 1948 with Rev. Ian Paisley as its Irish representative; shortly afterwards Porter became its secretary, with Paisley continuing as treasurer. This branch concentrated on a more general defence of the Protestant religion and culture, and, according to Anna Bryson, drew support from evangelicals in all Protestant denominations.[19] With reference to the 1937 constitution, the large crowds attending Maria Duce rallies, and the Tilson case, Ed Moloney has observed that 'in this cold war between Irish Protestantism and Catholicism, the NUP was only one of a plethora of politico-religious groups making up the Northern battle line'.[20] Paisley built up a reputation as one of the organisation's more forthright and colourful speakers as he spoke at open-air meetings throughout Northern Ireland on topics such as Sunday observance and the evils of mixed marriages.[21] Both Porter and Paisley forged notable political careers following this period of activism, with Porter elected in 1953 as MP to the Northern Ireland Parliament as an Independent Unionist for the Clifton ward, Belfast; Paisley had to wait until 1970 to be elected to the Westminster and Northern Ireland parliaments.

It is hardly a surprise that Porter took more than a passing interest in the plight of Ernest Tilson or, indeed, in the Tilson case.[22] In 1949 he wrote to the organisers of a series of lectures for all denominations to be held at the Clonard monastery Catholic church, Belfast, by Rev. G.J. Reynolds CSSR, warning that 'we feel it is our duty to meet what we consider a challenge to the Protestant Faith'. He enclosed a set of questions and asked that they be answered either at the lectures or later by post. One of his questions concerned mixed marriages: 'What is the attitude of your Church to mixed marriages, and is there anything to bind the non-member of your Church before consenting to the marriage?'[23]

The respondent from the church relied heavily on canon law 1060 and 1061.1 before remarking how Porter had added the following perspicacious comment beneath the formal question submitted: 'It is also well known that the Church of Rome has over-ruled the civil law in regard to marriage.' The respondent then continued: 'She [the Catholic Church] cannot take the civil law as the measure and rule of Christian duty in regard to marriage, since for all Christians marriage is above all a religious matter.'[24]

Ernest kept a low profile while staying in Oldcastle. After returning from very occasional visits to Dublin or elsewhere, he would disembark from the train and move furtively in the shadows along the narrow lanes from the station before making a final covert dash across Chapel Street to his parents' house.[25] His son Alan has corroborated these accounts, stating that his father explained many years later that fear of being recognised drove him to seek employment outside the state.[26] While Ernest explained his predicament to Giff, his letter of 30 September also shows how Giff and Porter had attempted to secure employment for him in Purdysburn Hospital in Belfast.[27]

> 8 Chapel Street,
> Oldcastle,
> Co Meath.
>
> 30.9.50
>
> Dear Mr. Giff,
>
> I received a letter in today's post informing me of the fact that Northern Ireland Protestants were given first preference for any vacancy in the Hospital [Purdysburn]. I need not stress how disappointed I am after all this writing, more especially since I am confined to the house and not been outside the door since the last time I called on you in Dublin. I have taken every precaution, as people here were continually making enquiries after me. It seems to have been fruitless as the letter came here addressed to me with a Belfast postmark, quite clearly on the envelope. I cannot say for certain if it has been interfered with. I must say it was very tactless on their behalf.
>
> My mother called on Mr. Kevin [the Church of Ireland rector in Oldcastle] who is to write to you. He also has the letter I received which he will forward when writing. I would have enclosed it in this letter but decided to write to you personally afterwards.
>
> I see no further point in seeking employment in N.I. [Northern Ireland] as valuable time is being wasted. I think the sooner I can

get to Canada the better as I am not staying here much further. They [Purdysburn Hospital] made a mess of things as I was asked to state my wife's address and place of birth. They may have gone so far as to get in touch with her ...

I should feel greatly obliged if you would kindly use your influence to get me out of the country as soon as possible, as I fear the worst.

Sorry for giving you so much trouble and thanking you so much for all you have done for me.

Yours Respectfully,

Ernest Tilson

On 2 October Giff's secretary forwarded to Porter a copy of Ernest's letter to Giff with a covering note asking, 'if you can do anything to help in the matter'.[28] Giff himself, however, appears to have wasted little time in finding alternative accommodation for Ernest. His 13 October letter to Sykes identifies his next refuge: 'The Tilson family in Oldcastle are having a very poor time, and I have thought it best to hide Tilson out for the present. Accordingly, I have put him out in the Children's Fold. He will share the cottage with our man-of-all-work and help him keep the place in order. There is plenty he can do on the grounds.'[29]

The Children's Fold in Boley, Monkstown, County Dublin, was a Protestant-run orphanage controlled by the Irish Church Missions in association with Mrs Smyly's Homes. It accepted children from the Protestant-run Bethany Home, a residential home in Dublin for Protestant women who had been convicted of petty theft, prostitution and infanticide, as well as women who were pregnant out of wedlock, and the children of these women.[30] It is deeply ironic that Ernest should end up in a Protestant orphanage, run by the Irish Church Missions in association with Mrs Smyly's Homes, so soon after his own children had been discharged from the Birds' Nest. The tables had well and truly turned.

It is unclear how long he remained there. We can be sure, however, that Giff and Porter continued to offer him assistance until he left for Belfast sometime before June 1951. On 27 June 1951 Giff wrote to Porter regarding Ernest's passport; on 5 July he wrote again and informed Porter that he had been in touch with the passport authorities. His letter also makes it clear that the NUP was his custodian in Belfast:

5 July 1951

Dear Norman,

<u>RE Ernest Tilson's Birth Certificate</u>

I have just been in touch with the passport authorities who had the Certificate. They say they posted it along with photographs to Mr. Tilson at the Children's Fold, Boley, Monkstown, and the Matron there tells me that she forwarded a large envelope about Friday last to him c/o N.U.P. Belfast. I take it therefore that Mr. Tilson must have received the Certificate by now ...

I hope to be in Belfast for the weekend and shall probably give you a ring if I arrive in time on Saturday.

Yours in the cause of life and liberty,

W.L.M. Giff[31]

After his arrival in Belfast Ernest secured employment as a guillotine operator in an engineering firm.[32] Giff's efforts to arrange a passport for him, almost a year after the court hearings, also suggests that there were plans for him to travel farther afield. After several months in Belfast, Ernest moved to London where he found accommodation in a flat in Rufford Street, Islington, and got employment as an administrator in a nearby firm. At home, Mary continued to raise her sons as Catholics, not in an overly devout manner, but, like most Catholics at this time, they attended mass on Sundays and on holy days and regularly received the sacraments.

In 1964, thirteen years after leaving, Ernest travelled to Ireland to attend the funeral of his father in Oldcastle. Passing through Dublin on his way back to London, he stopped off for a pint in Coles pub in Ballsbridge – a regular haunt of his in a past life – where he met his father-in-law, John Barnes.[33] After a few drinks, John convinced him to pay a visit to his children at Turner's Cottages, which was only a short walk away. Although he received a frosty reception from his wife and did not overstay, his visit nevertheless set in motion a series of letters between husband and wife, which culminated in her visit to him in London about six months later. Mary's own domestic circumstances were also changing at this time: her sister, Lily, with whom she had been living, was getting married and moving out, while three of her sons, Alan, Paul and Neville, had also married. Now in her early forties, for the first time in her life Mary faced the prospect of living alone. In the months that followed, she visited her husband on a few more occasions before moving to London to live with him on a permanent basis in 1967. Their reunion was greeted with the approval of their sons – Alan recalls: 'It was great, we were a family again.'[34]

In Islington Ernest continued in his clerical employment while his wife got a job as a cleaner in the offices of the *Islington Gazette* before securing a better job in a knitwear factory close to Chapel Market. She was soon promoted and enjoyed her career there until she reached retirement age. During those years in London, the couple would regularly go to local pubs together at weekends and attend occasional dinner dances. The Tilson sons and their families were frequent visitors, and the couple often visited Dublin to see their grandchildren. On one such visit to London, Judy Tilson recalled how her mother-in-law was appalled at the free availability of divorce in Britain, remarking that she was lucky in her own marital situation and did not have to worry about such matters.

The couple always hankered to live permanently in Ireland, and after their family had secured a Dublin Corporation flat for them in Ballyfermot, they returned to live there in 1990. A few months later they moved to a corporation house at Beech Hill Court in Donnybrook, closer to their sons. During this time the couple regularly attended Bohemians Football Club matches to watch one of their grandsons, David, play. Indeed, Judy Tilson has recalled that Ernest loved all his grandchildren and on one occasion offered to pay City & Guilds course fees for one of them. She has speculated that his fondness for them may have been rooted in the fact that he had missed being with his own children when they were growing up.[35]

Ernest was a heavy smoker and in 1991, was diagnosed with lung cancer, eventually being admitted to St James' Hospital. On his deathbed he expressed his profound regret at having placed his children in the Birds' Nest, telling his family, 'If I knew what was going to happen, the court cases and all of that, I would never have done it.' Perhaps hedging his bets, and to the wonder of his wife, he accepted Holy Communion from a Catholic priest who was visiting the sick, a day or two before he passed away. He died on 23 April 1991 and after a Church of Ireland service at St Mary's church, Anglesea Road, Ballsbridge he was laid to rest in Shanganagh Cemetery.

Following his death, Mary lived on her own at Beech Hill Court until she took ill suddenly in late July 1993 after suffering a brain haemorrhage; she passed away on 3 August at the nearby St Vincent's Hospital. After her funeral mass, which was held at the Church of the Sacred Heart in Donnybrook, she was buried alongside her husband, four months short of their fifty-second wedding anniversary.[36]

Conclusion

Although Mary and Ernest Tilson's dispute appeared to centre on the religious upbringing of their children, 'religion' or religious difference was not the *primum mobile* of their quarrel. It is important not to mistake cause for effect, and, in such a way, religious matters did not alone *cause* the division: Ernest did not strike his wife because she was a Catholic; equally, Mary did not 'desert' her husband because he was a Protestant. Their dispute originated as a domestic one and its causes were multiple: substandard living accommodation; living with the wife's in-laws; alcohol abuse; allegations of desertion; physical violence; money and religion. Allowing for their conflicting versions of events in their affidavits, and taking into account the views of Alan and Judy Tilson, when religion did arise as a source of conflict within the home, it stemmed from the circumstances of their marriage in 1941, from the eldest boy David's Holy Communion and, more conspicuously, from Mary's mother, Annie, who lived with the couple for many years. She was vehemently opposed to her daughter's marriage because Ernest was a Protestant, and then maintained her hostility towards him up to the time of her death. Both Mary and Ernest agreed in their affidavits that her parents had opposed the marriage and would not consent to it unless it was held in a Catholic church. Much more prominent than hostility over religious matters in the affidavits are the fractious domestic issues. Alan Tilson does not believe that the cause of his parents' marital breakdown was rooted in religion and is on the record as saying that if they'd had a house of their own, things might have worked out very differently.[1]

Although religious difference was not the only source of conflict in the household, religion was clearly used by Ernest as a means of agitation as he pursued his bitter quarrel with his wife. Claire Mitchell observes that religion or religious difference 'may remain beneath the surface of a society, ready to emerge in times of trouble, as has often been the case in Northern Ireland'.[2] It can be argued that this is what occurred in the Tilson household: Ernest and Mary were aware of their religious differences, but these remained largely *beneath* the surface for many years at Turner's

Cottages. As the domestic dispute intensified, the idea of using religion for antagonistic purposes appears to have occurred to Ernest in Oldcastle where he had taken his sons.

Removing the children to the Birds' Nest in Dún Laoghaire also solved the immediate problem of their accommodation and relieved Tilson's parents and sister of their caring duties. Rev. W.L.M. Giff's role in this manoeuvre cannot be underestimated: had Ernest turned up with his sons at the front door of the Birds' Nest of his own volition, it is probable that they would not have gained entry, for children were supposed to be destitute in order to be admitted. As discussed in Chapter 3, the Irish Church Missions existed in part to proselytise, and there is no doubt that Giff's interest in the matter was piqued at the prospect of winning three new souls. Mary had not deserted her children in the true sense, but Giff's assertion in writing on the three admission forms that 'the mother [has] deserted the children' circumvented Mrs Smyly's Homes' admission rules and enabled the children to be admitted.

There are good reasons why the dispute should not be interpreted solely as 'religious' in origin. First, Ernest took his three sons to his parents' house in Oldcastle because he was unsure of his next move in his domestic quarrel; at this point he had no intention of placing them in the Birds' Nest. The children remained in Oldcastle for six weeks, but this was only a temporary solution: his elderly parents and sister were busy attending to their tailoring business and had little time to care for three young children.[3] Turner's Cottages is less than one mile from Mrs Smyly's children's home in Grand Canal Street – where Ernest first took them after Oldcastle – and approximately five miles from the Birds' Nest. Had it been Ernest's intention to raise his children as Protestants in a Dublin orphanage, it made little sense to take them to Oldcastle, over fifty miles away. We have also seen how, in Oldcastle, Miss Frances Russell, a Protestant and active proselytiser, appears to have pointed Ernest in the direction of Mrs Smyly's Homes. Second, before taking his sons from their home, Ernest had allowed them to be raised as Catholics for all their formative years, which undercuts the claim in his affidavits that he was vehemently opposed to this arrangement. And third, Ernest and Mary's eventual reconciliation and twenty-four-year period together until their deaths in the 1990s hardly suggests that religion was a decisively contentious issue in their relationship. Moreover, during their time in London and Dublin, the couple appear to have been indifferent in their attitudes to their respective religious practices, with neither person regularly attending their own church.[4]

Ernest's extreme course of action came at a high cost: when his wife's solicitor issued a writ of *habeas corpus*, their quarrel suddenly assumed dimensions well beyond his control. When Rev. W.L.M. Giff took charge, appointing and funding a legal team, Ernest became little more than a bit player. Although Giff was instrumental in arranging the boys' admission to the Birds' Nest, and oversaw much of the subsequent legal proceedings, it would be wrong to conclude that what occurred was the result of an eccentric personal crusade on his part; numerous letters to *The Irish Times*, speeches by church figures such as Rev. J.A.F. Gregg, submissions by the West Cork Clerical Society to the Irish Church Missions, and the financial contributions made by Protestants across Ireland towards the legal costs show that the case attracted the support of the Church of Ireland and large numbers of its members.

Mary was primarily concerned with recovering her three children, but she was also relegated to a supporting role in the case. She earned only a modest weekly wage from the Swastika Laundry and had received no maintenance payments from her husband, but within days, if not hours, of discovering that her sons had been taken to the Birds' Nest, she had assembled a formidable legal team. Free legal aid did not exist in Ireland in 1950, and it is impossible not to speculate that she took the matter to her parish priest, who then raised it with those further up the hierarchy. It seems likely that the Catholic Church underwrote the significant legal costs. Indeed, that both churches, or their supporters, were footing the bill, and undoubtedly issuing instructions to their respective legal teams, underscores the notion that both Ernest and Mary had only supporting roles in the case.

Now before the courts, the Tilson case assumed national significance when it received widespread newspaper coverage. And notwithstanding the manifold causes of the dispute, it was interpreted by many as a battle between the Catholic and Protestant Churches for the souls of three children. Many in Ireland at the time identified themselves with either the Catholic or the Protestant combatant and closely followed the case's progress through the courts. Victory was important for both sides: the Catholic side was aghast at the prospect of losing three souls, particularly in the 'Holy Year' of 1950, while for the Protestant side a loss represented a fatal blow in their ongoing struggle to halt Protestant decline. In fact, according to Alan Tilson, the Tilson children all grew up in the belief that their parents' dispute was simply a conflict between both churches at a national level.[5]

Operating at multiple levels, what followed amounted to confessional antagonism, or what Caleb Wood Richardson has described as 'soft sectarianism'.[6] At an individual level it occurred when Ernest was supposedly treated as a pariah by Catholics in his workplace, or when his parents' tailoring business was boycotted, or when the parish priest at Oldcastle warned parishioners not to patronise the Protestant fundraising event. At a community level it occurred when the matter came before the High Court and the Supreme Court, or when Protestants and Catholics throughout Ireland identified themselves with one or other of the protagonists in the dispute and adapted a 'them' and 'us' mindset. In turn, this undoubtedly influenced social relations between both groups. Confessional antagonism was also fuelled by some reportage in national and local newspapers, by articles in Catholic and Protestant publications and by inflammatory speeches delivered by clerics such as Rev. W.L.M. Giff and Rev. J.A.F. Gregg.

Giff received a great many financial donations towards the cost of the court proceedings from Protestants throughout Ireland, and the letters accompanying these donations perhaps show that many Protestants felt compelled to support a quasi-war effort against the Catholic Church; or may be interpreted as part of a concerted effort to protect what they saw as their increasingly defenceless status in southern Ireland. These notions are given added support by the efforts of the West Cork Clerical Society, which sought to establish a more systematic or organised defence. Giff's widely reported 'monster meetings', arranged after the Supreme Court judgment, and his assertion that the Tilson case was 'a big onslaught on Protestantism in Ireland' also fomented confessional tensions.

Confessional antagonism also operated at an institutional and state level. Mr Justice Gavan Duffy could have ruled at the outset that Ernest estopped himself by allowing his children to be raised as Catholics for many of their formative years, deciding the case on that principle alone and thereby avoiding the subsequent controversy. Instead, he adjudged the matter in light of those articles of the constitution which were influenced by Catholic social teaching; this approach allowed him to lay heavy emphasis on the Catholic Church, which highlighted Ireland's confessional divisions and showed an anti-Protestant bias.

The Supreme Court then gave further oxygen to these matters by allowing the attorney general, Charles Casey – himself an ardently devout Catholic – to represent Mary Tilson. The attorney general gave an exposition on the sacrament of marriage during the court hearing and drew attention to the fact that 'the Catholic Church [claimed] to be the

One True Church'.[7] When delivering the judgment of the court, Mr Justice Murnaghan also added fuel by not offering an outright rebuttal of the language used by Gavan Duffy in the High Court, through his comments regarding the question of whether Catholics enjoyed constitutional privileges over people of other religions, and also through his denunciation of Ernest in his closing remarks.

After delivering judgment, Murnaghan could have left it at that, but instead referred to Ernest as 'intemperate', 'fond of drinking' and not accepting 'his obligations as a husband and father'. He speculated that Ernest's placing of his children in the Birds' Nest was 'an ingenious way of relieving himself of the payment' due to his wife under the District Court order. The judge's obiter comments were interpreted by some members of the Protestant community as a personal and unnecessary attack on Ernest Tilson. Instead, Murnaghan might have drawn attention to the fact that Ernest may have signed the prenuptial agreement under duress. Gerard Hogan has argued that the judge 'must also be faulted for having accepted at face value the validity of the undertaking extracted from Mr. Tilson having regard to the acute circumstances in which his consent to the rearing of children as Roman Catholics had been given'.[8] Indeed, the judge might also have highlighted the fact that it was the Catholic Church which insisted on the prenuptial agreement in the first place; the Protestant church imposed no such condition on its members or on whom they might marry. From a Protestant perspective, in other words, it was an uncompromising Catholic Church that appeared to be the architect of the imbroglio.

But for all this, there are two endings to the story of the Tilson case. The High Court and the Supreme Court made progressive decisions when they dispensed with paternal supremacy; as Mr Justice Black noted, it was 'an archaic law and a relic of barbarism' with no place in a modern society. The Guardianship of Infants Act (1964), the Succession Act (1965) and the unmarried mother's allowance (1973) are all examples of the state's acknowledgement that the actuality of family life could fall short of the idealisation of the family.[9] The Tilson judgment in the Supreme Court in 1950 predated all these statutes, but should be added to the list: the ruling significantly enhanced the rights of mothers and, by extension, the societal status of women in mid-twentieth-century Ireland when it revoked the automatic right of the father to the custody of legitimate children[10] and decided that it was the *parents*, rather than the father alone, who had a joint power and duty in regard to the education of their children. In fact, the Supreme Court decision accorded with the principle of joint guardianship later enshrined in the Guardianship of Infants Act (1964) and anticipated that act.[11] As minister for justice, Charles Haughey argued in the Seanad in 1964 that judgment in the Tilson case 'marked the establishment of the legal equality of the sexes in guardianship matters'.[12] Twenty years later Fine Gael TD Alan Shatter pointed out in the Dáil that 'the Tilson case ... should be part of the history of women's lib because it did not seek to support a religious divide but gave an equality of rights to mother and father or husband and wife of a nature which did not then exist in the United Kingdom or in many other countries'.[13]

On the other side of the coin, however, 'the pervasive fear of mixed marriages leading to the total extinction of the Southern Protestant community took an even stronger hold'[14] as the court decisions reinforced the perception that the southern state favoured Catholics over Protestants. With a dominant and influential Catholic Church to contend with, a largely acquiescent laity, and successive governments being disposed to papal encyclicals or Catholic teaching, or indeed encouraging or endorsing clerical influence, southern Protestant anxieties were already at a high pitch; the judgments in the Tilson case offered confirmation to some Protestants that the dice were loaded against them.

By extension to this, questions remain regarding *how* the case was handled by the courts. Article 44.2.3 of the constitution guaranteed that the state would 'not impose any disabilities or make any discrimination on the ground of religious profession, belief or status'. But did the judgments in the case shatter that pretence? Or more bluntly, when Ernest Tilson had his day in court, were the dice loaded against him simply because he was a Protestant? Given that the predominant raison d'être of the Catholic Church and the government at the time was the construction of a Catholic society, and the fact that Ernest Tilson was not only removing three children from the Catholic flock but, through this action, was undermining an essential pillar of that society – the family unit – had he started a fight that he could not possibly win? Notwithstanding the doubts expressed about the judgments by some parliamentarians in the past (as shown in Chapter 10), J.H. Whyte has observed that there was

> an element which might permit a nervous or suspicious observer to allege that there was a sectarian bias ... the outcome undoubtedly disquieted many members of the Church of Ireland. On the face of it, the courts had abandoned a rule of law which was impartial between denominations in favour of one which benefited the Roman Catholic Church.[15]

Conclusion

In the same vein, Gerard Hogan has argued that the High Court judgment was 'susceptible of giving the impression that the constitution and the law now favoured the Catholic in a mixed marriage',[16] while in a 2006 interview with Patsy McGarry, religious affairs correspondent of *The Irish Times*, the former Church of Ireland archbishop of Dublin, the Most Rev. John Neill, expressed his concern that 'some commentators were now saying the dominant Catholic ethos of the Constitution in the past had never been used in a negative way where other denominations were concerned'. The archbishop then cited the Tilson case and stated that 'the consequence of that case was social isolation for many Protestants ... those [Protestants] who grew up here in the 1950s did feel they lived in a confessional state'.[17] Meanwhile McGarry himself – one of the most vocal critics of *Ne Temere* – claimed in a subsequent letter to the *Irish Examiner* that the Supreme Court decision 'had been influenced by the earlier High Court judgment and the changed political climate with a new Government headed by the devout Catholic, John A. Costello. Certainly, that was the view among Irish Protestants who now saw the Ne Temere decree as having the full backing of the state.'[18]

Aside from the actual ruling, two aspects of the High Court case created a perception that the judgment was biased in favour of the Catholic party. First, the language used by Mr Justice Gavan Duffy was strongly Catholic in tone. The judge referred to the 'right of the Catholic Church' to Catholicism having a 'place of honour' in the constitution and to baptism being of 'transcendent importance' to Catholics. He also referred to the Christian content in the preamble to the constitution and to Articles 41 and 42 as being 'redolent ... of the great papal Encyclicals *in pari materia*'. Second, by relying on Articles 41, 42 and 44, Gavan Duffy's judgment appeared nebulous and lacking in a firm legal basis. Moreover, the ill-defined nature of the ruling should be considered in light of Gavan Duffy's reputation for being highly skilled on the bench and delivering 'leading' and 'impressive' decisions.[19] Did he struggle to find a solid legal basis for dispensing with the tradition of paternal supremacy?

The Supreme Court's handling of the case failed to ease perceptions of bias in the judicial process. As we have seen, the court relied on the narrow ground of Article 42.1 to show that paternal supremacy was to be replaced by joint paternal authority. Moreover, J.M. Kelly has persuasively argued that 'the very fact that the constitution did not expressly provide for such a radical change in the law was a fair indication that such a change was not intended'. And largely on that basis, the dissenting judge, Mr Justice Black, voiced serious concerns about the judgment. Mr Justice Murnaghan, as noted, also contributed to perceptions of bias by his refusal to state that the constitution did not grant the Catholic Church privileges denied to other religions.

Here we should also consider Archbishop McQuaid's letter to Cardinal Marchetti-Selvaggiani which clearly reveals the archbishop's *intentions* during this period. McQuaid claimed that he had previously accepted 'a commission' from Rome to have 'British law, with which the Republic [had] lived, effectively changed in favour of the prescriptions of the Church'. The cardinal's response appears to confirm that that was the case. Taking McQuaid's letter at face value, this initiative had its genesis in Rome, as McQuaid unambiguously stated: 'I was *directed* [by the Vatican] to take up the matter with the government.'[20] In his influential work *States of Ireland* (1972), Conor Cruise O'Brien argued that 'there is no known case of the Pope's interfering in the affairs of the Irish State',[21] but it appears from McQuaid's letter that the Vatican was actively engaged in an attempt to modify the civil laws of the Republic of Ireland during this period.

In the conclusion to *Church and State in Modern Ireland, 1923–1970* (1971), J.H. Whyte outlined some of the occasions when the Catholic hierarchy influenced state policy in Ireland. He lists a number of statutes, such as the Censorship of Films Act (1923), the Intoxicating Liquor (Amendment) Bill (1948) and the Adoption Act (1964), but qualifies his findings by pointing out that other important policy decisions bore the influence of bishops but were not embodied in statute. Whyte also points to occasions where consultations between government and hierarchy may have taken place but for which there is no evidence. Whyte concluded, 'it does not seem likely that contact between government and bishops at the level of policy is at all frequent'.[22]

Be that as it may, what Whyte was addressing here were representations being made during the period from the formation of the Free State to 1970 and which were being made on an ad hoc basis: the hierarchy made representations, as it saw fit, on matters in which the bishops took an interest. Many would rightly argue that, in the best moral interests of its flock, that was how the Catholic Church should conduct its affairs. It appears, however, that Archbishop McQuaid's 'commission' might have been more organised, systematic and a flagrant attempt to encroach into state matters. If we accept his letter to Cardinal Marchetti-Selvaggiani at face value, as we might also accept the cardinal's response, McQuaid unequivocally signed off by assuring the cardinal that he would use his 'best endeavours to secure respect for our holy Faith in all our legislation', while the cardinal, in his response, warned the archbishop to 'work and watch in the future so that the laws of this Republic adhere to the ecclesiastical laws to the best extent'.

We might also consider how mixed marriages appear to have been a pressing concern for monsignors Giovanni Montini and Domenico Tardini during this period. At their meeting with John A. Costello in Rome in January 1950, as outlined in Chapter 4, the 'mixed marriage situation in Ireland' came up for mention. Later in that year, as McQuaid's biographer John Cooney has noted, Tardini made enquiries about the Tilson case. It is plausible that the 'commission' was addressing the vexed issue of mixed marriages – a particularly thorny one for McQuaid – and that when Mary Tilson reported that her children had been placed in the Birds' Nest, the archbishop was compelled to move to action. In fact, as we have seen, he declared in his letter to Marchetti-Selvaggiani that he had 'waited for a favourable opportunity' and that 'opportunity [came] with the Tilson case'. Now firmly in his lap, did he view the case as a battle between church and state which had to be won at all costs, with his superiors in Rome watching over?

It is fair to conclude that McQuaid took an active role in the Tilson case and would have been prepared to use what influence he could to secure a favourable outcome. He stated that he 'was given the greatest assistance by the chief law officer of the Republic, the Attorney General' [Charles Casey] and had 'consulted for long with two members of the Judiciary whom [he] could trust'. It is possible that Casey or indeed the archbishop made overtures to Mr Justice Gavan Duffy about the matter, or that McQuaid is referring here to Mr Justice James Murnaghan, Mr Justice Cecil Lavery or to the chief justice, Conor Maguire. In fact, Ronan Keane has argued that Murnaghan's rise to senior judicial office in the newly established Irish Free State was due as much to his 'Catholic and nationalist background as to his academic distinctions'.[23] Maguire was also steeped in the Catholic tradition and had strong nationalist and republican sympathies.[24]

The trifurcated relationship between the interparty government, the Catholic Church and the judiciary at this time is another essential context within which to consider the court decisions. Chapter 4 drew attention to the church/state consensus in mid-twentieth-century Ireland and we saw how some parties in the coalition drew inspiration for their policies from papal encyclicals and, as noted, all the members of the cabinet were Catholics, while many were also members of the Knights of Saint

Columbanus. As we have seen, John A. Costello was a passionate Catholic and was, arguably, excessively deferential to the Catholic Church. In fact, as already noted, McQuaid claimed in his letter to Marchetti-Selvaggiani to have spoken with the 'head of government' about the Tilson case and reported that he was offered a 'very sympathetic' ear.[25] Moreover, Costello and Seán MacBride, as distinguished lawyers themselves, enjoyed personal friendships not only with Archbishop McQuaid but also with Mr Justice Gavan Duffy, Mr Justice Cecil Lavery and Mr Justice Murnaghan of the Supreme Court.[26]

Tom Garvin has argued that 'episcopal insistence of the Church's right to dictate policy in a broad range of social, cultural and intellectual and marital areas was maintained and successfully enforced among Irish Catholics until well into the late twentieth century'.[27] Garvin's claim may be something of an overstatement, but if the Catholic Church at the time saw itself as having a role well beyond ecclesiastical matters, by extension it is fair to say that there were some in the interparty government who might have been willing to acquiesce. After all, and as previously noted, the period of this government was the high-water mark of integralism in Ireland – integralism being the principle that the Catholic faith should be the basis of public law and public policy within civil society. It would hardly be an overreach to propose that some members of the interparty cabinet might have been prepared to use whatever influence they could to reclaim three Catholic children from a Protestant orphanage in the 'Holy Year' 1950.

Also, in terms of possible government involvement, the mother and child controversy might be considered because, as noted, it overlapped with the Tilson case. Although that clash between church and state was multi-layered, it showed how some members of the interparty cabinet were prepared to yield to episcopal influence. During the Dáil debate on Dr Noël Browne's resignation, Costello stated: 'I, as a Catholic, obey my Church authorities and will continue to do so.' In the same debate MacBride argued that 'those of us in this House who are Catholics, and all of us in the Government who are Catholics are, as such of course, bound to give obedience to the rulings of our Church and of our Hierarchy'.[28] Moreover, it is also established that McQuaid and Costello remained in close contact throughout the mother and child controversy; he told the Dáil, 'I was in close touch with His Grace the Archbishop ... during all that time. I kept in constant touch with His Grace.'[29] Would it be precipitant to suggest that they were in regular contact as the Tilson case progressed through the courts?

Conclusion

This book has also identified other factors which suggest that the case may have been subject to clerical or political interference:

1. The underwriting of Mary Tilson's legal fees by the church. If, as generally accepted, the Catholic Church underwrote the significant cost, this financial risk provided another sound reason for Archbishop McQuaid to use whatever influence he could to secure victory.
2. The dearth of archival material relating to the case. The four-page letter from McQuaid to Marchetti-Selvaggiani confirms that the Tilson case was uppermost in the archbishop's mind. It is therefore strange that the Dublin Diocesan Archives contains no substantial file on the matter, particularly since the same location has abundant material relating to lesser-known issues or controversies. On that note, it should be stated that McQuaid's letter was found only recently and then passed on to the archives. Furthermore, the Tilson marriage file, which should be stored at St Mary's church in Haddington Road where the couple were married, is missing. Contemporary Dáil debate records are silent on the matter, and the papers of John A. Costello, Seán MacBride and George Gavan Duffy are equally mute. Given the international profile of the case, it is inconceivable that a file does not exist somewhere in Ireland's archives or institutions. This raises the suspicion that an individual or organisation was determined to avoid leaving a paper trail and that certain material may have been destroyed.
3. The Frost case in 1945. As discussed in Chapter 5, this case was heard *after* the adoption of the 1937 constitution, which would have allowed the courts to extract similar interpretations of the relevant articles as the courts in the Tilson case. Instead, the Supreme Court in that case upheld the tradition of paternal supremacy and ordered that the children should continue with their Protestant upbringing in accordance with the wishes of the father.
4. Mr Justice Gavan Duffy's decision to hear the Tilson case as the sole judge. As president of the High Court, Gavan Duffy could have chosen to have heard the case with two colleagues; instead, he heard it alone, allowing him exclusive authority to rule in the case without consideration or interference from another judge.
5. The *Schlegel* v. *Corcoran and Gross* and *Cook* v. *Carroll* cases. As discussed in Chapter 7, the judgments handed down in these cases by Gavan Duffy suggest that he was not sufficiently impartial in cases involving religious matters. Some might point out that Gavan Duffy

showed judicial independence regarding these issues in the *McKenna* case of 1947 when he ruled in favour of the Protestant party,[30] but this was arguably a trivial issue, and when matters such as the preservation of the Catholic Church's dominance, or the embedding of the Catholic moral code in civil law was at stake, he ruled in favour of the Catholic party.

6. Ernest Tilson's removal of his three sons from Turner's Cottages to his parents' home in Oldcastle. Since Ernest's right to raise his children as Protestants was the fulcrum on which the case was likely to turn, it is odd that counsel for Mary Tilson did not see fit to question him about this crucial matter. If Ernest's most pressing concern was the religious upbringing of his children, why did they spend six weeks in Oldcastle *before* their formal Protestant education was initiated in the Birds' Nest? It is plausible that counsel for Mary were so sure of victory that they were simply going through the motions in court.

7. The letter, apparently sent by the Irish ambassador to the Holy See, Joseph Walshe, to Archbishop McQuaid after the judgments. Quoted by McQuaid's biographer John Cooney, this letter acknowledged that the 'Gavan Duffy decision' was 'brought about by [McQuaid's] patient and consistent work'. Read alongside McQuaid's letter to Marchetti-Selvaggiani, this suggests that the archbishop took an active role in the case.

And yet despite all these factors we cannot conclude that Gavan Duffy entertained overtures from McQuaid, Costello or anybody else; nor can we conclude that the Supreme Court came under the influence of the clerical or political establishment. Indeed, it may well have been the case that the relationship between the church, state and judiciary was so intertwined, and because many politicians and judges were themselves devout Catholics *and* nationalists, there was an unconscious assimilation of values and principles. In other words, the judgments may be seen as a manifestation of the collective Catholic nationalist conscience that pervaded among many at the time. In this light, a phone call or a tap on the shoulder and a quiet word before the case came before the courts would have been unnecessary.

In terms of the High Court ruling, for example, Gavan Duffy's own religiosity must be considered. His strong Catholic leanings and 'militant Catholicism'[31] were well known, and it is fair to say that he was an obsessive Catholic whose faith went well beyond what was routine for most lay Catholics in mid-twentieth-century Ireland. He was a founding and long-serving member of the Catholic lay organisation An Ríoghacht, which obliged him to 'propagate, promote and effect Catholic social principles in Irish public life'. Moreover, he was also an ardent nationalist, with ambitions to establish a distinctive Irish jurisprudence which departed from that of Britain.

Within this context, would it have been necessary to make overtures to him regarding the case? If nothing else, Archbishop McQuaid was a shrewd individual and would surely have known that approaching him about the matter, and thus calling into question his integrity, ran the risk of insulting the judge and perhaps receiving an unfavourable court decision. The archbishop may very well have decided that the wisest strategy was to stand back and allow the judge to follow his conscience. It is entirely plausible that Gavan Duffy firmly believed that the Catholic moral code or Catholic social teaching should be enshrined in the law of the land and that, by extension, his judgment in the Tilson case reflected that view. It is conceivable that as a Catholic judge in a predominantly Catholic country, he believed he was doing the right thing:

> In my opinion, an order of the Court designed to secure the fulfilment of an agreement, peremptorily required before a 'mixed marriage' by the Church whose special position in Ireland is officially recognised as the guardian of the faith of the Catholic spouse, cannot be withheld on any ground of public policy by the very State which pays homage to that Church.[32]

The same maxims, however, might not be as readily applied to the Supreme Court's ruling. It is plausible that McQuaid succeeded in persuading Charles Casey to represent Mary Tilson, though, given Casey's strong Catholic leanings, that may not have been too difficult. That, however, is likely to have been the extent of McQuaid's influence in that sphere. The Supreme Court may have failed to put more distance between the judiciary and the clerical and political establishments, but it also avoided obfuscating its judgment with references to Catholic teaching and maintained its independence by relying entirely on Article 42.1 of the constitution. In other words, the Supreme Court established a clear and unambiguous (if somewhat narrow) legal basis for its decision and, unlike Gavan Duffy, did not rely on Catholic teaching or ethereal matters.

But if Gavan Duffy was following his Catholic nationalist conscience and the Supreme Court was relying on Article 42.1, how do we explain the grand claims made by McQuaid in his letter to Marchetti-Selvaggiani? The answer might be simple. It is well established that the archbishop enjoyed power and influence and that he liked it to be well known that he had such authority. Was his letter to the Vatican an example of the archbishop exaggerating his importance to his superiors in Rome? Did he use the outcome of the Tilson case in a dissembling manner to enhance his own reputation? The answers to these questions, and many others posed, may finally be answered whenever the Vatican opens *its* file on the Tilson case – if indeed such a file exists.

The personal dimensions of the Tilson case have never been acknowledged by historians or other commentators. Ernest endured years of living alone in exile, while his wife had to face the onerous challenges of raising her four sons as a single mother on a very modest income without state benefits. Their children also experienced difficult times, having to grow to maturity in the absence of their father. Some might point out that Ernest was the author of his own downfall, or that the wounds on his Catholic family were inflicted by an irascible Protestant, but equally one might argue that when his troubles began in 1941 he was in an impossible bind: faced with the moral imperative of marrying his pregnant partner, but compelled to sign an objectionable written agreement issued by a church of which he was not even a member.

The Tilson case has been largely remembered among historians for Gavan Duffy's decision and the strong Catholic undertow of his language in the High Court. But should it be remembered for the couple at the centre of the case who, in 1941, chose to ignore church directives and social mores to marry outside their respective communities? Or for the same couple who later confounded the presuppositions of churches, society, historians and scholars by reconciling and happily living out their days with their sons nearby? David, Alan, Paul and Neville would agree. A Trinity College study – 'History of the Rising in Our Own Words' – has revealed how some people got on with their own lives during the 1916 Rising. One participant, Michael Gorman, has described how his Protestant mother and Catholic father continued to exchange love letters during this period of national trauma. 'They were not on any side,' he explained, 'they were on the "getting on with life" side.'[33]

Therein may lie the true legacy of the Tilson case. Mary and Ernest Tilson were bit players in what became an event of national importance, polarising the Protestant and Catholic communities, but they eventually

Conclusion

patched up their differences and got on with their lives. They survived and endured together, and their children grew to adults and they, in turn, had children of their own. Meanwhile, the narrow and moralistic ideologies of the powerful and self-important elites of the time – the hierarchy, the politicians and the judiciary – have long since been swept away. Blessed indeed are the meek, for they shall inherit the earth.

But a burning question remains as to why the Tilson case has largely faded in the memory of the general public, despite an enduring fascination with the Fethard-on-Sea boycott. Seán and Sheila Cloney, the couple at the centre of that controversy, lived at Dungulph Castle, a restored medieval dwelling on 116 acres. Sheila – the Protestant party – was also seen as a formidable woman who took a stand against the might of the Catholic Church in mid-twentieth-century Ireland. Feminism in Ireland in the 1950s might have been moribund, but could her actions be seen as a challenge to the ideological state pillars of marriage and the family? On the other hand, has the Tilson case been largely forgotten because Mary Tilson was working-class and pregnant, and quietly retreated to the traditional role ascribed to her as mother? Or was it because Ernest Tilson was also working-class and fond of alcohol and did not conform to the stereotypes of Protestants as respectable, upright and thrifty in lifestyle? Was there too much of the devil in the detail and, by extension, was the Tilson case ultimately a discomfort for Irish middle-class society? After all, it's a long way from Dungulph Castle to Turner's Cottages.

Notes

INTRODUCTION

1. Ernest Tilson was a member of the Church of Ireland. When I refer to Protestants, I am referring to members of the Reformed Church. Owing to the limited scope of this book, I do not differentiate between different Protestant denominations.
2. Mary Barnes described her mother in a High Court affidavit as 'a very religious and pious woman' (National Archives of Ireland, HC/1950 State Side 7/Tilson Infants (hereafter cited as NAIT) sworn affidavit, 11 July 1950). This was corroborated by her son Alan and daughter-in-law Judy in an interview with the author on 30 May 2019. Judy was married to Alan's brother Paul (now deceased) who was also placed in the Birds' Nest by his father.
3. John Whyte, 'Church, State and Society: 1950–70', in J.J. Lee (ed.), *Ireland 1945–70* (Dublin: Gill & Macmillan, 1979), pp. 73–82, at p. 80.
4. Olive C. Curran (ed.), *History of the Diocese of Meath 1860–1993*, vol. 2 (Mullingar: Most Rev. Michael Smith, Bishop of Meath, 1995), p. 731.
5. Interview with Oldcastle resident, 19 July 2019.
6. I described to one local resident how I had been to Loughcrew graveyard looking for the Tilson family grave. He responded: 'Ah, you were looking in the wrong place. Loughcrew? The Tilsons wouldn't have been allowed into Loughcrew! They're beside the paupers in Saint Bridget's!' (Interview with Oldcastle resident, 23 July 2019).
7. Interviews with Oldcastle residents, 23 July 2019.
8. Turner's Cottages were situated on Shelbourne Road, opposite where Ballsbridge Motors now stands. Mary Barnes' birth certificate shows her forename as Mary, even though family members always called her Maura.
9. Jeremy Williams, 'Turner, Richard', in James McGuire and James Quinn (eds), *Dictionary of Irish Biography*, vols 1–9 (Cambridge: Cambridge University Press, 2009) (hereafter cited as DIB), at https://www.dib.ie/biography/turner-richard-a8681 (accessed 12 July 2018).
10. 'The Late Mr George J. Crampton', *The Irish Times*, 3 December 1925, p. 4.
11. Turner's Cottages, Pembroke West, 1911 digitised census returns, http://www.census.national archives.ie/ (accessed February 2018).
12. Hugh Oram, 'An Irishman's Diary', *The Irish Times*, 25 April 2014, p. 15. Oram notes that, as Mary Tilson did, 'some of the women worked in the old Swastika Laundry, just across the road from the cottages'.
13. 'Local Government Board Inquiry', *The Irish Times*, 20 February 1913, p. 5.
14. 'Information Refused', *Evening Herald*, 14 April 1936, p. 6.
15. 'Charges of Breaking and Entering: Two sentences', *Irish Independent*, 26 May 1939, p. 11.
16. 'Dublin and District', *Irish Independent*, 2 March 1943, p. 2.
17. Interviews with Alan and Judy Tilson, 14 May 2019 and 30 May 2019.
18. The children were initially taken to Mrs Smyly's Home in Grand Canal Street, Dublin, and then to Mrs Smyly's Birds' Nest in Dún Laoghaire where they were to remain throughout the High Court and Supreme Court hearings.
19. Robbie McVeigh, 'Cherishing the Children of the Nation Unequally: Sectarianism in Ireland', in P. Clancy et al. (eds), *Irish Society: Sociological perspectives* (Dublin: Institute

of Public Administration in association with the Sociological Society of Ireland, 1995), pp. 620–51, at p. 638.
20 Claire Mitchell, *Religion, Identity and Politics in Northern Ireland: Boundaries of belonging and belief* (Aldershot: Ashgate, 2006), p. 3.
21 Jack White, *Minority Report: The Protestant community in the Republic of Ireland* (Dublin: Gill & Macmillan, 1975), p. 129.
22 Gerard Hogan, 'A Fresh Look at Tilson's Case', *Irish Jurist*, vol. 33, 1998, pp. 311–32, at p. 330.
23 Gerard Hogan, 'De Valera, the Constitution and the Historians', *The Irish Jurist*, vol. XL, 2005, pp. 293–6.
24 Marianne Elliott, *When God Took Sides: Religion and identity in Ireland – unfinished history* (Oxford: Oxford University Press, 2009), pp. 230–1.
25 Gerard Hogan, Gerry Whyte, David Kenny and Rachael Walsh (eds), *Kelly: The Irish constitution*, 5th edn (Dublin: Bloomsbury Professional, 2018), 7.9.27, p. 2467.
26 Paul Blanshard, *The Irish and Catholic Power: An American interpretation* (Boston: Beacon Press, 1953), p. 165.
27 James E. Carty, 'The Enforceability of Antenuptial Agreements for the Religious Instruction of Children', *Duke Bar Journal*, vol. 2, no. 1, 1951, pp. 70–89, at p. 81. James E. Carty argues that *Ramon v. Ramon* is the leading decision holding a prenuptial contract for the religious education of children as enforceable.
28 Padraig O'Malley, *The Uncivil Wars: Ireland today* (Belfast: Blackstaff Press, 1983), pp. 65–8.
29 Tim Fanning, *The Fethard-on-Sea Boycott* (Cork: Collins Press, 2010), pp. 68–9.
30 Patsy McGarry, 'Decree Likened to Social Genocide', *The Irish Times*, 9 May 1997, p. 12.
31 *The Irish Reports published under the Control of the Incorporated Council of Law Reporting for Ireland, containing Reports of Cases Argued and Determined by The Court of Appeal, The High Court of Justice, the Court for Crown Cases Reserved, in Ireland and the Irish Land Commission*, ed. William Green (1912), pp. 449–69. Hereafter cited as *IR*.

This dispute began with an interfaith relationship. William Arland Ussher then converted from Protestantism to Catholicism (albeit in unusual circumstances) and married the Catholic Mary Caulfield before the Rev. Joseph Fahy, a local Catholic parish priest. Ussher later took a civil action to obtain a declaration that his marriage to Caulfield was null and void because it had not been performed in accordance with the regulations of the Catholic Church as set out in the Council of Trent's *Tametsi* decree. In other words, his case was taken on the basis of an irregularity of canonical form; he argued that the validity of the marriage depended on whether or not it was considered to be so by the Catholic Church. The judge referred to *Tametsi* and *Ne Temere* and decided that neither decree had any standing in civil law. For a more comprehensive account, see David Jameson, 'The Religious Upbringing of Children in Mixed Marriages: The evolution of Irish law', *New Hibernia Review*, vol. 18, no. 2, 2014, pp. 65–83.
32 Kurt Bowen, *Protestants in a Catholic State: Ireland's privileged minority* (Kingston, Canada: McGill-Queen's University Press, 1983), p. 43.
33 Robin Bury, *Buried Lives: The Protestants of southern Ireland* (Dublin: History Press Ireland, 2017), p. 122.
34 Terence Brown, *The Irish Times: 150 years of influence* (London: Bloomsbury, 2015), p. 201.
35 *Jubilaeum Maximum* (26 May 1949) was the papal bull of Pope Pius XII announcing a Holy Year for 1950.
36 Although the attorney general, Charles Casey, appeared for Mary Tilson, to this day no law prohibits an attorney general from maintaining a private practice. See Alan Shatter's insightful article, 'Attorney General Should Not Maintain a Private Practice', *The Irish Times*, 6 October 2021, p. 10.

CHAPTER 1. **Historical Antecedents: Mixed-marriage disputes in Ireland**

1. Justine McCarthy, 'Interview with Geraldine Finucane: Breaking the glass ceiling', *Magill*, 10 January 2007, at magill.ie/archive/ (accessed February 2022).
2. Interview with John Finucane, 8 August 2018.
3. When referring to 'intermarriage', 'interchurch' or 'interfaith' relationships the author generally uses the stylistically convenient term 'mixed marriage'. This derives from the ecclesiastical term *matrimonia mixta*.
4. William Fanning, 'Mixed Marriage', in *The Catholic Encyclopedia*, vol. 9 (New York: Robert Appleton Company, 1910), http://www.newadvent.org/cathen/09698a.htm (accessed 23 April 2018).
5. Daithí Ó Corráin, *Rendering to God and Caesar: The Irish churches and the two states in Ireland, 1949–73* (Manchester: Manchester University Press, 2006), p. 185.
6. Louise Fuller, *Irish Catholicism since 1950: The undoing of a culture* (Dublin: Gill & Macmillan, 2002), p. 17.
7. 'Mixed Marriage Dangers: Church's attitude', *Irish Independent*, 20 December 1937, p. 7.
8. 'Evils of Mixed Marriages', *Strabane Chronicle*, 21 June 1941, p. 4.
9. Colin Barr and Daithí Ó Corráin, 'Catholic Ireland, 1740–2016', in Eugenio F. Biagini and Mary E. Daly (eds), *The Cambridge Social History of Modern Ireland* (Cambridge: Cambridge University Press, 2017), pp. 68–87, at p. 80.
10. 'A Bishop on Marriage', *Western People*, 8 March 1941, p. 8.
11. 'Archbishop Re-Affirms T.C.D. Ban', *The Irish Times*, 21 February 1944, p. 7. McQuaid continuously railed against mixed marriages in his Lenten pastorals throughout the 1940s and '50s.
12. 'Instruction Concerning Mixed Marriages', issued by John Charles McQuaid, archbishop of Dublin, primate of Ireland, 20 April 1966. This document is marked: 'Confidential: for the Clergy only'. From the papers of Father Aidan Lehane CSSp.
13. 'Class notes of Monsignor Frank Cremin, St Patrick's College, Maynooth (1950s)', from the papers of Father Aidan Lehane CSSp. Cremin was professor of moral and dogmatic theology and of canon law at St Patrick's College, Maynooth between 1939 and 1980.
14. Owen Dudley Edwards, *The Sins of Our Fathers: Roots of conflict in Northern Ireland* (Dublin: Gill & Macmillan, 1970), pp. 193, 196.
15. 'Mixed Marriages Condemned', *The Irish Times*, 1 November 1943, p. 3.
16. Donald Harman Akenson, *Small Differences: Irish Catholics and Irish Protestants, 1815–1922: An international perspective* (Kingston and Montreal: McGill-Queen's University Press, 1988), p. 115.
17. Valerie Morgan, Marie Smyth, Gillian Robinson and Grace Fraser, *Mixed Marriages in Northern Ireland: Institutional responses* (Centre for the Study of Conflict, Coleraine: University of Ulster Press, 1996), p. 9.
18. 'Primate Urges Prevention of Mixed Marriages', *The Irish Times*, 11 May 1946, p. 13.
19. Ibid.
20. Interview with Margaret MacCurtain, 12 March 2012.
21. Joseph Ruane, 'Comparing Protestant–Catholic Conflict in France and Ireland: The significance of the ethnic and colonial dimension', in John Wolffe (ed.), *Irish Religious Conflict in Comparative Perspective: Catholics, Protestants and Muslims* (London: Palgrave Macmillan, 2014), pp. 146–63, at p. 157.
22. Many Protestants did participate in Gaelic games; see Ida Milne's essay '"The jersey is all that matters, not your church": Protestants and the GAA in the rural republic', in Ian d'Alton and Ida Milne (eds), *Protestant and Irish: The minority's search for place in independent Ireland* (Cork: Cork University Press, 2019), pp. 171–90.

23 Ruane, 'Comparing Protestant–Catholic Conflict in France and Ireland', p. 157.
24 Ibid., pp. 156–7.
25 Robbie McVeigh, 'Cherishing the Children of the Nation Unequally', in Patrick Clancy et al. (eds), *Irish Society: Sociological perspectives*, pp. 620–51, at p. 639.
26 Mary Douglas, *Purity and Danger: An analysis of the concepts of pollution and taboo* (London: Kegan Paul, 1966, this edition 2002), pp. 122–4. Cited in John Fulton, *The Tragedy of Belief: Division, politics and religion in Ireland* (Oxford: Clarendon Press, 1991), p. 198.
27 R.F. Foster, *W.B. Yeats: A life II. The arch poet* (Oxford: Oxford University Press, 2003), pp. 618–19.
28 Alan Ford, 'Living Together, Living Apart: Sectarianism in early modern Ireland', in Alan Ford and John McCafferty (eds), *The Origins of Sectarianism in Early Modern Ireland* (Cambridge: Cambridge University Press, 2005), pp. 1–23, at p. 6.
29 Joseph Ruane and Jennifer Todd, *The Dynamics of Conflict in Northern Ireland: Power, Conflict and Emancipation* (Cambridge: Cambridge University Press, 1996), p. 22.
30 Ibid., p. 33.
31 Patrick MacGill, *Helen Spenser* (London: Herbert Jenkins Ltd., 1937), p. 55.
32 Ibid.
33 See Peter Hart, *The IRA at War, 1916–23* (Oxford: Oxford University Press, 2005), pp. 240–6.
34 'Court Story of a Mixed Marriage', *The Irish Times*, 10 January 1931, p. 9. *Irish Times* emphasis.
35 Ibid.
36 Interview with Alan Tilson, 11 June 2019. See also Ian d'Alton's observations on imputing sectarian motives on complex situations in '"No Country"? Protestant "belongings" in independent Ireland, 1922–49', in d'Alton and Milne (eds), *Protestant and Irish*, pp. 19–33, at pp. 23–4.
37 'Boycotting in County Cork. Alarming State of Affairs. Two Girls Abducted. Labourers Cottage Burned. Outrage at Protestant Church', *Daily Express*, 4 October 1911, p. 4.
38 'The Kilmurry Outrages', *Southern Star*, 21 October 1911, p. 2.
39 'Amusing Proceedings', *Southern Star*, 25 November 1911, p. 6.
40 'Boycott of Protestant Farmers. McCann Case Recalled. Extraordinary State of Affairs in County Cork', *The Irish Times*, 7 October 1911, p. 12.
41 'Kilmurry Scandal. Important Development. Another Outrage', *Cork Constitution*, 17 October 1911, p. 5.
42 'Alleged McCann Case in the South. Religion of Two Children. Facts of the Case', *The Irish Times*, 21 October 1911, p. 14.
43 Jonathan Shorten, 1911 digitised census returns, at http://www.census.nationalarchives.ie/ (accessed 13 March 2018).
44 The Eighty Club was a political gentlemen's club aligned with the British Liberal Party and boasted H.H. Asquith as its first secretary and David Lloyd George as a one-time president. Apparently, the club had sent a delegation to Ireland around this time to assess the possible impacts of home rule.
45 *Cork Examiner*, 9 October 1911, p. 4. At the parliamentary election held in 1880, Canon John O'Mahony came to widespread attention as a supporter of Charles Stewart Parnell. However, after William O'Shea divorced his wife following her adultery with Parnell, O'Mahony vociferously turned against him (C.J. Woods, 'O'Mahony, John', *DIB*, https://www.dib.ie/biography/omahony-john-a6879 (accessed 22 June 2018)).
46 *Cork Examiner*, 9 October 1911, p. 4.
47 'Portadown Mixed Marriage Case: A mother's allegations', *The Irish Times*, 2 November 1912, p. 6.
48 'Mother and Child: Charge against a nurse', *Belfast Evening Telegraph*, 28 October 1912, p. 5, *Evening Telegraph* emphasis.

49 'Mixed Marriages: Extraordinary allegations', *The Irish Times*, 22 November 1911, p. 10. David Boyd; Joseph Edward McKee, 1911 digitised census returns, http://www.census.nationalarchives.ie/ (accessed 13 March 2018). The household return form shows that McKee was employed at Boyd's drapery in Castleblayney, County Monaghan. David Boyd, the owner, is listed as a Presbyterian.
50 'County Monaghan Mixed Marriage Case: Husband's admission', *The Irish Times*, 27 January 1912, p. 5.
51 'Sequel to a Mixed Marriage', *The Irish Times*, 11 March 1912, p. 8.
52 'A Kidnapped Husband Who "Got Tired" of His Own Wife', *Ulster Herald*, 27 January 1912, p. 7.
53 James Harkins, General Register Office, digitised civil records at https://civilrecords.irishgenealogy.ie/ (accessed February 2018). Harkins' death certificate shows that he died on 27 October 1911 in Clonmel Workhouse. The cause of death is listed as 'scirrhus of stomach'.
54 'Workhouse Inmate's Religion: Remarkable case at Clonmel', *Cork Examiner*, 31 October 1911, p. 9.
55 Ibid.
56 'Regulations for the Archdiocese of Dublin', *Irish Independent*, 5 March 1962, p. 8.
57 'Daughter's Evidence in Suit To Have Will Established', *The Irish Times*, 20 November 1953, p. 8.
58 'Court Order for Will Suit Costs', *The Irish Times*, 28 November 1953, p. 11.
59 Interview with Oldcastle resident, 11 August 2019.
60 Rosemary Harris, *Prejudice and Tolerance in Ulster: A study of neighbours and 'strangers' in a border community* (Manchester: Manchester University Press, 1972), pp. ix, 143–9. Harris' study focuses on the small Northern Ireland village of 'Ballybeg'. Ballybeg was a pseudonym to disguise the identity of the place and the inhabitants.
61 Ian d'Alton, panel discussion after Roy Foster's paper 'Staying On or Staying Put', West Cork History Festival, 7 August 2021, at https://westcorkhistoryfestival.org/roy-foster-partition-and-left-overness/ (accessed 1 March 2022).
62 See Catherine O'Connor, '"My Mother wouldn't have been as hurt": Women and interchurch marriage in Wexford, 1945–65', in d'Alton and Milne (eds), *Protestant and Irish*, pp. 229–45, at p. 244.
63 Roy Foster, 'Staying On or Staying Put', paper presented at the West Cork History Festival, 7 August 2021. During the course of my research over the past twelve years, I have identified over eighty mixed-marriage disputes which occurred in Ireland, north and south, in the nineteenth and twentieth centuries.

CHAPTER 2. *Ne Temere*, the 'Promises' and the Dispensation
1 NAIT, sworn affidavit by Father Brendan Harley, 13 July 1950.
2 Ibid.
3 See Robin Bury's tendentiously titled chapter 'Grabbing the Children' in *Buried Lives: The Protestants of southern Ireland* (Dublin: History Press Ireland, 2017), pp. 120–37.
4 'Ne Temere', *The Irish Times*, 29 July 1950, p. 7.
5 'Ne Temere', *The Irish Times*, 17 August 1950, p. 5.
6 'Attorney General on Teaching of Church', *Irish Independent*, 14 February 1951, p. 7.
7 'Mixed Marriages and "Ne Temere"', *The Irish Times*, 6 January 2014, p. 15. Dr Ken Dunn argued that 'Ne Temere was applied enthusiastically by both clergy and politicians ... and marriages of long standing were broken up'.
8 Jonathan Bardon, *A History of Ulster* (Belfast: Blackstaff, 1992), p. 406; Mitchell, *Religion, Identity*, p. 16.

9 Alan Megahey, '"God will defend the right": The Protestant Churches and opposition to home rule', in D. George Boyce and Alan O'Day (eds), *Defenders of the Union* (London: Routledge, 2001), pp. 159–75, at p. 166.
10 Declan Kiberd, *Inventing Ireland: The literature of a modern nation* (London: Vintage, 1996), p. 421.
11 Thomas Bartlett, *Ireland: A history* (Cambridge: Cambridge University Press, 2010), p. 373.
12 F.S.L. Lyons, *Culture and Anarchy in Ireland 1890–1939* (Oxford: Clarendon Press, 1979), p. 144.
13 Patrick J. Corish, 'Catholic Marriage under the Penal Code', in Art Cosgrove (ed.), *Marriage in Ireland* (Dublin: College Press, 1985), pp. 67–77, at p. 73.
14 John Fulton, *The Tragedy of Belief: Division, politics and religion in Ireland* (Oxford: Clarendon Press, 1991), p. 205.
15 Gerald O'Donovan, *Waiting* (London: Macmillan & Co. Ltd., 1914), p. 188. O'Donovan was well qualified to depict the problems surrounding mixed marriages in his fiction. At the age of eighteen he entered the seminary at Maynooth and, after his ordination, was appointed as curate to a parish in County Galway. However, he left the priesthood in 1904 and later entered a mixed marriage himself when he married Beryl Verschoyle, a daughter of an Irish Protestant colonel.
16 'The New Legislation of the Catholic Church on the Betrothals & Marriage. Decree of the Sacred Congregation of the Council, Approved and Confirmed by His Holiness Pope Pius X', authorised translation (Dublin: Browne & Nolan Ltd., 1907), p. 7.
17 Ó Corráin, *Rendering to God and Caesar*, p. 185.
18 Michael Hurley, 'Mixed Marriages', *The Furrow*, vol. 17, no. 5, 1966, pp. 279–87, at p. 279.
19 'Mixed Marriages', *The Irish Times*, 8 February 1911, pp. 7–8.
20 *Church of Ireland Gazette*, 18 August 1950, p. 5.
21 Andrew Scholes, *The Church of Ireland and the Third Home Rule Bill* (Dublin: Irish Academic Press, 2010), p. 19.
22 'House of Commons; Debate on the Address; The Mixed Marriage Scandal', *Belfast Newsletter*, 8 February 1911, p. 8.
23 'Mixed Marriages in Ireland', 7 February 1911, *Hansard Parliamentary Debates*, 5th series, vol. 21, cc. 145–214.
24 'Mixed Marriages: The McCann case', *The Irish Times*, 1 March 1911, p. 7.
25 Scholes, *The Church of Ireland*, pp. 19–21.
26 Ian Ellis, *Vision and Reality: A survey of twentieth-century Irish inter-church relations* (Belfast: Institute of Irish Studies, Queen's University Belfast, 1992), p. 5.
27 Right Rev. C.F. D'Arcy, 'The Religious Difficulty under Home Rule: The church view', in S. Rosenbaum (ed.), *Against Home Rule: The case for the union* (Washington: Kennikat Press, 1912, this edition 1970), pp. 204–11, at p. 207.
28 Ibid., p. 206.
29 Bartlett, *Ireland: A history*, p. 373.
30 House of Commons Parliamentary Papers, vol. 46, cc. 611–12, 2 January 1913.
31 Desmond Bowen, *History and the Shaping of Irish Protestantism* (New York: Peter Lang, 1995), p. 373.
32 Paul Bew, *Ideology and the Irish Question: Ulster unionism and Ulster nationalism* (Oxford: Clarendon Press, 1994), p. 34.
33 'Mixed Marriages and the Papal Decree', *Church of Ireland Gazette*, 1 May 1908, p. 385.
34 'The "Ne Temere" Decree: Great Protest Meeting in Dublin', *Church of Ireland Gazette*, 3 February 1911, p. 105.
35 Ó Corráin, *Rendering to God and Caesar*, p. 13.

36 Rev. J.A.F. Gregg, 'The *Ne Temere* Decree. A Lecture Delivered before the Members of the Church of Ireland Cork Young Men's Association on 17 March 1911' (Dublin: Association for Promoting Christian Knowledge, 1911), p. 23.
37 Ibid., p. 10.
38 'Mixed Marriages – A Menace to the Church: Dr Gregg's address', *The Irish Times*, 10 November 1926, p. 5.
39 'Primate Urges Prevention of Mixed Marriages', *The Irish Times*, 11 May 1946, p. 13. Gregg also denounced *Ne Temere* at general synods in 1926 and 1951.
40 Hubert Butler, *Escape from the Anthill* (Mullingar: Lilliput Press, 1985), p. 138.
41 T. Lincoln Bouscaren, Adam C. Ellis and Francis N. Korth, *Canon Law: A text and commentary* (Milwaukee: Bruce, 1963), p. 522.
42 Edward Schillebeeckx, *Marriage: Secular reality and saving mystery. Vol. 2: Marriage in the history of the church*, trans. N.D. Smith (London: Sheed & Ward, 1965), p. 95.
43 Bouscaren et al., *Canon Law*, p. 523.
44 Ibid., p. 524.
45 Oliver P. Rafferty, *Catholicism in Ulster 1603–1983: An interpretative history* (London: Hurst, 1994), p. 140; Pope Benedict XIV, 'Magnae Nobis: Marriage impediments and dispensations', in Papal Encyclicals Online at https://www.papalencyclicals.net/ben14/b14magna.htm (accessed 8 November 2010).
46 Brian O'Higgins, 'Mixed Marriages: The "cautiones"', *Irish Theological Quarterly*, vol. 41, no. 3, 1974, pp. 205–21, at p. 216.
47 Brian O'Higgins, 'Mixed Marriages: The "cautiones II"', *Irish Theological Quarterly*, vol. 41, no. 4, 1974, pp. 274–88, at p. 285.
48 *IR*, R.A. Harrison (ed.), 1951, p. 16.
49 NAIT, sworn affidavit by Ernest Tilson, 19 June 1950.
50 Gerard Hogan, 'Law and Religion: Church–state relations in Ireland from independence to the present day', *The American Journal of Comparative Law*, vol. 35, no. 1, 1987, pp. 47–96, at pp. 59–60.
51 Hogan, 'A Fresh Look at Tilson's Case', p. 331.
52 M.E. Francis, *Dark Rosaleen* (New York: Kennedy, 1917), p. 238.
53 Ibid., p. 243.
54 Ibid., p. 347.
55 Barry Keane, Letters to the Editor, 'Mixed Marriages and "Ne Temere"', *The Irish Times*, 13 January 2014, p. 11.
56 Ó Corráin, *Rendering to God and Caesar*, p. 184.
57 Charles Townshend, *The Partition: Ireland divided, 1885–1925* (London: Allen Lane, 2021), p. 61.

CHAPTER 3. The Birds' Nest

1 Interview with Judy Tilson, 30 May 2019. While Mary Tilson's sister Lily passed on this version of events to Judy, Ernest Tilson offered a marginally different account in his affidavit to the High Court. There was also some debate in the courts about whether the children were admitted to Mrs Smyly's Homes on 13 May or 15 May 1950.
2 Deirdre Bryan, 'Smyly, Ellen', *DIB* at https://www.dib.ie/biography/smyly-ellen-a8165 (accessed 23 February 2018).
3 Ibid.
4 Vivienne Smyly, 'The Early History of Mrs. Smyly's Homes and Schools' (private publication, 1976). Vivienne Smyly was a granddaughter of Ellen Smyly.

Notes to pages 51 to 55

5 Ragged schools were common in Dublin from around the 1850s. Organisers recognised that many destitute children became involved in crime, and the schools were intended to dissuade children from criminal activities by offering them shelter and education.
6 *Erin's Hope*, March 1952.
7 Maria Luddy, *Women and Philanthropy in Nineteenth-century Ireland* (Cambridge: Cambridge University Press, 1995), p. 81.
8 Dún Laoghaire was then known as Kingstown. Miriam Moffitt describes how Mrs Whately and her daughter worked together, with Mrs Whately raising funds for the Mission Church in 1853 and her daughter sourcing funds for the Townsend Street ragged school. Miriam Moffitt, *The Society for Irish Church Missions to the Roman Catholics 1849–1950* (Manchester: Manchester University Press, 2010), p. 80.
9 'The Birds' Nest and Ragged Schools, Kingstown', *Belfast News Letter*, 9 June 1860, p. 2.
10 Ibid.
11 Ibid.
12 Douglas Bennett, *The Encyclopaedia of Dublin* (Dublin: Gill & Macmillan, 2005), p. 248.
13 'The Irish Church Missions – The Birds' Nest', *Cork Examiner*, 24 February 1864, p. 3.
14 'Birds' Nest Jubilee', *The Irish Times*, 6 February 1909, p. 5.
15 Moffitt, *The Society for Irish Church Missions*, p. 255.
16 George D. Williams, *Dublin Charities: A handbook including organisations in, or applicable to, Ireland* (Dublin: Association of Charities, 1902), 1903 edition cited in *Mother and Baby Homes Commission of Investigation Final Report*, 30 October 2020, 3.36.17.
17 1901 and 1911 digitised census returns, 19 York Street (1901), 19 York Road, Kingstown no. 1 (1911), http://www.census.nationalarchives.ie/ (accessed 4 April 2018).
18 *Erin's Hope*, August 1900, June 1952.
19 'Father Colohan and the Birds' Nest', *Evening Herald*, 19 November 1894, p. 4. Apparently Colohan had delivered his incendiary sermon on 11 November 1894.
20 Moffitt, *The Society for Irish Church Missions*, p. 116.
21 'Father Colahan's Sermon and "The Birds' Nest"', *Evening Herald*, 15 November 1894, p. 4.
22 Bryan, 'Smyly, Ellen', *DIB*.
23 Smyly Trust Services, Blackrock, County Dublin, at http://smylytrust.com/ (accessed 24 May 2018).
24 'The Birds' Nest; Deputation to the Kingstown Commissioners', *The Irish Times*, 4 December 1883, p. 6. Henry Fishe, 1901 digitised census returns, at http://www.census.nationalarchives.ie/ (accessed 12 March 2018). The household return form shows that Fishe was vicar of St Paul's church, Glenageary, County Dublin in 1901.
25 J.H. Whyte, *Church and State in Modern Ireland 1923–1970* (Dublin: Gill & Macmillan, 1971), p. 191n.
26 Moffitt, *The Society for Irish Church Missions*, p. 121.
27 'The Birds' Nest Again!', *The Freeman's Journal*, 4 May 1863, p. 4.
28 'The Cross and After; The Five per cent – 3', *The Irish Times*, 24 March 1965, p. 10.
29 James Joyce, *Ulysses* (London: The Bodley Head, 1986, this edition, 2002), p. 148.
30 Mary McAuliffe, 'Introduction', in Frances Taylor, *Irish Homes and Irish Hearts* (Dublin: UCD Press, 2013), p. xviii.
31 Taylor, *Irish Homes and Irish Hearts*, p. 94.
32 *Cork Examiner*, 15 April 1862, p. 2
33 *Cork Examiner*, 11 February 1864, p. 2.
34 'The Birds' Nest; Deputation to the Kingstown Commissioners', *The Irish Times*, 4 December 1883, p. 6.

35 Letter from Bishop James Staunton to Archbishop John Charles McQuaid, 25 January 1952. Papers of John Charles McQuaid, Dublin Diocesan Archives, XVIII/12/30.
36 Luddy, *Women and Philanthropy in Nineteenth-century Ireland*, pp. 77–8.
37 *The Irish Times*, 6 February 1909, p. 5.
38 Smyly, *Early History*, p. 16.
39 Bryan, 'Smyly, Ellen', *DIB*.
40 John Giff, General Register Office, digitised civil/church records, at https://civilrecords.irishgenealogy.ie/churchrecords/images/marriage_returns/marriages_1894/10550/5842896.pdf (accessed 1 June 2018).
41 *Clergy of Meath and Kildare, biographical successions list*, compiled by J.B. Leslie and updated by W.J.R. Wallace (Dublin: Columba Press, 2004), p. 491.
42 'Charged with Neglect of Children', *The Irish Times*, 14 October 1950, p. 3.
43 Irish Church Missions archive (hereafter cited as ICM, Tilson file).
44 Mrs Smyly's Homes archive (hereafter cited as MSH, Tilson file).
45 ICM, Tilson file. Author's emphasis.
46 NAIT, sworn affidavit by Mary Tilson, 17 May 1950.
47 Ibid.
48 Interview with Judy Tilson, 10 April 2019.
49 Interviews with Oldcastle residents, 10 July 2019.
50 Letter from Mabel Bird to T.G. McVeagh, 8 June 1950, MSH, Tilson file.
51 Interview with Alan Tilson, 3 April 2019.
52 NAIT, sworn affidavit by Ernest Tilson, 19 June 1950.
53 NAIT, sworn affidavit by Mary Tilson, 17 May 1950.
54 NAIT, sworn affidavit by Ernest Tilson, 19 June 1950.
55 NAIT, sworn affidavit by Ernest Tilson, 21 July 1950.
56 MSH, Tilson file, letter from Mabel Bird to Ernest Tilson, 20 June 1950.
57 MSH, Tilson file. Desmond de Courcy Wheeler MB, of Monkstown Castle, Monkstown, County Dublin was medical adviser to Mrs Smyly's Homes at the time, *Erin's Hope*, March 1948.
58 'Children's Religion: An issue in Dublin parents dispute', *Irish Independent*, 4 July 1950, p. 8.
59 MSH, Tilson file.
60 Ibid.
61 MSH, Tilson file. Letter from Bird to C.F. Kenny, Clonskeagh, Dublin, 24 November 1950. Author's emphasis. A handwritten note at the end of the letter reveals that Kenny had called to the Birds' Nest after the matter had been decided in the courts and had said that 'he considered this "proselytising"'.
62 *Erin's Hope*, June 1952.
63 *Erin's Hope*, June 1944.
64 NAIT, sworn affidavit by Francis T. Russell, 19 June 1950.
65 NAIT, sworn affidavit by Mary Tilson, 17 May 1950.
66 MSH, Tilson file, letter from T.G. McVeagh to Francis T. Russell, 17 June 1950.
67 NAIT, sworn affidavit by Francis T. Russell, 19 June 1950.
68 MSH, Tilson file, letter from Mabel Bird to Miss Holt, 17 May 1950.
69 MSH, Tilson file, High Court order contained therein dated 18 May 1950.
70 MSH, Tilson file, letter from Mabel Bird to T.G. McVeagh.
71 MSH, Tilson file, letter from T.G. McVeagh to George C. McGrath, 18 July 1950.
72 MSH, Tilson file, letter from Mabel Bird to T.G. McVeagh, 8 June 1950.
73 'Hollywood cake' was apparently sold by the Hollywood Bakery in Meath Street, Dublin in the 1940s and '50s.
74 Tilson family scrapbook.

75 Interview with Alan Tilson, 3 April 2019.
76 Interview with Judy Tilson, 10 April 2019.

CHAPTER 4. The Catholic Ethos and the Church/State Consensus
1 Fuller, *Irish Catholicism since 1950*, p. 19.
2 Brian Moore, *The Feast of Lupercal* (London: André Deutsch, 1958), p. 144.
3 Tom Garvin, *Preventing the Future: Why was Ireland so poor for so long?* (Dublin: Gill & Macmillan, 2004), p. 8.
4 Fearghal McGarry, 'Independent Ireland', in Richard Bourke and Ian McBride (eds), *The Princeton History of Modern Ireland* (Princeton: Princeton University Press, 2016), pp. 109–40, at p. 127.
5 Whyte, *Church and State*, p. 7.
6 Garvin, *Preventing the Future*, p. 3.
7 Bryan Fanning, *Racism and Social Change in the Republic of Ireland* (Manchester: Manchester University Press, 2002), p. 37.
8 'No Divorce in Free State', *The Irish Times*, 21 February 1925.
9 Michael Laffan, *The Partition of Ireland: 1911–1922* (Dublin: Dundalgan Press, 1983, this edition 1987), p. 117.
10 Tom Inglis, *Moral Monopoly: The Catholic Church in modern Irish society* (Dublin: Gill & Macmillan, 1987), p. 74.
11 Whyte, *Church and State*, p. 158.
12 Ibid.
13 Dermot Keogh, 'Ireland, the Vatican and the Cold War: the case of Italy, 1948', Irish Studies in International Affairs, vol. 3, no. 3, 1991, pp. 67–114, at p. 76.
14 Ibid., p. 77.
15 David McCullagh, *A Makeshift Majority: The first inter-party government, 1948–51* (Dublin: Institute of Public Administration, 1998), pp. 191–2.
16 Evelyn Bolster, *The Knights of Saint Columbanus* (Dublin: Gill & Macmillan, 1979), p. 34.
17 Ibid., p. 84.
18 Michael O'Leary, 'Corish, Brendan', DIB, at https://www.dib.ie/biography/corish-brendan-a2046 (accessed 29 May 2021).
19 Lawrence William White, 'Norton, William', DIB, at https://www.dib.ie/biography/norton-william-joseph-bill-a6239 (accessed 29 May 2021).
20 Ronan Fanning, 'Mulcahy, Richard', DIB, at https://www.dib.ie/biography/mulcahy-richard-a6029 (accessed 29 May 2021).
21 Pauric J. Dempsey, 'Blowick, Joseph', DIB, at https://www.dib.ie/biography/blowick-joseph-a0750 (accessed 29 May 2021).
22 Diarmaid Ferriter, 'Keyes, Michael', DIB, at https://www.dib.ie/biography/keyes-michael-john-a4532 (accessed 29 May 2021). The Irish Christian Front was a Catholic and anti-communist organisation co-founded by Patrick Belton, a veteran of the 1916 Rising. Although founded to raise funds for the nationalist side in the Spanish Civil War, it soon developed its own political agendas, usually opposing the Irish government of the time.
23 Maurice Manning, 'Dillon, James', DIB, at https://www.dib.ie/biography/dillon-james-mathew-a2602 (accessed 29 May 2021). The Ancient Order of Hibernians is an Irish Catholic organisation open to male Catholics only. It was founded at the end of the nineteenth century in response to the Protestant Orange Order.
24 Alvin Jackson, *Ireland 1798–1998: Politics and war* (Oxford: Blackwell Publishing, 1999, this edition 2003), pp. 306–7.
25 Bartlett, *Ireland: A history*, p. 475.
26 Jackson, *Ireland 1798–1998*, p. 312.

27 'Public Life in State of Decadence – Mr. MacBride', *Irish Independent*, 12 January 1948, p. 6.
28 Elizabeth Keane, *Seán MacBride: A life* (Dublin: Gill & Macmillan, 2007), p. 187.
29 Diarmaid Ferriter, *The Transformation of Ireland 1900–2000* (London: Profile Books, 2004), p. 512.
30 McCullagh, *A Makeshift Majority*, p. 200.
31 T.A. Finlay, 'Lavery, Cecil Patrick Linton', *DIB*, at https://www.dib.ie/biography/lavery-cecil-patrick-linton-a4699 (accessed 23 November 2018).
32 'Attorney-General on Teaching of Church', *Irish Independent*, 14 February 1951, p. 7.
33 J.J. Lee, *Ireland 1912–1985: Politics and society* (Cambridge: Cambridge University Press, 1989, this edition 2006), p. 316. Regarding reviving Fianna Fáil's proposed 1947 Health Act, Lee notes that Noël Browne met three bishops, including McQuaid, in October 1950.
34 Keogh, *Twentieth-century Ireland*, p. 216.
35 Henry Patterson, *Ireland Since 1939: The persistence of conflict* (Dublin, Penguin Books, 2007), p. 92.
36 Keogh, *Twentieth-century Ireland*, p. 215.
37 Patterson, *Ireland Since 1939*, p. 92.
38 Ronan Fanning, *Independent Ireland* (Dublin: Helicon Ltd., 1983), p. 185.
39 Diarmaid Ferriter, 'Everett, James', *DIB*, at https://www.dib.ie/biography/everett-james-a2970 (accessed 30 May 2021).
40 '12,000 Pilgrims for Rome', *Irish Press*, 31 March 1950, p. 3.
41 Dermot Keogh, *Ireland and the Vatican: The politics and diplomacy of church–state relations 1922–1960* (Cork: Cork University Press, 1995), p. 317.
42 'A Visit to Rome', *Munster Express*, 19 May, 1950, p. 8.
43 Keogh, *Ireland and the Vatican*, p. 315.
44 'Gift for the Holy Father', *Westmeath Independent*, 4 March 1950, p. 4.
45 'Cruiskeen Lawn', *The Irish Times*, 15 March 1950, p. 4, *Irish Times* emphasis.
46 'Cross Carried in Relays', *The Irish Times*, 10 July 1950, p. 5.
47 'Mantillas for Pilgrims to Rome during Holy Year Celebrations', Brown Thomas department store advertisement, *Irish Independent*, 11 January 1950, p. 10.
48 'Lenten Pastoral: Most Rev. Dr. Fogarty on Holy Year indulgence', *Nenagh Guardian*, 25 February 1950, p. 3.
49 'Instructions for Jubilee Indulgence', *The Irish Times*, 18 January 1950, p. 7.
50 Noël Browne, *Against the Tide* (Dublin: Gill & Macmillan, 1986), p. 145.
51 Ibid., p. 316.
52 'General Sean MacEoin', *Evening Echo*, 25 October 1950, p. 2.
53 NAI, DFA/24/66/1 B.
54 John Cooney, *John Charles McQuaid: Ruler of Catholic Ireland* (Dublin: O'Brien Press, 1999), p. 245.
55 Keogh, *Ireland and the Vatican*, pp. 320–1.
56 Bowen, *Protestants in a Catholic State*, p. 195.
57 Ó Corráin, *Rendering to God and Caesar*, pp. 20–1.
58 Ferriter, *The Transformation of Ireland*, p. 582.
59 Caleb Wood Richardson, *Smyllie's Ireland: Protestants, independence, and the man who ran the Irish Times* (Indiana: Indiana University Press, 2019), p. 6.
60 Deirdre Nuttall, *Different and the Same: A folk history of the Protestants of independent Ireland* (Dublin: Eastwood Books, 2020), pp. 263–4. Other illuminating accounts are provided by the same author in 'Count Us in Too: Wanting to be heard in independent Ireland', in d'Alton and Milne (eds), *Protestant and Irish*, pp. 82–98.
61 Interview with Judy Tilson, 22 April 2021. For analysis of the contrasting narratives of

the experience of southern Protestants since independence, see Joseph Ruane, 'Ireland's Mysterious Minority', in d'Alton and Milne (eds), *Protestant and Irish*, pp. 283–302.
62 Ian d'Alton, '"No Country"? Protestant "Belongings"', in d'Alton and Milne (eds), *Protestant and Irish*, pp. 19–33, at p. 27.
63 Andrew R. Holmes and Eugenio F. Biagini, 'Protestants', in Biagini and Daly (eds), *The Cambridge Social History of Modern Ireland*, pp. 88–111, at p. 106.

CHAPTER 5. Paternal Supremacy and the Irish Courts

1 In the cases dealt with before 1922, the 'state' refers to the British state under which Ireland was governed; thereafter, 'the state' refers to either the Irish Free State or the Republic of Ireland.
2 J.M. Kelly, *Fundamental Rights in the Irish Law and Constitution*, 2nd edn (Dublin: Allen Figgis & Co. Ltd., 1967), p. 221.
3 Raymond Byrne, J. Paul McCutcheon with Claire Bruton and Gerard Coffey (eds), *The Irish Legal System*, 6th edn (Dublin: Bloomsbury, 2009), p. 475.
4 Ibid., p. 476.
5 Tanya Ní Mhuirthile, Catherine O'Sullivan and Liam Thornton (eds), *Fundamentals of the Irish Legal System: Law, policy and politics* (Dublin: Round Hall, 2016), pp. 165–80.
6 Ibid., pp. 179–80.
7 Anne Crone, *Bridie Steen* (London: William Heinemann, 1949), p. 231.
8 'Court of Chancery: In re Meades Minors', *The Irish Times*, 13 January 1871, p. 4.
9 *IR*, John William Carleton (ed.) (1870–1), vol. V, pp. 98–139.
10 'Law Intelligence, Court of Chancery', *The Irish Times*, 24 December 1870, p. 2. This was outlined in court by Isaac Butt, counsel for Mary Ronayne.
11 *IR* (1870–1), vol. V, p. 103.
12 *IR*, William Green (ed.) (1902), vol. II, pp. 685–95.
13 'Religion of Children: Important Judgement', *The Irish Times*, 16 May 1902, p. 3.
14 *IR* (1902), vol. II, p. 695.
15 Margaret Frost's maiden name is not disclosed in *Irish Reports*, where she is referred to as 'the prosecutrix'.
16 *IR*, G.L. Dobbyn (ed.) (1947), pp. 3–29.
17 'High Court Decision Regarding Custody of Children', *The Irish Times*, 27 October 1945, p. 1.
18 *IR* (1947), p. 12.
19 'Court Refuses Mother's Claim to Children. Father's Right to Determine Religion Upheld', *The Irish Times*, 21 December 1945, p. 1.
20 Jean Blanchard, *The Church in Contemporary Ireland* (Dublin: Clonmore & Reynolds Ltd., 1963), p. 65.
21 'Judgment in Father's Application: Children to be transferred from Birds' Nest', *The Irish Times*, 22 October 1949, p. 9.
22 Ibid.
23 Ibid.
24 Ibid.

CHAPTER 6. The Affidavits and the High Court Case

1 An *ex parte* court application is one brought by one person in the absence of, and without representation by, or notification to, other parties.
2 'Oldcastle Father Ordered to Give Children to Wife', *Anglo-Celt*, 3 June 1950, p. 1.
3 *IR* (1951), p. 35.
4 ICM, Tilson file.

5 Alan Tilson remembers two guards calling to their home one day and a heated exchange taking place between his mother and father with each giving their own version of events. Interview with Alan Tilson, 3 April 2019.
6 NAIT, sworn affidavit by Mary Tilson, 17 May 1950. Apart from interviews with family members, all the information in this chapter regarding the personal lives or circumstances of Ernest and Mary Tilson's relationship from 1941 to 1950 has been sourced from their affidavits held at the National Archives of Ireland.
7 MSH, Tilson file.
8 *IR* (1951), pp. 1–47.
9 NAIT, sworn affidavit by Harriette Tilson, 19 June 1950.
10 'Put Children in the Birds' Nest', *Irish Press*, 4 July 1950, p. 5.
11 Interviews with Alan Tilson, 3 April 2019 and Judy Tilson, 23 May 2019.
12 Interview with Alan Tilson, 11 July 2019.
13 NAIT, sworn affidavit by Catherine Ryder, 13 July 1950.
14 NAIT, sworn affidavit by Francis Traynor, 14 July 1950.
15 'Custody of Children Disputed: Legal arguments on religious issue', *Irish Independent*, 25 July 1950, p. 8.
16 'Mother's Court Application', *Irish Press*, 25 July 1950, p. 2.
17 'Custody of Children: Eldest boy to attend court', *Irish Press*, 26 July 1950, p. 2.
18 In law, acquiescence occurs when a person knowingly stands by without raising any objection to the infringement of his or her rights, while someone else unknowingly and without malice aforethought acts in a manner inconsistent with their rights. As a result of acquiescence, the person whose rights are infringed may lose the ability to make a legal claim against the infringer.
19 Ernest Tilson's objections to his eldest son taking First Communion have been corroborated by Judy and Alan Tilson. Interview with Judy Tilson, 7 June 2019 and Alan Tilson, 11 June 2019.
20 *IR* (1951), pp. 1–47.
21 The family believe that all the correspondence received is in the family scrapbook. While some of the letters are anonymous, none are shown to have come from males.
22 Tilson family scrapbook. Names and addresses on these letters have been changed to protect the correspondents' identity. Author's emphasis.
23 Ibid.
24 Ibid.
25 Ibid.

CHAPTER 7. George Gavan Duffy
1 Gerard Hogan, 'Duffy, George Gavan', *DIB*, at https://www.dib.ie/biography/duffy-george-gavan-a2810 (accessed 20 June 2018).
2 F.S.L. Lyons, *Ireland Since the Famine* (London: Fontana Press, 1963, this edition 1971), pp. 109–10.
3 Papers of John Charles McQuaid, Dublin Diocesan Archives (hereafter cited as DDA), Folder 3, Lay Organisations, 35h and 36h.
4 Hogan, 'Duffy, George Gavan', *DIB*.
5 R.F. Foster, *Vivid Faces: The revolutionary generation in Ireland 1890–1923* (London: Allen Lane, 2014), p. 312.
6 Golding, G.M., *George Gavan Duffy 1882–1951* (Dublin: Irish Academic Press, 1982), pp. 15–16.
7 Hogan, 'Duffy, George Gavan', *DIB*.

8 George Gavan Duffy, Bureau of Military History, NAI, Witness Statement (381).
9 Colm Gavan Duffy, 'George Gavan Duffy', *Dublin Historical Record*, vol. 36, no. 3, 1983, pp. 90–106.
10 Ibid., p. 92.
11 F.S.L. Lyons, *Ireland Since the Famine*, p. 436.
12 *Dáil Éireann Debates*, 21 December 1921, at https://www.oireachtas.ie/en/debates/debate/dail/1921-12-21/2/ (accessed 14 June 2018).
13 Hogan, 'Duffy, George Gavan', *DIB*.
14 'Dublin and District', *Irish Independent*, 29 November 1926, p. 8. George Gavan Duffy is listed along with Edward Cahill and others as members of the first ard chomhairle elected.
15 C.J. Woods, 'Cahill, Edward', *DIB*, at https://www.dib.ie/biography/cahill-edward-a1364 (accessed 27 August 2018).
16 Dermot Keogh, 'Ireland', in David S. Wyman (ed.), *The World Reacts to the Holocaust* (Baltimore: Johns Hopkins University Press, 1996), pp. 642–69, at p. 648.
17 Neil R. Davison, *James Joyce, Ulysses, and the Construction of Jewish Identity: Culture, biography, and the 'Jew' in modernist Europe* (Cambridge: Cambridge University Press, 1996, this edition 1998), p. 55.
18 'Funeral of Rev. Edward Cahill. S.J.', *Irish Press*, 19 July 1941, p. 3.
19 J. Waldron, 'An Ríoghacht (The League of the Kingship of Christ): A retrospect', *The Irish Monthly*, vol. 78, no. 924, 1950, pp. 274–80.
20 Maurice Curtis, *A Challenge to Democracy: Militant Catholicism in modern Ireland* (Dublin: History Press of Ireland, 2010), p. 205.
21 Cited in Seán Faughnan's 'The Jesuits and the Drafting of the Irish Constitution of 1937', *Irish Historical Studies*, vol. 26, no. 101, 1988, pp. 79–102.
22 Waldron, 'An Ríoghacht', p. 279.
23 'Dublin and District: An Ríoghacht', *Irish Independent*, 29 November 1926, p. 8.
24 'Jesuit's Call', *Evening Herald*, 26 April 1937, p. 6.
25 Papers of Father Edward Cahill SJ, Irish Jesuit Archives, J55/107.
26 Waldron, 'An Ríoghacht', pp. 274–9.
27 Maurice Curtis, 'The Roots of Militant Catholicism', *History Ireland*, vol. 18, no. 5, 2010, pp. 34–7.
28 Dermot Keogh, *Jews in Twentieth Century Ireland* (Cork: Cork University Press, 1998), pp. 94–5. Keogh argues that Cahill was a 'strong proponent of the views held by Fahey'.
29 Enda Delaney, 'Political Catholicism in Post-war Ireland: The Revd Denis Fahey and Maria Duce 1945–54', *The Journal of Ecclesiastical History*, vol. 52, no. 3, 2001, pp. 487–511.
30 Terence Brown, *Ireland: A social and cultural history, 1922–2002* (London: Harper Perennial 2004), p. 115.
31 'Social Reform: Programme of An Ríoghacht', *Irish Independent*, 2 November 1936, p. 11. *Irish Independent* emphasis.
32 Curtis, *A Challenge to Democracy*, p. 134.
33 Papers of Father Edward Cahill SJ, Irish Jesuit Archives, J55/68(1) – (15).
34 Curtis, *A Challenge to Democracy*, p. 134.
35 Letter from Brian McCaffrey, president of An Ríoghacht, to Éamon de Valera, Papers of Father Edward Cahill SJ, Irish Jesuit Archives, J55/107.
36 Curtis, *A Challenge to Democracy*, p. 135.
37 Ibid.
38 Hogan, 'Duffy, George Gavan', *DIB*.
39 Gerard Hogan, *The Origins of the Irish Constitution 1928–1941*, with Eoin Kinsella (ed.) (Dublin: Royal Irish Academy, 2012), pp. 328–9.

40 Hogan and Kinsella (eds), *The Origins of the Irish Constitution*, pp. 438–41.
41 'Draft Constitution Praised by An Ríoghacht', *Irish Press*, 3 May 1937, p. 1.
42 Hogan, 'Duffy, George Gavan', *DIB*.
43 Gerard Hogan, 'The Sinn Féin Funds Judgment Fifty Years On', *The Bar Review*, vol. 2, no. 9, 1997, pp. 375–82.
44 Ibid.
45 Golding, *George Gavan Duffy*, p. 118.
46 Gerard Hogan and Gerry Whyte, *J.M. Kelly: The Irish Constitution*, 4th edn (Dublin: Butterworths, 2003), 7.8.74, cited in Ruth Cannon, 'The Bigoted Landlord: A re-examination of *Schlegel v. Corcoran and Gross*', *Dublin University Law Journal*, vol. 27, 2005, pp. 248–60, at p. 253.
47 1911 census returns, John Schlegel, 7 Harrington Street, http://www.census.nationalarchives.ie/ (accessed 20 February 2019). The return shows that the house was then owned by John Schlegel, a German-born watchmaker. All members of his family, including Hanly, are listed as Roman Catholics.
48 *IR*, Albert D. Bolton (ed.) (1942), p. 24.
49 Cannon, 'The Bigoted Landlord', p. 249.
50 Hogan, 'Duffy, George Gavan', *DIB*.
51 Golding, *George Gavan Duffy*, p. 130.
52 'Dublin Tenancy Case: Objection to a Jew: Before Mr. Justice Gavan Duffy', *The Irish Times*, 13 January 1942, p. 3.
53 *IR* (1942), pp. 25–6.
54 Ibid., p. 26.
55 Cannon, 'The Bigoted Landlord', p. 252.
56 For observations on Jesuit anti-Jewishness see Davison, *James Joyce, Ulysses, and the Construction of Jewish Identity*, pp. 55–7.
57 Cannon, 'The Bigoted Landlord', p. 252.
58 *IR*, Albert D. Bolton (ed.) (1945), pp. 515–25.
59 Gerard Hogan, Gerry Whyte, David Kenny and Rachael Walsh (eds), *Kelly: The Irish Constitution*, 5th edn (Dublin: Bloomsbury Professional, 2018), 7.9.30, p. 2468.
60 Golding, *George Gavan Duffy*, pp. 140–1.

CHAPTER 8. The High Court Judgment
1 ICM, Tilson file.
2 *IR* (1951), p. 2.
3 Ibid., p. 29.
4 Criminal Law Amendment Act 1935, Office of the Attorney General, at https://www.irishstatutebook.ie/eli/1935/act/6/section/2/enacted/en/html (accessed 14 October 2018).
5 NAIT, sworn affidavit by Mary Tilson, 11 July 1950.
6 *IR* (1951), p. 2. Author's emphasis.
7 Ibid.
8 Ibid., p. 3.
9 Ernest Tilson actually completed four forms – one for each of his four sons – but the court was not made aware of this.
10 *IR* (1951), p. 5.
11 Ibid., p. 9.
12 Ibid.
13 Hogan, 'A Fresh Look at Tilson's Case', p. 314.
14 *IR* (1951), p. 9.

15 Hogan, 'A Fresh Look at Tilson's Case', p. 313.
16 *IR* (1951), pp. 13–14.
17 'For the Glory of God and the Honour of Ireland'.
18 *IR* (1951), p. 14.
19 James E. Carty, 'The Enforceability of Antenuptial Agreements for the Religious Instruction of Children', *Duke Bar Journal*, vol. 2, no. 1, 1951, pp. 70–89, at p. 81. Carty argues that '*Ramon v. Ramon* is the leading decision holding an ante-nuptial contract for the religious education of children as enforceable'.
20 Hogan, 'A Fresh Look at Tilson's Case', p. 331.
21 Walter G. Gans, 'Enforceability of Antenuptial Agreements Providing for the Religious Education of Children', *Journal of Family Law*, vol. 1, no. 2, 1961, pp. 227–40, at p. 239.
22 'Mother Gets Back Children', *Irish Press*, 28 July 1950, p. 1.
23 'Ne Temere', *The Irish Times*, 29 July 1950, p. 7.
24 'Binding Force of Ante-Nuptial Agreement Upheld', *The Irish Catholic*, 3 August 1950, p. 8. *Irish Catholic* emphasis.
25 'CHILDREN NOT TO BE PROTESTANTS: Dublin judge rejects father's claim, quotes constitution', *Belfast Telegraph*, 28 July 1950, p. 4.
26 'Children of Mixed Marriage: Dublin court's order', *Manchester Guardian*, 28 July 1950, p. 5.
27 'High Court Upholds Nuptial Judgment', *The Representative* (Fox Lake, Wisconsin), 14 September 1950, p. 2.
28 'High Court Upholds Nuptial Judgment', *Oklahoma County Register* (Luther, Oklahoma), 7 September 1950, p. 8.
29 Patrick Maume, 'Devoy, John', *DIB*, at https://www.dib.ie/biography/devoy-john-a2562 (accessed 13 January 2018).
30 'Irish High Court Rules on Matter of Mixed Marriage', *Gaelic American*, 19 August 1950, p. 3.
31 'High Court Upholds Nuptial Agreement', *Freedom Call*, 14 September 1950, p. 6.
32 'Mother Wins Custody of Children', *Irish Independent*, 28 July 1950, p. 7.
33 'Appeal in Children Case', *The Irish Times*, 29 July 1950, p. 9.
34 Letter from John Charles McQuaid to Cardinal Francesco Marchetti-Selvaggiani, 4 September 1950, DDA, McQuaid Papers, AB8/B/XVIII/6.
35 Letter from Cardinal Francesco Marchetti-Selvaggiani to Archbishop John Charles McQuaid [Latin], 16 December 1950, DDA, McQuaid Papers, AB8/B/XVIII/6.
36 Cited in Cooney, *John Charles McQuaid*, p. 245. DDA, AB8,/B/XVIII/6. The author has been unable to locate the letter to which Cooney refers in the Dublin Diocesan Archives.

CHAPTER 9. The Supreme Court Appeal
1 Pauric J. Dempsey, 'Black, William Bullick', *DIB*, at https://www.dib.ie/biography/black-william-bullick-a0688 (accessed 23 November 2018).
2 'Children's Religion Issue in Appeal by Father', *The Irish Times*, 1 August 1950, p. 3.
3 Hogan, 'A Fresh Look at Tilson's Case', p. 321.
4 'Children Supreme Court Appeal', *Irish Press*, 1 August 1950, p. 2.
5 Ibid.
6 'Custody of Children: Father appeals against High Court order', *Irish Independent*, 1 August 1950, p. 3.
7 'Children's Religion Is Issue in Appeal by Father', *The Irish Times*, 1 August 1950, p. 3.
8 'Legal Submissions on Father's Rights in Tilson Case', *The Irish Times*, 2 August 1950, p. 3.
9 'Argument in Tilson Children Appeal Case', *Irish Press*, 2 August 1950, p. 6.
10 'Custody of Children Disputed: Law unchanged by constitution', *Irish Independent*, 2 August 1950, p. 4.

11 Pauric J. Dempsey, 'Casey, Charles Francis ("Charlie")', *DIB*, at https://www.dib.ie/biography/casey-charles-francis-charlie-a1534 (accessed 20 April 2020). See also Dr Macdara Ó Drisceoil's 'Catholicism and the Judiciary in Ireland, 1922–1960', *Irish Judicial Studies Journal*, vol. 4, no. 1, 2020, pp. 1–24, at p. 16.
12 J.P. Casey, *The Office of the Attorney General in Ireland* (Dublin: Institute of Public Administration, 1980), p. 216, n. 78.
13 DDA, McQuaid to Marchetti-Selvaggiani.
14 ICM, Tilson file. Author's emphasis.
15 'Attorney-General States Case for Mrs Tilson', *The Irish Times*, 3 August 1950, p. 3.
16 'Custody of Children Disputed: Supreme Court hears case for mother', *Irish Independent*, 3 August 1950, p. 3.
17 Ibid.
18 'Attorney General States Case for Mrs. Tilson', *The Irish Times*, 3 August 1950, p. 3.
19 Bureau of Military History, NAI, Witness Statement (1511).
20 'Citizens' Rights', *The Irish Times*, 7 August 1950, p. 7.
21 'Judgment Reserved in Custody of Children Appeal', *The Irish Times*, 4 August 1950, p. 3.
22 Ibid.
23 'Custody of Children Disputed: Supreme Court to give judgment tomorrow', *Irish Independent*, 4 August 1950, p. 3.
24 'Tilson Appeal Arguments End', *Irish Press*, 4 August 1950, pp. 5–6.
25 'Judgment Reserved in Custody of Children Appeal', *The Irish Times*, 4 August 1950, p. 3.
26 Ibid.
27 'Court Judgments in Tilson Case Tomorrow', *Irish Press*, 4 August 1950, pp. 5–6.
28 The alteration on Ernest Tilson's affidavit invites the question: was this done to correct a typographical error or did Ernest Tilson or others have a reason to alter the date?
29 'Custody of Children Disputed: Supreme Court to give judgment tomorrow', *Irish Independent*, 4 August 1950, p. 3.
30 Ibid.
31 'Tilson Case Judgment Reserved', *The Irish Times*, 4 August 1950, p. 7.
32 Ibid.
33 *Irish Independent*, 4 August 1950, p. 3.
34 *IR* (1951), p. 23.
35 Ibid., p. 25.
36 Tilson family scrapbook.
37 *IR* (1951), p. 29.
38 Ibid., p. 31.
39 Ibid., pp. 31–2.
40 Ibid., p. 32. Author's emphasis.
41 Ibid., pp. 32–3.
42 Ibid., p. 34.
43 Ibid., p. 35.
44 Ibid.
45 Ibid.
46 Ibid., p. 36.
47 Ibid.
48 Ibid.
49 Ibid.
50 Ibid., pp. 37–9.
51 Ibid., p. 38.

Notes to pages 155 to 169

52 Ibid.
53 Ibid., p. 32.
54 Ibid., 37.
55 Ibid., pp. 39–40. *Irish Reports* emphasis.
56 Ibid., p. 41.
57 Ibid., p. 42.
58 Kelly, *Fundamental Rights*, p. 229.
59 Ibid., p. 44.
60 *IR* (1951), p. 44.
61 Ibid., p. 46.
62 'Five Children To Be Brought up as Roman Catholics – High Court Ruling', *The Irish Times*, 13 June 1957, p. 9.
63 DDA, McQuaid to Marchetti-Selvaggiani.
64 Hogan, 'A Fresh Look at Tilson's Case', p. 325.
65 Interview with Judy Tilson, 30 May 2019; interview with Oldcastle residents, 23 July 2019.
66 MSH, Tilson file.

CHAPTER 10. Reaction to the Court Judgments
1 DDA, McQuaid to Marchetti-Selvaggiani.
2 DDA, Marchetti-Selvaggiani to McQuaid. 'Secret.' is short for 'Secretary'.
3 'Mother Gets Her Children', *Sunday Press*, 6 August 1950, p. 1. *Sunday Press* emphasis.
4 Brown, *The Irish Times*, p. 201.
5 'Ne Temere', *The Irish Times*, 7 August 1950, p. 7.
6 'The Tilson Case', *Nenagh Guardian*, 12 August 1950, p. 5.
7 'Against Public Policy', *Meath Chronicle*, 19 August 1950, p. 5.
8 *Belfast Telegraph*, 5 August 1950, p. 5; *Derry Journal*, 7 August 1950, p. 2; *Belfast News Letter*, 7 August 1950, p. 3.
9 'Tilson Appeal Dismissed by Majority Decision', *Londonderry Sentinel*, 8 August 1950, p. 2.
10 'Father Must Give Up His Sons, Judges Rule', *Sunday Dispatch*, 6 August 1950, p. 3.
11 Press cuttings of the case from the *Sunday Express*, *Daily Mail*, *News Chronicle* and *Sunday Dispatch* are contained in the Tilson family scrapbook. No dates or page numbers feature on the cuttings.
12 'Religious Education of Children: Ante-nuptial agreement upheld', *The Times*, 8 August 1950, p. 2.
13 'Parents' Rights in Religious Upbringing of Children: Eire decision restores three boys to mother', *Manchester Guardian*, 7 August, 1950, p. 7.
14 'In Mixed Marriages: Irish court decision recalls American rulings on offspring's religious training', *Cincinnati Catholic Telegraph Register* (Cincinnati), 18 August 1950, p. 10.
15 'Irish Court Upholds Pre-Nuptial Pacts', *Rochester Catholic Courier and Journal* (Rochester), 17 August 1950, p. 6.
16 'In Mixed Marriages: Irish court decision recalls American rulings on offspring's religious training', *Catholic Advance* (Wichita, Kansas), 18 August 1950, p. 8.
17 'U.S. Courts Also Uphold Pre-Marriage Agreements', *Standard*, 18 August 1950, p. 1.
18 'Ruling on Parent's Promise Upheld: Supreme Court finds for mother in claim for children', *Sydney Catholic Weekly*, 31 August 1950, p. 9.
19 Ian d'Alton, 'A Careful Contrarianism: How *The Irish Times* and the *Church of Ireland Gazette* approached the Tilson case and the dogma of the Assumption in 1950', unpublished conference paper, 2012.
20 'The Tilson Case', *Church of Ireland Gazette*, 11 August 1950, p. 1. *Gazette* emphasis.

21 Rev. W.L.M. Giff, 'The Tilson Case', *The Church of Ireland Gazette and Family Newspaper*, 11 August 1950, pp. 1–2. See also Marie Coleman, 'The *Church of Ireland Gazette*'s Perspective of Life in 1950s Ireland', at https://www.ireland.anglican.org/news/9935/the-church-of-ireland-gazettes (accessed 12 July 2022).
22 'Notes of the Week', *Church of Ireland Gazette*, 11 August 1950, p. 6.
23 'A Decisive Judgment', *Standard*, 11 August 1950, p. 6.
24 Ibid.
25 'Archaic Law', *Irish Catholic*, 10 August 1950, p. 1.
26 'Irish Law and English Law', *Irish Catholic*, 10 August 1950, p. 2.
27 Ibid.
28 Ibid.
29 *Fiat*: Published in the Service of the Social Rights of Christ the King (Dublin: Key Publishing Society, March 1949), p. 3. '*Fiat*' translates: 'Let it be done'.
30 'The Tilson Case and Article 44', *Fiat*, no. 24, October 1950. *Fiat* emphasis.
31 Ibid. *Fiat* emphasis.
32 'Ne Temere', *The Irish Times*, 16 August 1950, p. 5.
33 'Unmixed Marriages', *The Irish Times*, 31 August 1950, p. 5.
34 'Ne Temere', *The Irish Times*, 16 August 1950, p. 9.
35 'Ne Temere', *The Irish Times*, 12 September 1950, p. 5.
36 'Ne Temere', *The Irish Times*, 25 August 1950, p. 5.
37 'Ne Temere', *The Irish Times*, 11 August 1950, p. 5.
38 'Ne Temere', *The Irish Times*, 17 August 1950, p. 5.
39 'Ne Temere', *The Irish Times*, 25 August 1950, p. 5.
40 'Ne Temere', *The Irish Times*, 5 August 1950, p. 9.
41 Interview with Alan Tilson, 3 April 2019; interview with Judy Tilson, 23 May 2019.
42 'Mother Gets Back Children: Judge holds religion promise is binding', *Irish Press*, 28 July 1950, p. 1.
43 'Appeal Dismissed in Tilson Children Case', *The Irish Times*, 7 August 1950, p. 6.
44 Private correspondence with Gerard Hogan, 20 January 2020.
45 ICM, Tilson file.
46 Ibid.
47 'Correspondence', *Church of Ireland Gazette and Family Newspaper*, 4 August 1950, p. 8.
48 'Notes of the Week', *Church of Ireland Gazette and Family Newspaper*, 11 August 1950, p. 6. I am grateful to Ian d'Alton for bringing this to my attention.
49 ICM, Tilson file.
50 Ibid.
51 Ibid.
52 Ibid.
53 Mitchell, *Religion, Identity*, p. 98.
54 Ibid.
55 Ruane and Todd, *The Dynamics of Conflict*, pp. 47–60.
56 Ferriter, *The Transformation of Ireland*, p. 368; Elizabeth Keane, *An Irish Statesman and Revolutionary: The nationalist and internationalist politics of Seán MacBride* (London: Tauris, 2006), p. 67.
57 Jackson, *Ireland 1798–1998*, p. 311.
58 Lee, *Ireland 1912–1985*, p. 301.
59 Keogh, *Twentieth-century Ireland*, pp. 197–8.
60 Jackson, *Ireland: 1798–1998*, p. 358.
61 Patterson, *Ireland since 1939*, pp. 129–30.

Notes to pages 182 to 194

62 Lee, *Ireland 1912–1985*, p. 300.
63 'Northern Critics of Southern Law', *The Irish Times*, 6 September 1950, p. 1.
64 '"Police State" Preferred to Republic by Northern M.P.', *The Irish Times*, 28 August 1950, p. 7.
65 'Northern Critics of Southern Law', *The Irish Times*, 6 September 1950, p. 1.
66 'M.P.'s Fears for Justice under Republic', *The Irish Times*, 30 September 1950, p. 1.
67 'Proposed Public Debate, National Union of Protestants v. Minister for External Affairs', NAI, DFA/305/14/161. There is no doubt that MacBride was well informed about the Tilson case; Norman Ruddock has described how Ernest's mother, Harriette, wrote to him about the matter but did not receive a reply. Norman Ruddock, *The Rambling Rector* (Dublin: Columba Press, 2005), p. 58.
68 ICM, Tilson file, letter from Norman Porter to W.L.M. Giff, 10 October 1950.
69 Tilson family scrapbook.
70 These letters are all contained in the Tilson family scrapbook.
71 Inglis, *Moral Monopoly*, pp. 188–207.
72 Benedict Anderson, *Imagined Communities: Reflection on the origin and spread of nationalism* (London: Verso, 1983, this edition 2003), p. 6.
73 Tilson family scrapbook.
74 Ibid. Letter writer's emphasis.
75 Ibid.
76 MSH, Tilson file.
77 Ibid.
78 'Church Notices', *The Irish Times*, 5 September 1950, p. 7.
79 'Diocesan News', *Church of Ireland Gazette and Family Newspaper*, 22 September 1950, p. 4.
80 ICM, Tilson file. Letter dated 13 September 1950.
81 'Canon Law Criticised by Speaker at Youth Conference', *The Irish Times*, 8 November 1950, p. 1.
82 'Home Tragedies', *The Irish Times*, 8 November 1950, p. 1.
83 ICM, Tilson file.
84 'Protestants Hit by Mixed Marriage Problem', *The Irish Times*, 16 September 1950, p. 1.
85 ICM, Tilson file, letter dated 24 October 1950.
86 ICM, Tilson file, letter dated 2 November 1950.
87 DDA, McQuaid papers, XV/10/28.
88 St Patrick's College Maynooth Archives, Canon Law Faculty minutes B5/4/4 in R8.
89 In conversation and correspondence with canon lawyer Monsignor Maurice Dooley, 22 and 29 November 2019.
90 ICM, Tilson file, letter dated 24 October 1950.
91 ICM, Tilson file, letter dated 9 November 1950.
92 ICM, Tilson file, resolution dated 25 November 1950 and signed by H.G. Johnson (hon. sec.).
93 'Church of Ireland Warning Against Mixed Marriages', *The Irish Times*, 9 May 1951, p. 1.
94 Ibid.
95 *Seanad Éireann Debates*, 2 December 1959, vol. 51, no. 14, at https://www.oireachtas.ie/en/debates/debate/seanad/ (accessed 23 March 2022). Sheehy Skeffington was speaking during a Court of Justice Bill (1959) debate.
96 *Dáil Éireann Debates*, 2 November 1972, vol. 263, no. 3, at https://www.oireachtas.ie/en/debates/ (accessed 23 March 2022).
97 *Seanad Éireann Debates*, 3 November 1972, vol. 73, no. 9, at https://www.oireachtas.ie/en/debates/debate/seanad/ (accessed 23 March 2022). Keery was also speaking during the Fifth Amendment debate.

98 *Seanad Éireann Debates*, 3 November 1972, vol. 73, no. 9. FitzGerald was speaking during the Fifth Amendment debate. According to Garret FitzGerald, Alexis FitzGerald had 'an exceptional reputation for legal skills' and became an 'informal adviser to John A. Costello after he was elected taoiseach'. See Garret FitzGerald, 'FitzGerald, Alexis James Oliver', *DIB*, at https://www.dib.ie/biography/fitzgerald-alexis-james-oliver-a3132 (accessed 28 March 2022).

99 *Seanad Éireann Debates*, 9 October 1981, vol. 96, no. 2, at https://www.oireachtas.ie/en/debates/debate/seanad/ (accessed 23 March 2022). Murphy was speaking during a Constitutional and Legislative Review debate.

CHAPTER 11. Reconciliation

1 'Father on Child Neglect Charges', *Evening Herald*, 13 October 1950, p. 2.
2 Nearly two months later, on 1 December 1950, Mary Tilson applied to the District Court to have the neglect charges against her husband withdrawn. Since there were no objections, Justice Mangan marked the case dismissed. See 'Neglect Charge Dismissed', *Meath Chronicle*, 2 December 1950, p. 6.
3 'Father on Child Neglect Charges', *Evening Herald*, 13 October 1950, p. 2.
4 Letter from W.L.M. Giff to W. Dodgson Sykes, 13 October 1950, ICM, Tilson file.
5 Interviews with local resident, 19 July 2019.
6 Ibid.
7 Interview with Judy Tilson, 23 May 2019. Fuller, *Irish Catholicism since 1950*, p. 9.
8 Ruddock, *The Rambling Rector*, pp. 58–9.
9 Letter from Ernest Tilson to W.L.M. Giff, 30 September 1950, ICM, Tilson file. The boycott of the Tilson family tailoring business was corroborated by some Catholic residents of Oldcastle who were interviewed in July 2019.
10 Rev. James Johnson, Rev. Mathew Gilsenan and Rev. Patrick Leogue were the curates in Oldcastle parish at the time.
11 ICM, Tilson file, letter from Harriette Tilson to Rev. W.L.M. Giff, 21 November 1950. It is interesting that Harriette Tilson name-checked 'Miss Russell' in this letter; she is the same person who, according to Oldcastle residents, suggested to Ernest Tilson that he place his children in the Birds' Nest.
12 'The Morality of "Boycotting" Non-Catholic Merchants', *Irish Ecclesiastical Record: A monthly journal under episcopal sanction*, vol. XXIX, 1953, pp. 220–3.
13 Ibid.
14 Andrew Atherstone, 'Evangelicalism and Fundamentalism in the Inter-war Church of England', in David W. Bebbington and David Ceri Jones (eds), *Evangelicalism and Fundamentalism in the United Kingdom during the Twentieth Century* (Oxford: Oxford University Press, 2013), pp. 57–75, at p. 66.
15 'Church Notices', *The Irish Times*, 8 May 1951, p. 5; 'Church Notices', *The Irish Times*, 29 April 1953, p. 5.
16 ICM, Tilson file. Letter from W.L.M. Giff to W. Dodgson Sykes, 13 October 1950.
17 Dennis Cooke, *Persecuting Zeal: A portrait of Ian Paisley* (Dingle, Co. Kerry: Brandon, 1996), p. 134.
18 'National Church: Doctrine and practice', *The Times*, 13 January 1944, p. 6. *Times* emphasis.
19 Anna Bryson, 'Porter, Norman', *DIB*, at https://www.dib.ie/biography/porter-norman-a7437 (accessed 1 August 2019).
20 Ed Moloney, *Paisley: From demagogue to democrat?* (Dublin: Poolbeg Press, 2008), p. 23.
21 Ibid., p. 20.

22 Richard Lawrence Jordan has noted Porter's work for the Catholic Evangelical Fellowship to convert Catholics to evangelical Christianity in the 1950s. See Richard Lawrence Jordan, *The Second Coming of Paisley: Militant fundamentalism and Ulster politics* (New York: Syracuse University Press, 2013), pp. 111–12.
23 *Catholic Answers to Questions Posed by the National Union of Protestants* (Dublin: The Catholic Truth Society of Ireland, 1950), pp. 17–18.
24 Ibid.
25 Interviews with Oldcastle residents, 19 July 2019.
26 Interview with Alan Tilson, 3 April 2019.
27 Purdysburn Hospital opened in 1906 as Belfast City Infectious Diseases Hospital but was generally known as Purdysburn Fever Hospital or colloquially as 'the Burn'. It was later renamed the Northern Ireland Fever Hospital and Radiotherapy Centre and then Belvoir Park Hospital, until it closed in 2006.
28 ICM, Tilson file.
29 Ibid., letter from Rev. W.L.M. Giff to W. Dodgson Sykes, 13 October 1950.
30 For more on the Bethany Home and an account of W.L.M. Giff's involvement in controversy involving an eight-year-old girl at the Children's Fold, see Niall Meehan's article in *History Ireland*, vol. 18, no. 5, September–October 2010. Alan Tilson recalls that while he was staying in the Birds' Nest, he and some other children were often taken on an afternoon walk to a nearby orphanage where they would play. This was most likely the Children's Fold.
31 ICM, Tilson file. Letter from W.L.M. Giff to Norman Porter, 5 July 1951.
32 Interview with Alan Tilson, 3 April 2009.
33 Coles pub later became 'Bellamy's' and is now 'The Bridge'.
34 Interview with Alan Tilson, 11 June 2019.
35 David is the son of Judy and the late Paul Tilson. Paul was placed in the Birds' Nest by his father. David was a star player in the League of Ireland in the 1990s, is a graduate of University College Dublin's Soccer Scholarship system and has a degree in commerce. Interview with Judy Tilson, 23 May 2020.
36 Interview with Judy Tilson, 30 May 2019; interview with Alan Tilson, 14 May 2019. Alan is the only surviving member of the family. David, the eldest, passed away on 2 September 2012; Neville, the youngest, on 11 November 1997, aged fifty-one, and Paul, eighteen days later, on 29 November 1997, aged fifty-three.

CONCLUSION

1 Interview with Alan Tilson, 11 June 2019.
2 Mitchell, *Religion, Identity*, p. 3.
3 Harriette Tilson was aged seventy-five at the time of the court hearings.
4 Interview with Judy Tilson, 25 March 2020.
5 Interview with Alan Tilson, 7 July 2019.
6 Richardson, *Smyllie's Ireland*, p. 6.
7 'Attorney-General States Case for Mrs. Tilson', *The Irish Times*, 3 August 1950, p. 3.
8 Hogan, 'A Fresh Look at Tilson's Case', p. 331.
9 Lindsey Earner-Byrne and Diane Urquhart, 'Gender Roles in Ireland since 1940', in Biagini and Daly (eds), *The Cambridge Social History of Modern Ireland*, pp. 312–26, at p. 324.
10 Yvonne Scannell, 'The Constitution and the Role of Women', in Brian Farrell (ed.), *De Valera's Constitution and Ours* (Dublin: Gill & Macmillan, 1998), pp. 123–36.
11 Kennedy, Finola, *Cottage to Creche: Family change in Ireland* (Dublin: Institute of Public Administration, 2001), p. 94.

12 *Seanad Éireann Debates*, 4 March 1964, vol. 57, no. 8. Haughey was speaking during the debate on the Guardianship of Infants Bill.
13 *Dáil Éireann Debates*, 17 February 1983, vol. 340, no. 3. Shatter was speaking during a debate on the Eighth Amendment to the Constitution Bill, 1982. This amendment was passed recognising the equal right to life of the pregnant woman and the unborn.
14 Foster, *Modern Ireland*, p. 544.
15 J.H. Whyte, 'Political Life in the South', in Michael Hurley SJ (ed.), *Irish Anglicanism 1869–1969: Essays on the role of Anglicanism in Irish life presented to the Church of Ireland on the occasion of the centenary of its disestablishment by a group of Methodist, Presbyterian, Quaker and Roman Catholic scholars* (Dublin: Allen Figgis Limited, 1970), pp. 143–53, at p. 147n, p. 148.
16 Hogan, 'A Fresh Look at Tilson's Case', p. 328.
17 Patsy McGarry, 'Dr Neill Not Worried if Reference to God Is Not Left Out: Constitution should be "secular" says archbishop', *The Irish Times*, 10 January 2006, p. 7.
18 Patsy McGarry, 'Letters to the Editor', *Irish Examiner*, 21 January 2006, p. 16.
19 Hogan, 'Duffy, George Gavan', *DIB*.
20 DDA, McQuaid to Marchetti-Selvaggiani.
21 Conor Cruise O'Brien, *States of Ireland* (London: Hutchinson, 1972), p. 107.
22 Whyte, *Church and State*, pp. 364–5.
23 Ronan Keane, 'Murnaghan, James Augustine', *DIB*, at https://www.dib.ie/biography/murnaghan-james-augustine-a6066 (accessed 24 January 2019).
24 Marie Coleman, 'Maguire, Conor Alexander', *DIB*, at https://www.dib.ie/biography/maguire-conor-alexander-a5354 (accessed 18 August 2020). Coleman describes how Conor Maguire's mother wrote prayer books and other religious books for the Catholic Truth Society.
25 DDA, McQuaid to Marchetti-Selvaggiani.
26 Seán MacBride, *That Day's Struggle: A memoir 1904–1951* (Dublin: Currach Press, 2005). For MacBride on George Gavan Duffy, see pp. 44–7; on Cecil Lavery see p. 159. Caitriona Lawlor, custodian of Seán MacBride's papers, has also opined that 'Seán MacBride and Cecil Lavery were the greatest of friends', personal correspondence, 22 July 2022.
27 Garvin, *Preventing the Future*, p. 163.
28 *Dáil Éireann Debates*, vol. 125, no. 5, 12 April 1951.
29 Ibid.
30 The McKenna case of 1947 concerned a bequest of £4,000 payable to Mary Priscilla Higgins by her Protestant father, on the condition that she would never marry a Roman Catholic, which she duly did. Mr Justice Gavan Duffy ruled in favour of the Protestant party when he upheld the validity of the clause in the will disinheriting her. *IR* (1947), pp. 277–90.
31 Hogan, 'A Fresh Look at Tilson's Case', p. 329. Hogan cites Golding, *George Gavan Duffy*, pp. 140–1.
32 *IR* (1951), pp. 9–19.
33 Peter Murtagh, 'History of the Rising in Our Own Words: A project at Trinity College Dublin invites people to share family stories and documents and help put ordinary faces on the tumult of the early 20th century', *The Irish Times*, 2 November 2013, p. 5 ('Review' section).

Bibliography

PRIMARY SOURCES

Private material/publications
Tilson family scrapbook, entitled 'The Tilson Case'; Vivienne Smyly, 'The Early History of Mrs. Smyly's Homes and Schools' (privately published, 1976); Papers of Father Aidan Lehane CSSp

Interviews
Alan Tilson; Judy Tilson; residents of Oldcastle, County Meath; residents of Dublin 4; Monsignor Maurice Dooley; John Finucane MP; Mr Justice Gerard Hogan; Father Aidan Lehane CSSp; Edna Longley; Margaret MacCurtain; Father Peter McVerry; Imogen Stuart

Archives
Dublin Diocesan Archives, Drumcondra, Dublin 9: Papers of John Charles McQuaid, AB8/B/XVIII/6, XVIII/12/30
General Register Office, Werburgh Street, Dublin 2: Birth, Marriage and Death Certificates
Irish Church Missions Archives, Bachelor's Walk, Dublin 1: Tilson file
Jesuit Archives, Leeson Street, Dublin 2: Papers of Edward Cahill SJ
Mrs Smyly's Homes Archives, Blackrock, Co. Dublin: Tilson file
National Archives of Ireland, Bishop Street, Dublin 8: HC/1950 State Side 7/Tilson Papers; Bureau of Military History; Department of the Taoiseach; Department of Foreign Affairs, Holy See Embassy Records
Ó Fiaich Memorial Library & Archive, Armagh: Papers of Cardinal John D'Alton
St Patrick's College, Maynooth Archives, Maynooth, Co. Kildare: Papers of Monsignor Edward J. Kissane; Canon Law Faculty minutes
University College Dublin, Archives Department, Belfield, Dublin 4: Papers of John A. Costello; Papers of George Gavan Duffy

Annual reports

Catholic Truth Society of Ireland Annual Report 1927; Mrs Smyly's Homes Annual Report 1950; Birds' Nest Annual Report 1914–15; Society for Irish Church Missions to the Roman Catholics and Associated Homes Annual Report 1950

Official publications

Bunreacht na h-Éireann/The Irish Constitution, 1937 (Dublin: Stationery Office)

The Irish Reports: containing reports of cases argued and determined in the Chancery Divisions of the High Courts of Justice and by the Irish Land Commission, and on appeal therefrom in the Courts of Appeal in the Irish Free State and in Northern Ireland (Dublin: Incorporated Council of Law Reporting in Ireland, 1867–)

'The New Legislation of the Catholic Church on the Betrothals & Marriage. Decree of the Sacred Congregation of the Council, Approved and Confirmed by His Holiness Pope Pius X', authorised translation (Dublin: Browne & Nolan Ltd., 1907).

Hansard Parliamentary Debates, 'Mixed Marriages in Ireland', 5th series, vol. 21, cc. 145–214, 7 February 1911

Census of Ireland 1901/1911

Hansard Parliamentary Debates, vol. 46, cc. 611–12, 2 January 1913

Mother and Baby Homes Commission of Investigation, Final Report, 30 October 2020

Online resources

Biographical information:
https://www.dib.ie/

Catholic Encyclopedia:
https://www.newadvent.org/cathen/

Census of Ireland, 1901/1911:
http://www.census.nationalarchives.ie/

Dáil Debates; Seanad Debates:
https://www.oireachtas.ie/

Bibliography

Newspapers and magazines:
https://archive.irishnewsarchive.com/
https://www.proquest.com/hnpirishtimes/
https://www.britishnewspaperarchive.co.uk/
https://newspaperarchive.com/
https://www.newspapers.com/
https://magill.ie/archive/magazine-archive

Office of the Attorney General:
https://www.irishstatutebook.ie/

Papal Encyclicals:
https://www.papalencyclicals.net/

Records of Birth, Marriages and Death:
https://www.nationalarchives.ie

West Cork History Festival:
https://westcorkhistoryfestival.org/

Newspapers

Anglo-Celt
Belfast Evening Telegraph
Belfast News Letter
Catholic Advance (Wichita, Kansas)
Church of Ireland Gazette
Cincinnati Catholic Telegraph Register
Cork Constitution
Cork Examiner
Daily Express
Daily Mail
Derry Journal
Drogheda Independent
Erin's Hope
Evening Herald
Evening Press
Fiat
Freedom Call (Freedom, Oklahoma)
Freeman's Journal
Furrow
Gaelic American
Guardian
Irish Catholic
Irish Ecclesiastical Record
Irish Independent
Irish Jurist
Irish Press
Irish Times
Londonderry Sentinel
Manchester Guardian
Meath Chronicle
Munster Express
Nenagh Guardian
News Chronicle
Oklahoma County Register (Luther, Oklahoma)

Representative (Fox Lake, Wisconsin)
Rochester Catholic Courier and Journal (Rochester, New York)
Southern Star
Standard
Sunday Despatch
Sunday Express
Sunday Independent
Sunday Press
Sydney Catholic Weekly (Sydney)
Times (London)
Ulster Herald
Westmeath Independent

SECONDARY SOURCES

Books, journal articles and periodicals

Akenson, Donald Harman, *Small Differences: Irish Catholics and Irish Protestants, 1815–1922. An international perspective* (Kingston and Montreal: McGill-Queen's University Press, 1988)

Anderson, Benedict, *Imagined Communities: Reflection on the origin and spread of nationalism* (London: Verso, 1983, this edition, 2003)

Atherstone, Andrew, 'Evangelicalism and Fundamentalism in the Inter-war Church of England', in David W. Bebbington and David Ceri Jones (eds), *Evangelicalism and Fundamentalism in the United Kingdom during the Twentieth Century* (Oxford: Oxford University Press, 2013), pp. 55–75

Bardon, Jonathan, *A History of Ulster* (Belfast: Blackstaff, 1992)

Barritt, Denis P., and Charles F. Carter, *The Northern Ireland Problem: A study in group relations* (Oxford: Oxford University Press, 1972)

Bartlett, Thomas, *Ireland: A history* (Cambridge: Cambridge University Press, 2010)

Bennett, Douglas, *The Encyclopaedia of Dublin* (Dublin: Gill & Macmillan, 2005)

Bew, Paul, *Ideology and the Irish Question: Ulster unionism and Ulster nationalism* (Oxford: Clarendon Press, 1994)

Biagini, Eugenio F., and Mary E. Daly (eds), *The Cambridge Social History of Modern Ireland* (Cambridge: Cambridge University Press, 2017)

Blanchard, Jean, *The Church in Contemporary Ireland* (Dublin: Clonmore & Reynolds Ltd., 1963)

Blanshard, Paul, *The Irish and Catholic Power: An American interpretation* (Boston: Beacon Press, 1953)

Bolster, Evelyn, *The Knights of Saint Columbanus* (Dublin: Gill & Macmillan, 1979)

Bourke, Richard, and Ian McBride (eds), *The Princeton History of Modern Ireland* (Princeton: Princeton University Press, 2016)

Bouscaren, T. Lincoln, Adam C. Ellis and Francis N. Korth (eds), *Canon Law: A text and commentary* (Milwaukee: Bruce, 1963)

Bowen, Desmond, *History and the Shaping of Irish Protestantism* (New York: Peter Lang, 1995)

Bowen, Kurt, *Protestants in a Catholic State: Ireland's privileged minority* (Kingston and Montreal, Canada: McGill-Queen's University Press, 1983)

Boyce, D. George, and Alan O'Day (eds), *Defenders of the Union* (London: Routledge, 2001)

Brown, Terence, *Ireland: A social and cultural history, 1922–2002* (London: Harper Perennial, 2004)

—, *The Irish Times: 150 years of influence* (London: Bloomsbury, 2015)

Browne, Noël, *Against the Tide* (Dublin: Gill & Macmillan, 1986)

Bury, Robin, *Buried Lives: The Protestants of southern Ireland* (Dublin: History Press Ireland, 2017)

Butler, Hubert, *Escape from the Anthill* (Mullingar: Lilliput Press, 1985)

Byrne, Raymond, and J. Paul McCutcheon with Claire Bruton and Gerard Coffey (eds), *The Irish Legal System*, 6th edn (Dublin: Bloomsbury, 2009)

Cahill, Rev. E., 'Ireland's Peril' (Dublin: M.H. Gill & Son, 1930)

—, *The Framework of a Christian State: An introduction to social science* (Dublin: Gill & Sons Ltd., 1932)

Cannon, Ruth, 'The Bigoted Landlord: A re-examination of *Schlegel* v. *Corcoran and Gross*', *Dublin University Law Journal*, vol. 27, 2005, pp. 248-260

Carty, James E., 'The Enforceability of Antenuptial Agreements for the Religious Instruction of Children', *Duke Bar Journal*, vol. 2, no. 1, 1951, pp. 70-89

Casey, J.P., *The Office of the Attorney General in Ireland* (Dublin: Institute of Public Administration, 1980)

Catholic Answers to Questions Posed by the National Union of Protestants (Dublin: The Catholic Truth Society of Ireland, 1950)

Catholic Encyclopedia (The), vol. 9 (New York: Robert Appleton Company, 1910)

Clancy, Patrick, Sheelagh Drudy, Kathleen Lynch and Liam O'Dowd (eds), *Irish society: Sociological Perspectives* (Dublin: Institute of Public

Administration in association with the Sociological Society of Ireland, 1995)

Cooke, Dennis, *Persecuting Zeal: A portrait of Ian Paisley* (Dingle, County Kerry: Brandon, 1996)

Cooney, John, *John Charles McQuaid: Ruler of Catholic Ireland* (Dublin: O'Brien Press, 1999)

Corish, Patrick J., *The Irish Catholic Experience: A historical survey* (Dublin: Gill & Macmillan, 1985)

Cosgrove, Art (ed.), *Marriage in Ireland* (Dublin: College Press, 1985)

Crone, Anne, *Bridie Steen* (London: William Heinemann Ltd., 1949)

Cruise O'Brien, Conor, *States of Ireland* (London: Hutchinson, 1974)

Cunningham, T.P., 'Mixed Marriages in Ireland before *Ne Temere*', *The Irish Ecclesiastical Record*, vol. CI (Dublin: Browne & Nolan Ltd., 1964), pp. 53–6

Curran, Olive C. (ed.), *History of the Diocese of Meath 1860–1993*, vol. 2 (Mullingar: Most Rev. Michael Smith, Bishop of Meath, 1995)

Curtis, Maurice, *A Challenge to Democracy: Militant Catholicism in modern Ireland* (Dublin: History Press of Ireland, 2010)

—, 'The Roots of Militant Catholicism', *History Ireland*, vol. 18, no. 5, 2010, pp. 34–7

d'Alton, Ian, 'A Careful Contrarianism: How *The Irish Times* and the *Church of Ireland Gazette* approached the Tilson case and the dogma of the Assumption in 1950', unpublished paper read at the Newspaper and Periodical History Forum of Ireland 2012 Conference, University of Kingston, UK, 17 November 2012

d'Alton, Ian, and Ida Milne (eds), *Protestant and Irish: The minority's search for place in independent Ireland* (Cork: Cork University Press, 2019)

D'Arcy, Rev. C.F., 'The Religious Difficulty under Home Rule: The church view', in S. Rosenbaum (ed.), *Against Home Rule: The case for the union* (Washington: Kennikat Press, 1912, this edition, 1970), pp. 204–11

Davison, Neil R., *James Joyce, Ulysses, and the Construction of Jewish Identity: Culture, biography, and the 'Jew' in modernist Europe* (Cambridge: Cambridge University Press, 1996; this edition, 1998)

de Bhaldraithe, Eoin, 'Mixed Marriages and Irish Politics: The effect of "Ne Temere"', *Studies: An Irish quarterly review*, vol. 77, no. 307, 1988, pp. 284–99

Delaney, Enda, 'Political Catholicism in Post-war Ireland: The Rev. Denis Fahey and Maria Duce 1945–54', *The Journal of Ecclesiastical History*, vol. 52, no. 3, 2001, pp. 487–511

Douglas, Mary, *Purity and Danger: An analysis of the concepts of pollution and taboo* (London: Kegan Paul, 1966, this edition 2002)

Edwards, Owen Dudley, *The Sins of Our Fathers: Roots of conflict in Northern Ireland* (Dublin: Gill & Macmillan, 1970)

Elliott, Marianne, *When God Took Sides: Religion and identity in Ireland – unfinished history* (Oxford: Oxford University Press, 2009)

Ellis, Ian, *Vision and Reality: A survey of twentieth-century Irish inter-church relations* (Belfast: Institute of Irish Studies, Queen's University Belfast, 1992)

Erin's Hope (monthly publication of Mrs Smyly's Homes, 1852–)

Faloon, W. Harris, *The Marriage Law of Ireland* (Dublin: Hodges, Figgis & Co., 1881)

Fanning, Bryan, *Racism and Social Change in the Republic of Ireland* (Manchester: Manchester University Press, 2002)

Fanning, Ronan, *Independent Ireland* (Dublin: Helicon Limited, 1983)

Fanning, Tim, *The Fethard-on-Sea Boycott* (Cork: Collins Press, 2010)

Fanning, William, 'Mixed Marriage', in *The Catholic Encyclopedia*, vol. 9 (New York: Robert Appleton Company, 1910)

Farrell, Brian (ed.), *De Valera's Constitution and Ours* (Dublin: Gill & Macmillan, 1988)

Faughnan, Seán, 'The Jesuits and the Drafting of the Irish Constitution of 1937', *Irish Historical Studies,* vol. 26, no. 101, 1988, pp. 79–102

Ferriter, Diarmaid, *The Transformation of Ireland: 1900–2000* (London: Profile Books, 2005)

Fitzpatrick, David, *The Two Irelands 1912–1939* (Oxford: Oxford University Press, 1998)

Fletcher, Dudley, *Rome and Marriage: An examination of the recent papal decree*, Ne Temere (Dublin: Church of Ireland Printing & Publishing Co., Ltd., 1911)

—, *Rome and Marriage: A warning* (Dublin: Church of Ireland Printing & Publishing Co., Ltd., 1936)

Ford, Alan, and John McCafferty (eds), *The Origins of Sectarianism in Early Modern Ireland* (Cambridge: Cambridge University Press, 2005)

Foster, R.F., *Modern Ireland: 1600–1972* (London: Penguin Books, 1988)

—, *Vivid Faces: The revolutionary generation in Ireland 1890–1923* (London: Allen Lane, 2014)

—, *W.B. Yeats: A life II. The arch poet* (Oxford: Oxford University Press, 2003)

Francis, M.E., *Dark Rosaleen* (New York: Kennedy, 1917)

Fuller, Louise, *Irish Catholicism since 1950: The undoing of a culture* (Dublin: Gill & Macmillan, 2002)

Fulton, John, *The Tragedy of Belief: Division, politics and religion in Ireland* (Oxford: Clarendon Press, 1991)

Gans, Walter G., 'Enforceability of Antenuptial Agreements Providing for the Religious Education of Children', *Journal of Family Law*, vol. 1, no. 2, 1961, pp. 227–40

Garvin, Tom, *Preventing the Future: Why was Ireland so poor for so long?* (Dublin: Gill & Macmillan, 2004)

Gavan Duffy, Colm, 'George Gavan Duffy', *Dublin Historical Record*, vol. 36, no. 3, 1983, pp. 90–106

Golding, G.M., *George Gavan Duffy 1882–1951* (Dublin: Irish Academic Press, 1982)

Gregg, Rev. J.A.F., 'The *Ne Temere* Decree': A lecture delivered before the members of the Church of Ireland Cork Young Men's Association on 17 March 1911 (Dublin: Association for Promoting Christian Knowledge, 1911)

Harris, Rosemary, *Prejudice and Tolerance in Ulster: A study of neighbours and 'strangers' in a border community* (Manchester: Manchester University Press, 1972)

Hart, Peter, *The IRA at War, 1916–23* (Oxford: Oxford University Press, 2005)

Hogan, Gerard, 'A Fresh Look at Tilson's Case', *The Irish Jurist*, vol. 33, 1998, pp. 311–32

—, 'de Valera, the Constitution and the Historians', *The Irish Jurist*, vol. XL, 2005, pp. 293–320

—, 'Law and Religion: Church–state relations in Ireland from independence to the present day', *The American Journal of Comparative Law*, vol. 35, no. 1, 1987, pp. 47–96

—, 'The Sinn Féin Funds Judgment Fifty Years On', *The Bar Review*, vol. 2, no. 9, 1997, pp. 375–82

—, and Eoin Kinsella (eds), *The Origins of the Irish Constitution 1928–1941* (Dublin: Royal Irish Academy, 2012)

—, and Gerry Whyte, *J.M. Kelly: The Irish constitution*, 4th edn (Dublin: Butterworths, 2003)

—, Gerry Whyte, David Kenny and Rachel Walsh (eds), *Kelly: The Irish constitution*, 5th edn (Dublin: Bloomsbury Professional, 2018)

Hurley, Michael, 'Mixed Marriages', *The Furrow*, vol. 17, no. 5, 1966, pp. 279–87

Inglis, Tom, *Moral Monopoly: The Catholic Church in modern Irish society* (Dublin: Gill & Macmillan, 1987)

—, 'Religion, Identity, State and Society', in Joe Cleary and Claire Connolly (eds), *The Cambridge Companion to Modern Irish Culture* (Cambridge: Cambridge University Press, 2005), pp. 59–77

Irish Ecclesiastical Record: A monthly journal under episcopal sanction, vols 1–10 (Dublin: Browne & Nolan, 1865–1968)

Jackson, Alvin, *Ireland 1798–1998: Politics and war* (Oxford: Blackwell Publishing, 1999, this edition 2003)

Jameson, David, 'Norah Hoult and Temple Lane's Novels of Mixed Marriages in the Early Free State', *New Hibernia Review*, vol. 22, no. 3, 2018, pp. 110–23

—, 'The Religious Upbringing of Children in Mixed Marriages: The evolution of Irish law', *New Hibernia Review*, vol. 18, no. 2, 2014, pp. 65–83

Jordan, Richard Lawrence, *The Second Coming of Paisley: Militant fundamentalism and Ulster politics* (New York: Syracuse University Press, 2013)

Joyce, James, *Ulysses* (London: The Bodley Head, 1986, this edition 2002)

Keane, Elizabeth, *An Irish Statesman and Revolutionary: The nationalist and internationalist politics of Seán MacBride* (London: Tauris, 2006)

—, *Seán MacBride: A life* (Dublin: Gill & Macmillan, 2007)

Kelly, J.M., *Fundamental Rights in the Irish Law and Constitution*, 2nd edn (Dublin: Allen Figgis & Co. Ltd., 1967)

Kelly, J.M., G.W. Hogan and G. Whyte, *The Irish Constitution*, 4th edn (Dublin and London: Butterworths, 2003)

Kennedy, Finola, *Cottage to Creche: Family change in Ireland* (Dublin: Institute of Public Administration, 2001)

Keogh, Dermot, *Ireland and the Vatican: The politics and diplomacy of church–state relations, 1922–1960* (Cork: Cork University Press, 1995)

—, 'Ireland, the Vatican and the Cold War: the case of Italy, 1948', *Irish Studies in International Affairs*, vol. 3, no. 3, 1991, pp. 67–114

—, 'Ireland', in David S. Wyman (ed.), *The World Reacts to the Holocaust* (Baltimore: Johns Hopkins University Press, 1996), pp. 642–69

—, *Jews in Twentieth-century Ireland* (Cork: Cork University Press, 1998)

—, *Twentieth-century Ireland: Revolution and state building* (Dublin: Gill & Macmillan, 2005)

—, and Andrew J. McCarthy, *The Making of the Irish Constitution 1937: Bunreacht na hÉireann* (Cork: Mercier Press, 2007)

Kiberd, Declan, *Inventing Ireland: The literature of a modern nation* (London: Vintage, 1995)

Laffan, Michael, *The Partition of Ireland: 1911–1922* (Dublin: Dundalgan Press, 1983, this edition 1987)

Lane, Temple, *The Trains Go South* (London: Jarrolds, 1938)

Lee, J.J., *Ireland 1912–1985: Politics and society* (Cambridge: Cambridge University Press, 1989, this edition 2006)

— (ed.), *Ireland 1945–70* (Dublin: Gill & Macmillan, 1979)

Leslie, J.B., compiled by, and updated by W.J.R. Wallace, *Clergy of Meath and Kildare: Biographical successions list* (Dublin: Columba Press, 2004)

Luddy, Maria, *Women and Philanthropy in Nineteenth-century Ireland* (Cambridge: Cambridge University Press, 1995)

Lyons, F.S.L., *Culture and Anarchy in Ireland 1890–1939* (Oxford: Clarendon Press, 1979)

—, *Ireland Since the Famine* (London: Fontana Press, 1963, this edition 1971)

MacBride, Seán, *That Day's Struggle: A memoir 1904–1951*, Caitriona Lawlor (ed.) (Dublin: Currach Press, 2005)

MacGill, Patrick, *Helen Spenser* (London: Herbert Jenkins Ltd., 1937)

McCarthy, J. (Rev.), 'The Morality of "Boycotting" Non-Catholic Merchants', *Irish Ecclesiastical Record: A monthly journal under episcopal sanction* (Dublin: Browne & Nolan, 1953) vol. XXIX, pp. 220–3

McCullagh, David, *A Makeshift Majority: The first inter-party government, 1948–51* (Dublin: Institute of Public Administration, 1998)

McGuire, James, and James Quinn (eds), *Dictionary of Irish Biography*, vols 1–9 (Cambridge: Cambridge University Press, 2009)

Meehan, Niall, 'Church and State and the Bethany Home', *History Ireland*, vol. 18, no. 5, September–October 2010 (supplement), pp. 1–12

Megahey, Alan, *The Irish Protestant Churches in the Twentieth Century* (Basingstoke: Macmillan, 2000)

Miller, David W., 'Varieties of Irish Evangelicalism', *Field Day Review*, vol. 3, 2007, pp. 215–23

Mitchell, Claire, *Religion, Identity and Politics in Northern Ireland: Boundaries of belonging and belief* (Aldershot: Ashgate, 2006)

Moffitt, Miriam, *Soupers and Jumpers: The Protestant missions in Connemara, 1848–1937* (Dublin: Nonsuch, 2008)

—, *The Society for Irish Church Missions to the Roman Catholics 1849–1950* (Manchester: Manchester University Press, 2010)

Moloney, Ed, *Paisley: From demagogue to democrat?* (Dublin: Poolbeg Press, 2008)

Moore, Brian, *The Feast of Lupercal* (London: André Deutsch, 1958)

Moore, Frank Frankfort, *The Ulsterman: A story of today* (London: Hutchinson, 1914)

Morgan, Valerie, Marie Smyth, Gillian Robinson and Grace Fraser, *Mixed Marriages in Northern Ireland: Institutional responses* (Centre for the Study of Conflict, Coleraine: University of Ulster Press, 1996)

Moxon-Browne, Edward, *Nation, Class and Creed in Northern Ireland* (Aldershot: Gower, 1983)

Ní Mhuirthile, Tanya, Catherine O'Sullivan and Liam Thornton (eds), *Fundamentals of the Irish Legal System: Law, policy and politics* (Dublin: Round Hall, 2016)

Nuttall, Deirdre, *Different and the Same: A folk history of the Protestants of independent Ireland* (Dublin: Eastwood Books, 2020)

Ó Corráin, Daithí, *Rendering to God and Caesar: The Irish churches and the two states in Ireland, 1949–73* (Manchester: Manchester University Press, 2006)

O'Donovan, Gerald, *Waiting* (London: Macmillan & Co., Ltd., 1914)

Ó Drisceoil, Macdara, 'Catholicism and the Judiciary in Ireland, 1922–1960', *Irish Judicial Studies Journal*, vol. 4, no. 1, 2020, pp. 1–24

O'Higgins, Brian, 'Mixed Marriages: The "cautiones"', *Irish Theological Quarterly*, vol. 41, no. 3, 1974, pp. 205–21

—, 'Mixed Marriages: The "cautiones II"', *Irish Theological Quarterly*, vol. 41, no. 4, 1974, pp. 274–88

O'Malley, Padraig, *The Uncivil Wars: Ireland today* (Belfast: Blackstaff Press, 1983)

Patterson, Henry, *Ireland Since 1939: The perspective of conflict* (Dublin: Penguin Books, 2007)

Preston, Margaret, *Charitable Words: Women, philanthropy and the language of charity in nineteenth-century Dublin* (London: Praeger Publishers, 2004)

Rafferty, Oliver P., *Catholicism in Ulster 1603–1983: An interpretative history* (London: Hurst, 1994)

Richardson, Caleb Wood, *Smyllie's Ireland: Protestants, independence, and the man who ran the Irish Times* (Indiana: Indiana University Press, 2019)

Ruane, Joseph, 'Comparing Protestant–Catholic Conflict in France and Ireland: The significance of the ethnic and colonial dimension', in

John Wolffe (ed.), *Irish Religious Conflict in Comparative Perspective: Catholics, Protestants and Muslims* (London: Palgrave Macmillan, 2014), pp. 146–63

—, 'Long Conflict and How it Ends: Protestants and Catholics in Europe and Ireland, *Irish Political Studies*, vol. 36, no. 1, 2021, pp. 109–31

—, and Jennifer Todd, *The Dynamics of Conflict in Northern Ireland: Power, Conflict and Emancipation* (Cambridge: Cambridge University Press, 1996, this edition 1998)

Ruddock, Norman, *The Rambling Rector* (Dublin: Columba Press, 2005)

Schillebeeckx, Edward, *Marriage: Secular reality and saving mystery. Vol 2: Marriage in the history of the church*, trans. N.D. Smith (London: Sheed & Ward, 1965)

Scholes, Andrew, *The Church of Ireland and the Third Home Rule Bill* (Dublin: Irish Academic Press, 2010)

Shatter, Alan Joseph, *Family Law in the Republic of Ireland* (Dublin: Wolfhound Press, 1977)

Taylor, Frances, *Irish Homes and Irish Hearts* (Dublin: UCD Press, 2013)

Townshend, Charles, *The Partition: Ireland divided, 1885–1925* (London: Allen Lane, 2021)

Waldron, J., 'An Ríoghacht (The League of the Kingship of Christ): A retrospect', *The Irish Monthly*, vol. 78, no. 924, 1950, pp. 274–80

White, Jack, *Minority Report: The Protestant community in the Irish Republic* (Dublin: Gill & Macmillan, 1975)

Whyte, J.H., *Church and State in Modern Ireland: 1923–1970* (Dublin: Gill & Macmillan, 1971)

—, 'Church, State and Society: 1950–70', in J.J. Lee (ed.), *Ireland 1945–70* (Dublin: Gill & Macmillan, 1979), pp. 73–82

—, 'Political Life in the South', in Michael Hurley SJ (ed.), *Irish Anglicanism 1869–1969: Essays on the role of Anglicanism in Irish life presented to the Church of Ireland on the occasion of the centenary of its disestablishment by a group of Methodist, Presbyterian, Quaker and Roman Catholic scholars* (Dublin: Allen Figgis Limited, 1970), pp. 143–53

Williams, George D., *Dublin Charities: A handbook including organisations in, or applicable to, Ireland* (Dublin: Association of Charities, 1902)

Index

References to the picture section are in **bold**.

adoption, 68, 141–2, 212
Ahern, Maureen C., 175
Akenson, Donald, 22
Ancient Order of Hibernians, 71
Anderson, Benedict, 185
Anglo-Celt, 89
Anglo-Irish Treaty, 108, 117
Anti-Partition League (APL), 181–2
anti-Semitism, 109, 111, 115–17
Asquith, Herbert Henry, 43
assimilation, 76, 216
Atherstone, Andrew, 199
Australia, 8, 52, 168

bail, 57, 196
Ballina, Co. Mayo, 71
Ballisodare, Co. Sligo, 57
Ballybunion, Co. Kerry, 75, 117–18
Banna Strand, Co. Kerry, 107
baptism, 4, 13, 26, 30–31, 37, 46, 47, 87, 125, 130, 140, 211
Bardon, Jonathan, 39
Barnes, Annie (née Drum), 1, 2, 4, 35, 205
Barnes, Berna, 2
Barnes, Ena, 2
Barnes, Joe, 2
Barnes, John, 2, 3–4, 203
Barnes, Lily, 2, 50, 59, 62, 159, 203
Barnes, Mary *see* Tilson, Mary Josephine (née Barnes)
Barnes, Phyllis, 2
Bartholomew, Paul, 8
Bartlett, Thomas, 8, 39, 43
Beech Hill Court, Donnybrook, 204
Behan, W.J., 117

Belfast, 19, 27–8, 41–3, 74, 182–3, 189–90, 199–203
Belfast News Letter, 51, 132, 167
Belfast Telegraph, 132, 167
Belloc, Hilaire, 111
Benedict XIV, 40, 46–7
Bethany Home, Dublin, 202
Beveridge Plan, 71
Biagini, Eugenio F., 8, 78
Bible Churchmen's Missionary Society College, 199
Bird, Mabel, 60, 61–2, 63, 64–5, 91–2, 95, 188
Birds' Nest orphanage, Dún Laoghaire
  admission forms, 7, 13, 62–3, 121, 122–3, 137–8, 148–9, 158
  Ernest removes children to, 1, 4–5, 13, 56–66, 89, 91–2, 94–6, 103, 122–4, 129, 148–50, 154, 158, 206–7
  Frost children placed in, 85
  history, 13, 50–56
  Keenan children placed in, 87–8
  letters received after Supreme Court case, 187–8
  Mary brings children home from, 159–60, 165, **p9**
  Mary visits children at, 64–6, 103, 148
  pictured, **p1**
  and proselytism, 53–6, 60, 63, 137, 206
  role of Irish Church Missions, 13, 53–4, 56–8, 63
Black, William, 90, 136, 140, 143–6, 154–8, 166, 167, 194, 209, 211–12

255

Blanshard, Paul, 10–11
Blowick, Joseph, 71
Bourke, Richard, 8
Bowen, Desmond, 43
Bowen, Kurt, 8, 12
boycotts, 6, 9, 15–16, 36, 196, 197–9, 208, 219
Boyne, battle of the, 25
Bradford Observer, 167
Brady, Mary, 28–30
Bray Head, Co. Wicklow, 75
Breen, Dan, 110
Bridie Steen (Crone), 82
Britain, 8, 28, 42–4, 52, 68, 71, 106–8, 132, 167, 181–2, 199, 203
British army, 31, 56, 76
British law, 11, 125, 155, 164, 169, 171–2, 212, 217
Brown, Terence, 12, 111, 165
Brown Thomas department store, 75
Browne, Noël, 73, 75, 214
Browne case, 124
Bryan, Deirdre, 56
Bryson, Anna, 200
Buckley, Margaret, 114
Buckley v. *Attorney General* case, 114–15
Budd, F.G.O., 92
burial, 2, 28–30, 33, 35
Burke, Edmund, 169
Burke, Richard, 193
Bury, Robin, 12
Byrne, John, 4

Cahill, Edward, 8, 109–10, 111, 117, 126, 172
Campbell, J.H., 42
Canada, 179–80, 202
Canavan, J., 110
Cannon, Ruth, 117
canon law, 10, 38–9, 44, 46, 49, 112–13, 128, 138–9, 141, 157, 171–2, 189–94, 198, 200
Carrauntoohil, Co. Kerry, 75
Carson, W.H., 14, 92, 101–2, 122
Carter, Elizabeth Florence, 34

Carter, William, 34
Casement, Roger, 107–8
Casey, Charles, 15, 38, 72, 76, 136, 141–4, 155, 183, 208–9, 213, 217, p2
Casey, J.P., 8, 142
Cashel ecclesiastical province, 40
Castleblayney, Co. Monaghan, 31–2
Catholic Advance, 168
Catholic Bulletin, 15
Catholic emancipation, 24
Catholic Encyclopedia, 20
Catholic ethos, 13, 68, 76–7, 111, 211
Catholic Social Welfare Bureau, 106
censorship, 68, 110, 212
census data, 3, 29, 31, 51–2, 76
Chamberlain, Austin, 108
child abduction, 28–30
child welfare, 14, 81, 83, 88, 100, 101, 129, 130, 136, 138–40, 147
Childers, Erskine, 71
Children's Fold orphanage, Monkstown, 202, 203
Christmas raid, 114
Church of Ireland Diocesan Youth Conference, 189
Church of Ireland Gazette, 8, 15, 41–2, 168–70, 178, 188–9, 194–5
Church of the Sacred Heart, Donnybrook, 204
Cincinnati Catholic Telegraph Register, 168
civil law, 11, 14, 42, 44, 81, 112–13, 159, 171, 172, 189, 201, 212, 216
Civil War, 25, 26, 81–3, 87–8, 108, 114
Clann na Poblachta, 70, 71, 181
Clann na Talmhan, 70
Clarkin, Andy, 184
class *see* social class
Clogherhead, Co. Louth, 75
Cloney, Seán, 219
Cloney, Sheila, 15–16, 219
Clonmel, Co. Tipperary, 33
Coles' pub, Ballsbridge, 4, 203
Colohan, Rev. Mr., 52
colonialism, 5, 19, 24, 49, 53

Index

common law, 11, 81–2, 86, 124, 128, 139, 152, 155–6, 167, 169, 173
Communion, 95, 98, 100, 102, 123, 152, 205
communism, 109, 111
Connell, James C., 168
Connellan, Thomas, 54
Connemara, 53
Connor, Thomas, 54
Constitution of Ireland
    Article 40, 114
    Article 41, 10, 15, 86, 113, 126, 128, 137, 152, 154–7, 173, 211
    Article 42, 10, 12, 15, 86, 126, 128, 137, 152–9, 166, 173, 211, 217
    Article 44, 10, 12, 15, 69, 112, 116, 118, 126, 128, 137, 142, 150, 152, 154–7, 172–3, 193–4, 210, 211
    Article 45, 113
    Article 50, 153
    Catholic influence upon, 68–9, 110, 111–14
    constitutional privilege, 15, 116, 154, 157–8, 169, 173, 174, 209, 210–12
    on family and education, 10, 12, 69, 86, 112, 126–7, 137, 150–59, 173
    and George Gavan Duffy, 106, 113–14, 118, 125–8, 193–4, 208, 211
    and paternal supremacy, 87, 88, 100–102, 124–7, 130, 137, 139–41, 145–7, 150–59, 166, 167, 169, 173, 211–12, 215
    Preamble, 125, 133, 146, 154, 155–6, 173, 211
    special position of Catholic Church, 10–12, 69, 112, 118, 126, 140–41, 150, 172–3, 193–4
contracaption, 68
conversion, 29, 33–4, 35, 53–6, 83–4
Cook v. Carroll case, 115, 117–18, 215
Cooney, John, 76, 213, 216
Corcoran, John, 115
Corcoran, Kevin, 115
Corish, Brendan, 70–71
Cork, 28, 38, 44–6
Cork Examiner, 51, 55, 131, 165; *see also Irish Examiner*
Cork Young Men's Association, 44
Corkery, William, 41
Cosgrave, W.T., 69
Costello, John A., 9, 13–14, 36, 69–73, 76, 134, 141, 142, 181, 182, 211, 213–16, **p3**
Council of Trent, 39–40
Crampton, George, 3
Cremin, Frank, 21
criminality, 3–4, 52
Cromwell, Oliver, 25
Crone, Anne, 82
Crowley, Diarmuid, 109
cultural identity, 76, 111
cultural nationalism, 106
Cumann na mBan, 106
Cumann na nGaedheal, 70
Curtis, Maurice, 109, 113
Cusack Smith, Thomas, 124

Dáil Courts, 109
Dáil Éireann, 9, 69, 73, 108–9, 193–4, 195, 210, 214, 215
Daily Express, 28, 51
Daily Mail, 167
Dallas, Alexander, 53
D'Alton, Ian, 35–6, 77–8, 168–9
D'Alton, John, 7–8, 74
Daly, Mary E., 8
D'Arcy, Charles, 42
Dark Rosaleen (Francis), 48–9
Darling, Sydney, 4
Davison, Neil R., 109
Davitt, Cahir, 86, 158
de Valera, Éamon, 69, 70, 75, 108, 111, 113, 175, 181, 182
Declaration of Independence, 108, 144
Delaney, Enda, 111
Derry, 182
Derry Journal, 167
Desmond Rebellion, 25
Devoy, John, 133
Dictionary of Irish Biography, 8

Dillon, James, 71
disestablishment (of Church of Ireland), 76, 82
dispensations (for mixed marriage), 12, 13, 37, 41, 46–9, 85, 89, 93, 97, 100, 123–4, 152
District Court, 3, 4, 59, 90, 94, 122, 150, 154, 158, 196, 209
divorce, 69, 113, 126, 132, 204
Dixon, Kevin, 89, 92, 93
Donegan, William, 4
Donegan, Winifred, 3–4
Donoughmore, Richard Hely-Hutchinson, 6th earl, 42
Dooley, Maurice, 191
Douglas, Mary, 23–4
Dowling, Noelle, 9
Dowra, Co. Cavan, 57
Doyle, Michael Francis, 107
Drogheda, Co. Louth, 189
Dublin Corporation, 2, 60, 74, 77, 94, 176, 196
Dublin Diocesan Archives, 9, 215
Dudley, Owen, 111
Dudley Edwards, Owen, 21–2
Duggan, Éamon, 108

Easter Rising, 106, 107, 144, 218
Eighty Club, 29
Elliott, Marianne, 10
emigration, 49, 68, 76, 78
Erin's Hope, 64
Eucharistic Congress, 69
evangelicalism, 24
Evening Echo, 166
Evening Herald, 52, 110, 131, 166
Everett, James, 74
Exsequendo Nunc, 46

Faculty of Canon Law, Maynooth, 8, 9, 190–91
Fahey, Denis, 111
Fanning, Brian, 68
Fanning, Ronan, 73
Fanning, Tim, 11
far right, 111

Farrell, Mairead, 19
Faulkner, R.B., 175
Feast of Lupercal, The (Moore), 67
feminism, 219
Fermanagh Herald, 167
Ferriter, Diarmaid, 72
Fethard-on-Sea boycott, 9, 11, 15–16, 36, 219
Fianna Fáil, 70, 73, 75, 110, 136, 181, 184, 193–4
Fiat, 15, 170, 172–3
Fine Gael, 193, 194, 210
Finucane, John, 19
Finucane, Pat, 19
Fishe, Henry, 53, 56
FitzGerald, Alexis, 194
Fitzsimons, E.S., 65, 92
Fleming, Robert, 31–2
Fogarty, Michael, 75
Foster, Roy, 8, 24, 36, 107
Francis, M.E., 48–9
Freedom Call, 132–3
Freeman's Journal, 54
Freemasonry, 109, 111
Frost, Charles, 85–6
Frost, Margaret, 85–6, 88
Frost case, 81, 85–7, 88, 124, 130, 140, 153, 156, 166, 215
Fuller, Louise, 20

Gaelic American, 132–3
Gaelic Athletic Association (GAA), 23, 74–5
Garda Síochána, 59
Garvin, Tom, 8, 68, 214
Gavan Duffy, Charles, 106, 133
Gavan Duffy, George
  appointment as High Court judge, 114
  archive of papers, 9, 215
  background and family, 106
  and the constitution of 1937, 106, 113–14, 118, 125–8, 193–4, 208, 211
  education, 106
  hearing of Tilson case, 14, 57–8, 92, 96, 100–103, 215

Index

key High Court judgements,
  114–18, 215–16
nationalism, 14, 106–7, 108, 126–7,
  134, 164, 217
pictured, **p4**
political career, 108–9
represents Roger Casement, 107–8
An Ríoghacht membership, 14,
  109–14, 125–7, 134, 216–17
Tilson judgement, 10–12, 14–15, 105,
  120–35, 152, 157, 173, 193–5, 208,
  211, 216–18
Gavan Duffy, Louise, 106
Gavan Duffy, Máire, 106
Gavan Duffy, Margaret (née Sullivan),
  106
general synods, 44, 45, 58, 193
Germany, 52, 107
Gibbon, Edward, 169
Giff, Esther (née Egar), 56
Giff, John, 56
Giff, W.L.M.
  assists Ernest after Supreme Court
    case, 179–80, 196, 197–8, 199,
    201–3
  background and family, 56–7
  as bail person for Ernest, 57, 196
  cooperates with Norman Porter of
    NUP, 183–4, 189–90, 199, 201–3
  correspondence with West Cork
    Clerical Society, 190, 191–3, 208
  countersigns admission forms, 7, 13,
    63, 94, 123, 137–8, 148–9, 206
  fundraising for legal costs, 7, 57,
    176–80, 208
  letters and articles in the press,
    168–70, 178, 194–5
  pictured, **p5**
  public meeting addresses, 188–90,
    195, 208
  role in bringing children to Birds'
    Nest, 60, 63, 65, 137–8, 148–9,
    206, 207
  role in Irish Church Missions, 7, 13,
    57–8, 177–9, 188–9

role in legal proceedings, 57–9, 90,
  105, 120, 142, 207
Glencree Reformatory, 52
Glenvar, Co. Donegal, 107
Gloucestershire Echo, 167
Glynn, Joseph, 110
Golding, G.M., 8, 116, 118
Gorman, Michael, 218
Government of Ireland Act, 39, 43, 181
Great Famine, 53, 54
Great Northern Railway, 1, 96
Gregg, J.A.F., 13, 22, 38, 44–6, 49, 193,
  195, 207, 208
Grey, Charlotte (née Callan), 83–4
Grey, Henry, 83–4
Grey case, 83–5
Griffith, Arthur, 106, 117
Gross, Nathaniel, 115
Guardianship of Infants Act, 155, 209,
  210

habeas corpus, 14, 65, 84, 85, 89–92,
  106, 130, 136, 157, 207
Hamill, W.I., 92, 96, 133, 136
Hammersmith ironworks, Ballsbridge,
  2–3
Handbook of Dublin Charities, 52
Hannon, T.B., 92
Hanrahan, Margaret, 30
Harkins, James, 33
Harley, Brendan, 37, 47, 95, 97, 98, 100,
  102, 120
Harmony Row ragged school, 50–51
Harris, Rosemary, 35
Haugh, Kevin, 87–8
Haughey, Charles, 210
Hawkins, Anna Maria, 34
healthcare, 62, 63, 68, 69, 72–3, 77
Hearne, John, 10
Heavey, James R., 89, 92, 136
High Court
  case heard by one judge instead of
    three, 121, 215
  Ernest's affidavits, 4, 7, 14, 48, 61,
    92–6, 99–100, 123–4, 148, 152

High Court (continued)
   Ernest's representation, 7, 14, 92, 96, 101–2, 122, 133
   Francis T. Russell's affidavit, 63–4, 93
   habeas corpus proceedings, 14, 65, 89–92, 130, 207
   Harriette Tilson's affidavit, 93, 96
   judgement, 10–12, 14–15, 38, 105, 120–35, 152, 157, 173, 193–4, 195, 208, 211, 216–18
   key judgements by Gavan Duffy, 114–18, 215–16
   legal costs, 7, 8, 12, 57, 130, 176–80, 215
   Mary brings case to, 1, 14, 65, 92
   Mary's affidavits, 4, 7, 14, 89–93, 96–9, 101, 120–21, 122, 123, 152
   Mary's representation, 14, 92, 96, 100–101
   May case judgement, 158
   teachers' affidavits, 93, 100, 103, 123
Hill v. *Hill* case, 124
Hobson, Bulmer, 106
Hogan, Gerard, 8, 10, 48, 107, 113, 114, 115, 124, 125, 131, 137, 209, 211
Hollis, Christopher, 111
Holmes, Andrew R., 78
Holt, Miss (matron, Birds' Nest), 62, 64–5, 95
Holy Year, 1, 14, 73–8, 207, 214
home rule, 26, 29, 39, 41–3, 45, 49, 182
House of Commons, 42, 44
House of Lords, 42, 44
Hull Daily Mail, 167
Hunter, Alexander, 182
Hyde, Douglas, 114

iconography, 67, 98–9
illegitimacy, 27, 44
indulgences, 75
infant mortality, 73
Inglis, Tom, 69, 184–5
integralism, 69, 214
internment, 114
Irish Catholic, 131–2, 170, 171–2

Irish Christian Front, 71
Irish Church Missions, 7, 13, 53–4, 56–8, 63, 120, 160, 177–9, 188, 199, 202, 206, 207
Irish Club, 106
Irish Ecclesiastical Record, 198–9
Irish Examiner, 211; see also *Cork Examiner*
Irish Free State, 68, 69, 76–8, 142, 181, 213
Irish Independent, 7, 38, 92, 110, 131, 165
Irish Monthly, 109
Irish Nation, 133
Irish Newspaper Archives, 8
Irish Press, 89, 92, 113–14, 131, 165, 176
Irish Reports, 8
Irish Republican Army (IRA), 19, 114
Irish Republican Brotherhood (IRB), 144
Irish Society for the Prevention of Cruelty to Children, 59, 90, 196
Irish Times
   advertisements and notices, 188, 199
   letters to, 15, 144, 174–6, 207
   reporting, 8, 11, 13, 22, 28–9, 38, 41, 49, 74–5, 89, 92, 131, 165–6, 176, 189–90
Irvine, George, 144–5
Islington Gazette, 204

Jackson, Alvin, 8, 71, 181
James II, 25
Jesuit Archives, Dublin, 8
Johnson, Stafford, 71
joint guardianship, 209–10
Jones, Thomas Artemus, 107
Jones, W.M.A., 174
Jordan, Henry, 27–8
Jordan, Sarah, 27–8
Joyce, James, 54
Judaism, 109, 115–17, 146, 168

Kanturk, Co. Cork, 75
Keane, Ronan, 213
Keenan, Cornelius, 87–8

Index

Keenan, Sarah, 87–8
Keenan case, 14, 87–8
Keery, Neville, 193–4
Kelly, J.M., 8, 81, 115, 155–6, 211
Keogh, Dermot, 70, 181
Keyes, Michael, 71
Kiberd, Declan, 39
Kilbohane, Co. Cork, 28
Killucan, Co. Westmeath, 57
Kilmeague, Co. Kildare, 34
Kilmurry, Co. Cork, 28–30
King's Inns, Dublin, 72, 108, 141
Kingstown Commissioners, 53, 55
Knife, The (O'Donnell), 25
Knights of Saint Columbanus, 71, 74, 111, 213–14
Kylemore Abbey, Co. Galway, 72

Labour Party, 70, 71
land reform, 76
Lavery, Cecil, 72, 121, 136, 137, 139, 148–50, 213, 214, **p6**
Lee, J.J., 8
legal costs, 7, 8, 12, 57, 130, 176–80, 196, 207, 208, 215
legal precedent, 11, 14, 81–2, 88
Legion of Mary, 74, 111
Leicester Evening Mail, 167
Lennon, M.J., 110
Lenten pastorals, 21, 34, 75
Leo XIII, 40
Leonard, R.G.L., 136, 137–41, 146–51, 158
Lincolnshire Echo, 167
Liston, T.K., 14, 92, 96, 100–101, 136, 145–6, 151, 157
Locke, John, 169
London, 106–7, 203
Londonderry Sentinel, 167
Loughcrew Protestant graveyard, Oldcastle, 2
loyalism, 19, 39, 42, 43, 181
Luddy, Maria, 51, 56
Lunn, Arnold, 111
Lunney, Thomas, 31–2
Lyons, F.S.L., 39, 108

McBride, Ian, 8
MacBride, Seán, 8–9, 70, 71–2, 74, 75, 110, 141, 181, 183–4, 214, 215, **p6**
MacCabe, Edward, 55
McCann, Agnes, 41–3
McCann, Alexander, 41–3
McCann case, 41–3, 182
McCarthy, Justine, 19
McCarthy, Rev. J., 198–9
MacCathmhaoil, Patrick, 175
MacCurtain, Margaret, 23
McEntee, Seán, 136
MacEoin, Seán, 76
McGarry, Patsy, 11, 211
McGrath, George, 65, 92, 136, 160, 165, 196, **p9**
McKee, Bertha, 31–3, 35
McKee, Joseph, 31–3, 35
McKenna case, 216
MacManaway, J.G., 182
Mc Neill, Kenneth, 58–9, 189–90
McQuaid, John Charles, 9, 15, 21, 34, 55–6, 71–6, 106, 134–5, 142, 159, 163–4, 212–18, **p7**
McVeagh, T.G., 60, 64, 65, 91, 92
McVeigh, Robbie, 5
Mageean, Rev. Dr., 21
Magnae Nobis, 46–7
Maguire, Conor, 136, 147–8, 149, 152, 213
maintenance payments, 4, 27, 28, 59, 87, 90–91, 94, 150, 154, 158, 196, 207, 209
Manchester Guardian, 132, 167
Mansion House, Dublin, 108
Marchetti-Selvaggiani, Francesco, 9, 15, 134, 142, 159, 163–4, 212–16, 218
Maria Duce, 111, 170, 172, 200
Markievicz, Constance, 106
mass attendance, 5, 29, 67, 68, 95, 98, 99, 203
Mateer, Herbert J., 189
Mawhinney, Geraldine, 19
May case, 158
Maynooth Statutes, 191

Meade, Alice (*née* Ronayne), 82
Meade, Robert, 82–3
Meade case, 14, 82–3, 88, 124, 155
Meath Chronicle, 89, 166
Meath Clerical Union, 189
Megahey, Alan, 39
Metropolitan Hall, Dublin, 44
Micks, E.C., 136
minority rights, 77
miscarriage, 59, 90, 94
Mrs Smyly's Home, Grand Canal Street, 50, 60–61, 62, 95, 206
Mrs Smyly's Homes organisation, 7, 52–3, 56, 60, 62, 65, 89, 91–3, 160, 187, 202
Mitchell, Claire, 5, 39, 180, 205
Moloney, Ed, 200
Montini, Giovanni, 76, 213
Moore, Alexander, 30–31
Moore, Brian, 67
Moore, Ellen, 30–31
Morgan, J.H., 107
Morrisroe, Rev. Dr., 21
Mothel, Co. Waterford, 75
mother and child scheme, 72–3, 214
Moynihan, Maurice, 10, 70, 110
Mulcahy, Richard, 70–71, **p3**
Munster Express, 74
Murnaghan, James, 90, 120, 136–7, 139, 146–7, 149–55, 157–8, 166, 171, 209, 212–14
Murphy, Ciaran P., 194
Murphy, T.J., 71

na gCopaleen, Myles, 74–5
Nation, 106
National Archives of Ireland, 7, 9
National Catholic Welfare Council (NCWC), 168
national identity, 68
National Labour, 70
National Union of Protestants, 9, 183–4, 189–90, 199–203
nationalism, 14, 19, 68, 106–8, 111, 117, 126–7, 134, 163, 164, 181–2, 213, 216–17

Nationalist and Leinster Times, 166
Ne Temere decree, 10, 11, 12, 13, 27, 37–46, 49, 78, 83, 169, 174–6, 188, 211
Neill, John, 211
Nenagh Guardian, 166
Netherlands, 40
New York, 11, 130–31, 168
News Chronicle, 7, 167
newspapers *see* press
North Atlantic Treaty Organisation (NATO), 181
Northern Ireland, 19, 35, 39, 82, 132, 163–4, 167, 181–4, 199–203
Northern Whig, 132
Norton, William, 70–71
Nuttall, Deirdre, 77

O'Brien, Conor Cruise, 212
O'Brien, Peter, Lord, 84–5
O'Byrne, John, 136, 138, 139
Ó Corráin, Daithí, 44, 76
O'Donnell, Peadar, 25
O'Donovan, Gerald, 40
O'Faoláin, Seán, 111
O'Farrell, Fr., 196, 198
Offences Against the State Act, 114
O'Hagan, Thomas, Lord, 83, 155
O'Hegarty, P.S., 106
O'Higgins, Brian, 47
O'Kelly, Seán T., 75
Oklahoma County Register, 132–3
Oldcastle, Co. Meath
  boycotts, 6, 16, 196–9, 208
  confessional antagonism, 1–2, 198–9, 208
  Ernest brings children to, 12, 50, 59–60, 94–5, 122, 123, 149, 206, 216
  Ernest grows up in, 1–2
  Ernest 'holidays' at, 90, 94, 99
  Ernest lives at after court case, 196–202
  Ernest returns for father's funeral, 203
  ostracism of Tilsons, 196–9, 201–2, 208

press reporting, 89
proposed as alternative home for children, 96, 101–2, 103, 123, 129
social class, 2
O'Mahony, Rev. Canon, 29–30
O'Malley, Padraig, 11
'One True Church' claims, 24, 143, 172–3, 208–9
O'Neill, Desmond, 2
Orange Order, 24, 77
O'Rourke, John, 54

Paisley, Ian, 200
papal encyclicals, 46–7, 71, 109, 111, 112, 126, 210, 211, 213
partition, 15, 68, 76, 111, 181–4
paternal supremacy, 12, 14–15, 81–8, 96, 100–102, 124–7, 130, 137–41, 145–7, 150–59, 166, 167, 169, 173, 188–9, 209–12, 215
Peacocke, Joseph, 44
penal laws, 25, 76
Pennefather, Rev., 190, 191–3
Pentonville Prison, London, 107
Phoenix Park, Dublin, 114
pilgrimage, 67, 74–5
Pius VI, 40, 46
Pius X, 37, 111
Pius XI, 109, 111
Pius XII, 70, 73, 74, 76, 134
Plunkett, George Oliver, 109
Plunkett, Joseph, 106
police *see* Garda Síochána
Portadown, Co. Armagh, 30–31
Porter, Norman, 9, 183–4, 190, 199–203
prayer, 7, 15, 67, 98, 99, 103–5, 159, 184–6
prenuptual agreements
 Browne case, 124
 and canon law, 190–92
 and duress, 48–9, 175–6, 209
 Ernest's pledge, 1, 13, 37, 46–9, 91, 93, 100–101, 123–8, 130, 136–8, 145–7, 150–55, 159, 169–70, 174–6, 209, 218

Frost case, 85–6, 88
High Court judgement on, 15, 123–5, 127–8, 130–32, 136–7, 145
Hill v. *Hill* case, 124
legal status, 11, 15, 83, 85–6, 88, 100–101, 124–8, 130–32, 136–8, 141, 145–7, 150–55, 159, 167–76
Meade case, 83, 88, 124
and the *Ne Temere* decree, 11, 46, 49, 169
Ramon v. *Ramon* case, 11, 130–31, 178
required to obtain dispensation, 13, 37, 46–9, 93, 123–4, 132, 209
Supreme Court judgement on, 152–5, 159, 167–76, 209, 218
Presbyterianism, 31, 41, 42
press, 1, 8, 13, 15, 26–9, 38, 51–2, 55, 74–5, 89, 92, 110, 131–3, 165–76, 188–90, 194, 207–8
processions, 67, 68
proselytism, 11, 30, 45, 53–6, 60, 63, 137–8, 142, 206
Protestant population decline, 76–8, 174, 207, 210
Purdysburn Hospital, Belfast, 201–2
Purgatory (Yeats), 24

Quas Primas, 109
Queen's University Belfast, 56

Rafferty, Oliver P., 46–7
Ramon v. *Ramon* case, 11, 130–31, 168
Rathmolyon, Co. Meath, 57
Reformation, 19, 24, 118, 128
religious freedom, 38, 39, 42, 131, 169
Repeal campaign, 24
Representative, 132
Reynolds, G.J., 200
Richardson, Caleb Wood, 77, 208
Richardson, W.H., 90, 92, 136, 148, 196
Ríoghacht, An, 14, 109–14, 125–7, 134, 216–17
Robb, J.C., 22

Rochester Catholic Courier and Journal, 168
Rome, 74–6, 134, 159, 164, 212–13, 218
Ronayne, Mary, 82–3
Rooke, W.W.L., 175
rosaries, 15, 67, 76, 159, 184–5, 197
Ruane, Joseph, 8, 23
Ruddock, Norman, 197
Russell, Frances, 60, 206
Russell, Francis T., 62, 63–4, 93, 148
Ryan, Louis, 20
Ryder, Catherine, 93, 100, 103

sacerdotal privilege, 117–18
sacraments, 5, 20, 29, 31, 46, 69, 143, 203
Sacred Heart orphanage, Drumcondra, 87–8
St Bridget's Cemetery, Oldcastle, 2
St Brigid's Orphanage, Dublin, 51, 52
St John Lateran basilica, Rome, 75
St Mary Major basilica, Rome, 75
St Mary's church, Anglesea Road, 204
St Mary's church, Haddington Road, 1, 9, 37, 47–8, 89, 97, 215
St Michael's church, Blackrock, 44
St Patrick's College, Maynooth, 8, 21, 190
St Paul's basilica, Rome, 75
St Peter's basilica, Rome, 74, 75
Schlegel, Teresa, 115–17
Schlegel v. Corcoran and Gross case, 115–17, 215
Scholes, Andrew, 42
Seanad Éireann, 184, 193, 195, 210
Second Vatican Council, 20
Second World War, 76
1798 Rebellion, 25–6
Shatter, Alan, 8, 210
Sheehy Skeffington, Owen, 193
Shorten, Jonathan, 28–30, 35
Sinn Féin, 19, 106, 108–9, 114–15, 117, 136, 141
Sinn Féin Funds Act, 114–15, 141
Skehan, Cornelius, 37
Smyllie, R.M., 38

Smyly, Annie Dallas, 51
Smyly, Ellen (née Franks), 50–53, 54, 56
Smyly, Ellen (daughter of the above), 51
Smyly, Josiah, 50
Smyly, Vivienne, 56
social class, 2, 5–6, 24, 35, 77–8, 179, 184, 219
social norms, 23–4, 34, 218
Southern Star, 28
Spain, 10, 40
special position (Catholic Church), 10–12, 69, 112, 118, 126, 140–41, 150, 172–3, 193–4
sport, 23, 52
Standard, 15, 168, 170–71
State (Burke) v. Lennon case, 114
Staunton, James, 55–6, 73
Steinbrink, Meier, 168
Stonyhurst College, 106
Stormont Parliament, 181–2, 200
Strabane Chronicle, 21, 167
Succession Act, 209
Sullivan, A.M., 107
Sullivan, C.J., 86, 153
Sunday Dispatch, 7, 167
Sunday Express, 167
Sunday Independent, 165
Sunday Press, 7, 165
Supreme Court
    Ernest appeals case to, 1, 72, 133
    Ernest's representation, 7, 136, 137–41, 146–51
    Frost case appeal, 86–7, 88, 124, 136, 215
    judgement, 10–12, 152–60, 173, 194–5, 208–12, 217
    judges, 72, 90, 136, 213, 214
    legal costs, 7, 8, 12, 57, 176–80
    Mary's representation, 15, 72, 136, 141–6, 151, 153–4, 208–9, 217
    reliance on Article 42 of Constitution, 10, 12, 152–8, 166, 173, 211, 217
Swastika Laundry, Ballsbridge, 59, 90, 92, 95, 97, 154, 176, 207

Index

Sybil Hill Lodge, Clontarf, 89–90, 93–4, 97, 99, 121
Sydney Catholic Weekly, 168
Sykes, W. Dodgson, 196, 199, 202

Tamesti decree, 39–40
Tardini, Domenico, 76, 213
Taylor, Frances (Fanny), 54–5
Tierney, Michael, 110
Tilson, Alan, 4, 6, 50, 58–66, 91–103, 122–4, 129–30, 159–60, 165, 176, 201, 203–5, 207, 218, **p8, p9**
Tilson, David (father of Ernest), 1–2, 50, 59–60, 96, 101, 102, 105, 197–8, 203, 206
Tilson, David (grandson of Ernest), 204
Tilson, David (son of Ernest), 4, 7, 50, 58–66, 91–103, 122–4, 129–30, 140, 152, 159–60, 165, 205, 218, **p8, p9**
Tilson, Ernest Neville
    affidavits, 4, 7, 14, 48, 61, 92–6, 99–100, 123–4, 148, 152, 205
    alleged assault of Mary, 4, 31, 32, 59, 90, 91, 94, 99, 205
    alleged drinking, 89–90, 94, 97, 101, 122, 154, 205, 209
    appeals case to Supreme Court, 1, 133
    arrested for neglect of children, 57, 196
    background and family, 1–2
    completes Birds' Nest admission forms, 7, 13, 62–3, 121, 122–3, 137–8, 148–9, 158
    employment with Dublin Corporation, 2, 60, 74, 77, 152, 176, 196
    High Court representation, 7, 14, 92, 96, 101–2, 122, 133
    illness and death, 204
    interview with parish priest, 37, 47, 100, 120
    marriage difficulties, 4–5, 89–91, 92–5, 101, 121–2, 205–6
    marriage to Mary, 1, 4, 20, 89, 91, 93, 96–7, 99, 152
    moves back to Dublin, 204
    moves to London, 203–4
    ostracised in Oldcastle, 196–9, 201–2, 208
    pictured, **p11**
    prenuptial agreement signed by, 1, 13, 37, 46–9, 91, 93, 100–101, 123–8, 130, 136–8, 145–7, 150–55, 159, 169–70, 174–6, 209, 218
    reconciliation with Mary, 6, 12, 203–4, 206, 218
    religious observance, 5, 91, 98
    removes children to Birds' Nest, 1, 4–5, 13, 56–66, 89, 91–2, 94–6, 103, 122–4, 129, 148–50, 154, 158, 206–7
    seeks dispensation for marriage, 37, 47–8, 97, 100, 152
    seeks employment outside the state, 201–2
    summoned for maintenance, 4, 59, 90–91, 94, 150, 154, 158, 209
    Supreme Court representation, 7, 136, 137–41, 146–51
Tilson, Harriette (née Forsyth), 1–2, 9, 59–60, 93, 96, 101, 102, 105, 197–8, 206
Tilson, Judy, 4, 6, 77, 96, 176, 197, 204, 205
Tilson, Martha (Mitty), 1–2, 6, 96, 197, 206
Tilson, Mary Josephine (née Barnes)
    affidavits, 4, 7, 14, 89–93, 96–9, 101, 120–21, 122, 123, 152, 205
    age at marriage, 120–21
    background and family, 2–4
    brings case to High Court, 1, 14, 65, 92
    brings *habeas corpus* proceedings, 14, 65, 89–92, 130, 207
    discovers Ernest has taken children, 59, 91, 122

Tilson, Mary Josephine (née Barnes) (*continued*)
  employment at Swastika Laundry, 59, 90, 92, 95, 97, 154, 176, 207
  High Court representation, 14, 92, 96, 100–101
  illness and death, 204
  letters of support received by, 7, 15, 103–5, 151–2, 184–6, 195
  marriage difficulties, 4–5, 89–91, 92–5, 101, 121–2, 205–6
  marriage to Ernest, 1, 4, 20, 89, 91, 93, 96–7, 99, 152
  moves back to Dublin, 204
  moves to London, 203–4
  pictured, **p9**, **p11**
  pregnancy at time of marriage, 1, 35, 37, 46, 48, 93, 120–21, 218
  reconciliation with Ernest, 6, 12, 203–4, 206, 218
  regains custody of children, 160, 165, **p9**
  religious observance, 5, 91, 95, 98, 99, 123
  seeks dispensation for marriage, 37, 47–8, 97, 100
  suffers miscarriage, 59, 90, 94
  summons Ernest for maintenance, 4, 59, 90–91, 94, 150, 154, 158, 209
  Supreme Court representation, 15, 72, 136, 141–6, 151, 153–4, 208–9, 217
  visits children at Birds' Nest, 64–6, 103, 148
Tilson, Neville, 4, 50, 59, 62, 66, 95, 96, 100, 103, 122, 129–30, 203, 218
Tilson, Paul, 4, 6, 50, 58–66, 90, 91–103, 122–4, 129–30, 159–60, 165, 203, 218, **p8**, **p9**
Tilson, Tom, 1–2, 96
Times, The, 167, 199–200
Townshend, Charles, 49
Traynor, Francis, 93, 100, 103
Trinity College Dublin, 19, 163–4, 218
Troubles, 19, 35
Tuam ecclesiastical province, 40
Turner, Richard, 2–3
Turner's Cottages, 2–4, 6, 28, 50, 59–60, 62, 66, 67, 77, 89–90, 93–103, 121–3, 129, 137, 149, 159, 203, 205–6, 216

Ulster Herald, 167
Ulster plantation, 25
Ulster Rebellion, 25
Ulysses (Joyce), 54
unionism, 24, 29, 39, 42, 43, 49, 181–3, 195
United States, 8, 11, 52, 131–3, 168, 186
unmarried mother's allowance, 209

Vatican II *see* Second Vatican Council
Viney, Michael, 54

Waiting (O'Donovan), 40
Waldron, J., 110
Wale, George, Mrs, 51
Wall, Rev. Dr., 37
Walshe, Joseph, 76, 134–5, 216
War of Independence, 25, 26, 110
Warnock, J. Edward, 183
Waters, Berthon, 110
Weekly Irish Times, 8
West Cork Clerical Society, 190, 192–3, 207, 208
Whately, George, Mrs, 51, 54
Wheeler v. *Le Marchant*, 118
Whelan, James, 4
White, Jack, 5
Whyte, J.H., 8, 68, 210, 212
William III, 25
wills, 34, 35, 85–6
Wogan, Miss (ISPCC), 59, 90, 94, 196
Wood, Ernest, 34
Worldwide Missionary Convention, 58–9, 189–90

Yeats, W.B., 24
Young Ireland movment, 106